LITURGICS FOR ORTHODOX LITURGICAL SINGING

VOLUME 2

In Memory of

Fr. John Meyendorff

(+ 1992),

and

Dedicated to

Fr. Peter DeFonce.

Liturgics for Orthodox Liturgical Singing Volume 2

By

David Barrett

Foreward by

Father Sergei Glagolev

Orthodox Liturgical Press
Southbury, Connecticut
January 2016

Library of Congress Cataloging-in-Publication Data

Barrett, David
1956 –

Liturgics for Orthodox Liturgical Singing • Volume 2

LITURGICS FOR ORTHODOX LITURGICAL SINGING • VOLUME 2

Copyright © 2015 by
David Barrett

Orthodox Liturgical Press
Southbury, CT 06488

All Rights Reserved.

ISBN 978-0-9915905-2-0

Printed in the United States of America by
Lightning Source Inc.
1246 Heil Quaker Boulevard
La Vergne, TN 37086 – 3515

CONTENTS

[For the liturgics for Vespers; Matins; the Divine Liturgy; Sacramental Services; and, Non-Sacramental Services; please see Volume 1!]

FOREWORD   xi

   PREFACE   xiii

6. FUNERAL, INTERMENT, AND MEMORIAL   431

   A. FUNERAL FOR A LAY PERSON   431

   B. FUNERAL FOR A PRIEST   452

   C. FUNERAL FOR A CHILD   486

   D. FUNERAL FOR BRIGHT WEEK   495

   E. INTERMENT   499

   F. MEMORIAL   502

7. LENTEN SERVICES 515
    A. PRE – LENTEN WEEKS 515
    B. FORGIVENESS VESPERS 526
    C. KANON OF ST ANDREW OF CRETE 539
    D. THE LITURGY OF THE PRESANCTIFIED GIFTS 556
    E. AKATHIST TO THE THEOTOKOS 577
    F. LITTLE COMPLINE 596

8. HOLY WEEK, PASCHA, AND BRIGHT WEEK 605
    A. LAZARUS SATURDAY AND PALM SUNDAY 605
    B. BRIDEGROOM MATINS 628
    C. MATINS OF HOLY THURSDAY 649
    D. VESPERAL LITURGY OF HOLY THURSDAY 670
    E. MATINS OF HOLY FRIDAY 688
    F. ROYAL HOURS OF HOLY FRIDAY 719
    G. VESPERS OF HOLY FRIDAY 739

H. MATINS OF HOLY SATURDAY	752
I. VESPERAL LITURGY OF HOLY SATURDAY	777
J. NOCTURNS OF HOLY SATURDAY	800
K. PASCHAL MATINS	807
L. PASCHAL DIVINE LITURGY	826
M. PASCHAL VESPERS	844
N. PASCHAL HOURS	854
O. BRIGHT WEEK	858
BIBLIOGRAPHY	869

FOREWARD

Coming to church, we enter into holiness. What we see and hear, and what we sing, is holy. What we offer as our liturgical life is holy: "Holy Things for the holy!"

Our worship is "iconic." "We confess and proclaim our salvation in words and images." (Kontakion of the Sunday of Orthodoxy). The words we sing give voice to the liturgical prayer-life of our Holy Church. They give structure to the time and place of our holy worship.

God bless David Barrett for his love of liturgics!

Fr Sergei Glagolev
East Meadow, NY
November 2015

Fr Sergei Glagolev is a renowned music teacher and composer of Orthodox liturgical music.

PREFACE

This book is intended as an outline or a guide for choir directors in the Orthodox Church who wish to understand the structure and *liturgics* (rules regarding the celebration of the divine services). The basic book that is followed for this is the *Typikon*, which is the liturgical book that contains instructions about the order of the various Church services, in the form of a perpetual calendar. The Typikon arose within the monastic movements of the early Christian era as a way to regulate the life a monastery. Two monastic centers have influenced the services of the Orthodox Church more than any other: the Holy Lavra of Saint Savvas (or, Sabbas) the Sanctified near Jerusalem, and the Monastery of Saint John (Studium) in Constantinople.[1] The development of these two forms of the Typikon is as follows.

The Orthodox Church recognizes ***The Typikon of Saint Savvas - formally The Typikon of the Church Service of the Holy Lavra at Jerusalem of our God-Bearing Father St. Sabbas*** - as the standard of monastic usage. The original Typikon of Saint Savvas was developed to organize the lavra (monastic

---

[1] The Internet site, "Wikipedia," under "Typikon."

community) that St Sabbas the Sanctified founded in Jerusalem in the year 484 AD. It incorporated the practices and customs of existing Christian monastic communities in Palestine, Egypt, and Asia Minor, and was influenced by the Cathedral Office (services) in Jerusalem. The Typikon of Saint Sabbas was expanded in the 7th and 8th centuries to include large amounts of ecclesiastical poetry. It is also sometimes called the **Sabbaite** or **Jerusalem Typikon**.

Another Typikon, the Palestinian Typikon, was brought to the monasteries of Constantinople during the iconoclastic controversies of the 8th century, and was adopted and expanded for use in the Monastery of Stoudios. The Monastery's synthesis incorporated additional poetry and elements of the Cathedral Office of Constantinople. In the 11th century, the Studite usage was revised and updated. From this effort, a new version of the Typikon of Saint Savvas was created.

The newly revised Typikon of Saint Savvas became adopted widely, and by the 15th century had displaced both the Cathedral Office of Constantinople and the prior synthesis of the Studite Monastery, and had become the standard Typikon for all the Orthodox world. Its usage was further solidified when it was published in 1545, the first printed Typikon. It is still in widespread use among most Orthodox monastic communities, and in large areas of the Orthodox world, including Russia.

By the 19th century, the Ecumenical Patriarchate in Constantinople, headquartered at one time at Hagia Sophia, **The Great Church of Christ**, recognized that the monastic strictures of the Typikon of Saint Savvas, while eminently useful in a monastic or cathedral setting, were not suitable for typical parish life as experienced by most Orthodox Christians. It published a new Typikon with the goal of creating an order of services that could be celebrated in a typical parish. Thus, ***The Ecclesiastical Typikon According to the Style of the Great Church of Christ** (Τύπικον της εκκλησιάστικον κατα το Ήφος της του Χριστού Μεγάλης Εκκλήσιας [Typikon Ekklisiastikon kata to ifos tis tou Christou Megalis Ekklisias])* (Konstantinos Protopsaltis, Constantinople, 1839) was created. Subsequent corrections and revisions were published with the new title, ***The Typikon of the Great Church of Christ** (Τύπικον της του Χριστού Μεγάλης Εκκλήσιας [Typikon tis tou Christou Megalis Ekklisias])* (George Violakis, Constantinople, 1888).[2] This Typikon was soon adopted by the Ecumenical Patriarchate, and is

---

[2] Bogdanos, Theodore, ***The Byzantine Liturgy: Hymnology and Order***, Greek Orthodox Diocese of Denver Choir Federation, 1993, p. xviii.

now in use by all churches under the direct jurisdiction of the Ecumenical Patriarchate (for example, the Greek Orthodox Archdiocese of North America) and most Greek-speaking churches (including the Church of Greece and the Church of Cyprus), as well as in some other Orthodox jurisdictions.[3]

For clarity of thought and presentation, in the remainder of this book, the liturgics will be presented according to the "Slavic" or "Russian" tradition as followed in the Orthodox Church in America. Whenever the liturgics from the other traditions are according to **both** the Greek **and** the Antiochian practices, they will be referred to as the "Byzantine tradition" or the "Byzantine practice". Whenever the Greek and Antiochian practices differ from each other (that is, they stand alone), then they will be referred to by their own designation ("Greek tradition [or practice]" and "Antiochian tradition [or practice]").

This author frequently gets frustrated when, perusing specifics in a reference volume on the appropriate page and section, the book says, "See such-and-such back on page so-and-so." Therefore,

---

[3] Mother Mary and Ware, Kallistos (Timothy), **The Festal Menaion** (3rd printing), 1969, St. Tikhon's Seminary Press, p. 543.

each separate service presented here will give the essential details completely, even if they have been presented in another section for another service. So, for example, the details regarding the Augmented Litany for a Great Vespers does **not** say, "Refer to the discussion on the Augmented Litany in the section on Resurrectional Vespers," but gives, **_again_ in the section on Great Vespers**, the full details necessary for the celebration of the Augmented Litany in that particular service. In fact, the **only** times I made reference to previous pages was when I presented the sections on Baptismal and Matrimonial Divine Liturgies, where, calling for the celebration of two prokeimena, I footnoted the reader to the section above on the celebration of two prokeimena in the Divine Liturgy section proper. The other occasion was, when concluding the discussion of the Funeral Divine Liturgy, I referenced that the rubrics for Interment at the cemetery were to be found in the chapter on Funerals (as separate from the Divine Liturgy) and Interments. Again, since this is a totally separate service (and at a totally different location [the cemetery, instead of the church]), this again is not a violation of the policy. Everywhere else, the rubrical information is re-presented in full for each and every liturgical service.

Another point to keep in mind regarding this book is the following. In addition to presenting the basic outline and shape (or, "***ordo***") of the various services, as well as the liturgics concerning them, mention will be made of various popular or widely practiced liturgical customs. To cite an example: when Resurrectional or Great Vespers is served with a Vigil, "Rejoice, O Virgin!" is often used as the concluding troparion of Vespers. When either of these forms of Vespers is served alone, a dismissal is celebrated at the end of the service, and, therefore, the ***dismissal*** troparion will either be the Resurrectional or festal troparion. However, in popular practice, many parishes that serve Resurrectional or Great Vespers alone will sing "Rejoice, O Virgin!" twice, and then either the Resurrectional or festal troparion. The essential point to remember is this: liturgical practices are ***not*** "written in stone," so to speak, but are flexible and varied from parish to parish. In the Orthodox Church, the main celebrant (whether it be the parish priest, a "substitute" priest filling in, a diocesan bishop, or the Metropolitan) makes all final decisions regarding the pattern of elements taken or deleted from the customary parish practice. It behooves the choir director to sit down with the main celebrant and discuss the order of the liturgical services, to determine what liturgical elements will be celebrated and what elements will be omitted. As with everything in our life in Christ, all things must be done, as St Paul reminds us, "decently and in order" (1 Corinthians 14:40), with the love, compassion, and cooperation that come from God.

Another item of note: Despite the increasingly-common use of reading prayers, hymns, and Scripture readings in the style of using a regularly spoken voice (as though reading aloud an article or editorial from a newspaper) borrowed from the Western churches, it has consistently been the official practice in the Orthodox Church throughout the centuries to use a chanting voice (usually on one note that may go up or down for emphasis, ***not*** being sung on a melody, however) for celebrating these prayers, hymns, and Scripture readings. Therefore, throughout this work, the word "chanting" will refer to the proper reading by a celebrant or reader on one note, and the word "singing" will refer to the celebration of hymns sung to melodies by a choir and the people. Whatever the local practice is within a given parish or jurisdictional tradition can be reinterpreted or adjusted accordingly.

This work is in two volumes. Volume 1 covers Vespers; Matins; the Divine Liturgy; Sacramental Services (Holy Baptism, Holy Chrismation, Holy Matrimony, and Holy Unction); and, in the last chapter, Non-Sacramental Services (the Hours, the Lenten Hours, the Royal Hours, Grand Compline, Thanksgiving, Churching of Women, New House Blessing, and House Blessing). Volume 2 covers Funerals, Interments, and Memorials; Lenten Services; and, in the last chapter, Holy Week, Pascha, and Bright Week.

May you find this liturgical guide to be of help to you and make the understanding of our liturgical services clear and easy as you serve Christ in this wonderful and rewarding ministry of singing praises, worship, and thanksgiving to God, for the salvation of the world and to the glory of His eternal Kingdom.

6

FUNERAL, INTERMENT, AND MEMORIAL

A. FUNERAL FOR A LAY PERSON

When a funeral is celebrated separately from the Divine Liturgy, its order is as follows.[4] Here, we will present the funeral for a lay person. After that will be presented sections discussing the particulars of a funeral for a priest, a child, and those who die at Pascha or during Bright Week. The Memorial is usually celebrated the evening before, at what is colloquially known as "the wake."[5]

If the body of the newly-departed in his or her casket has not yet been brought into the church, the singers stand vigilantly on the sidewalk in the front of the church. When the hearse drives up and the

---

[4] Hapgood, pp. 368-393 (laymen), pp. 394-423 (priests), pp. 424-434 (children), and pp. 435-436 (those who die at Pascha or during Bright Week). For a Funeral Divine Liturgy, cf. *Volume 1*, pp. 232-239.

[5] For the service of the Memorial, cf. below, pp. 498-509.

body of the departed is wheeled into the church, the singers lead the procession, singing the *slow* Processional "Holy God!" ("Holy God! Holy Mighty! Holy Immortal! Have mercy on us!") *repeatedly* until the casket of the departed is in the center of the church.

Doxology, the Trisagion Prayers, and the Lord's Prayer

The service begins with the doxology, "Blessed is our God!" The *people* respond by *singing*, "Amen.", then (*except* in the Antiochian tradition [where they go right into Psalm 90] *and* in the Greek practice [where they go right to the 1st Stasis]) sing the Trisagion ("Holy God! Holy Mighty! Holy Immortal! Have mercy on us!") *three* times. A *reader* then reads the Trisagion Prayers ("O Most Holy Trinity, have mercy on us!"; a *triple* "Lord, have mercy."; and a full "Glory,...now and ever...!"), followed by the Lord's Prayer. After the exclamation "For, Yours are the Kingdom, and the power, and the glory,...!", the reader chants, "Amen.", and then a full "Come, let us worship God, our King!...".

Funeral, Interment, and Memorial

Psalm 90

The reader then ***immediately*** chants Psalm 90 ("He who dwells in the shelter of the Most High,...!"). At the conclusion of the Psalm (***except*** in the Antiochian tradition, where they now chant the Evlogitaria ["Blessed are You, O Lord! Teach me Your statutes!"] in tone 5), the reader chants a full "Glory,...now and ever...!", and "Alleluia! Alleluia! Alleluia! Glory to You, O God!" ***three times***.

1ˢᵗ Stasis

The three stases and Little Litanies that follow are ***not*** done in the Antiochian tradition.

In the Greek practice, the priest chants verses 1, 12, 20, 28, 36. 53, and 63; after each verse, he sings "Alleluia!" in tone 6; at the end, he chants a full "Glory,...now and ever...!" and "Alleluia!"; at the end of the 1ˢᵗ Stasis, the Litany for the Departed is celebrated and, omitting the prayer, "O God of spirits and all flesh...!", goes directly to "For, You are the Resurrection...!".

In the Slavic tradition, the priest then chants the first verses of the 1st Stasis of Psalm 118 ("Blessed are You, O Lord! Teach me Your statutes! Blessed are those whose way is blameless, who walk in the Law of the Lord! Blessed are those who keep His testimonies, who seek Him with their whole heart!"). After each set of verses, the people sing a *single* "Alleluia!" After the priest chants a full "Glory,... now and ever...!", the people sing a *single* "Alleluia!" one final time.

[Little Litany]

Even though the service books call for the celebration of the Little Litany at this point, in *most* parishes it is *omitted*.

2nd Stasis

In the Greek practice, the priest chants verses 73, 83, 94, 102, 112, and 126; after each verse, he sings, "Be merciful to me, O Lord...!" or "Have mercy on me, O Lord,...!" in tone 5, concluding with a full "Glory,...now and ever...!" and "O Lord, O Lord, have mercy on me!"

In the Slavic tradition, the priest chants the first verses of the 2nd Stasis of Psalm 118 ("Your hands have made and fashioned me! Give me understanding, that I may learn Your commandments! Those who fear You will see me and rejoice, because I have hoped in Your Word! I know, O Lord, that Your judgments are right, and that, in faithfulness, You have afflicted me!"). After each set of verses, the people sing, "Have mercy upon Your servant!" After the priest chants a full "Glory,... now and ever...!", the people sing, "Have mercy upon Your servant!" one final time.

[Little Litany]

Even though the service books call for the celebration of the Little Litany at this point, in **most** parishes it is **omitted**.

3rd Stasis

In the Greek practice, the priest sings, "And have mercy on me! Alleluia!", followed by verses 132, 141, 149, 161, 175, and 176, after which the service proceeds immediately to the Evlogitaria

("Blessed are You, O Lord! Teach me Your statutes!").

In the Slavic tradition, the priest chants the first verses of the 1st Stasis of Psalm 118 ("Look on me and be merciful to me, as is Your good pleasure towards those who love Your Name! Order my steps according to Your promise, and let no iniquity have dominion over me! Make Your face to shine on Your servant, and teach me Your statutes!"). After each set of verses, the people sing a **single** "Alleluia!" After the priest chants a full "Glory,… now and ever…!", the people sing a **single** "Alleluia!" one final time.

"Blessed Are You, O Lord" and Stikhera

Following the 3rd Stasis of Psalm 118, the people **immediately** sing the refrain, "Blessed are You, O Lord! Teach me Your statutes!", and the subsequent stikhera. These conclude with the singing of, "Alleluia! Alleluia! Alleluia! Glory to You, O God!" **three** times. Usually, in **most** parishes, there is a great censing of the church done during the singing of this refrain and these stikhera. In the Greek practice, this is followed by the Kontakion for the Departed in tone 8, and then the Stikhera for the

Departed of St John of Damascus: eight basic hymns (one in each tone), plus alternatives for tones 2, 4, and 7, and "Glory,...now and ever...!" verses for the principal hymn in tone 8 ("I weep and I wail...!"). After this, the Greek service books call for going *directly* to the singing of the Beatitudes, although the singing of the Beatitudes is *omitted* in some Greek parishes.

Little Litany

At this point, a Little Litany *is* celebrated (*except* in the Greek practice) in most parishes. The order for a Little Litany is as follows.

Deacon:	Again and again, in peace, let us pray to the Lord.
People:	Lord, have mercy.
Deacon:	Furthermore, we pray for the soul of the servant of God, _____, departed this life, that [he, she] may be pardoned all of [his, her] sins, both voluntary and involuntary.
People:	Lord, have mercy.

Deacon:	That the Lord our God may establish [his, her] soul where the just repose.
People:	Lord, have mercy.
Deacon:	The mercies of God, the Kingdom of Heaven, and the remission of [his, her] sins, let us entreat of Christ, our immortal King and God.
People:	Grant it, O Lord.
Deacon:	Let us pray to the Lord.
People:	Lord, have mercy.

There follows then a prayer chanted by the priest that begins, , "O God of spirits and of all flesh,…!", concluding with the exclamation, "For, You are the Resurrection, and the Life, and the Repose of Your servant,…!" The people then respond with "Amen." **<u>Note</u>:** In **many** parishes (and in the Antiochian tradition), the prayer that begins, "O God of spirits and of all flesh,…!" is **omitted**, and **only** the concluding exclamation, "For, You are the Resurrection, and the Life, and the Repose of Your servant,…!" is chanted.

Kathisma Hymns

The people then sing a set of Kathisma Hymns, in tone 5. They are: "Give rest with the just, O our Savior…!"; a full "Glory,… now and ever…!"; and "O Christ our God, from a Virgin, You shone forth to the world,…!"

[Psalm 50]

At this point, the service books call for a reader to chant Psalm 50 ("Have mercy on me, O God, according to Your steadfast love,…!"). In *many* parishes, however, this is *omitted*. The decision, as always, rests with the main celebrant.

The Kanon

The Kanon is now celebrated. Even though the service books call for the celebration of all of the odes (odes 1, 3-9), in *almost all* parishes *only* odes 1, 3, 6, and 9 are celebrated (the Antiochians *omit* ode 1). Therefore, that is what is presented here. This Kanon is in tone 6.

Also, in most parishes, the order for celebrating these odes is as follows: the ode is sung, then the priest chants, "Give rest, O Lord, to the soul of Your servant who has fallen asleep!" The people then sing this same petition ("Give rest, O Lord,...!"). The priest then chants, "Glory to the Father, and to the Son, and to the Holy Spirit!" The people then sing, "Now and ever and unto ages of ages! Amen.", followed by the next ode. **However**, **many** parishes are starting to revive the ancient practice of restoring some, if not all, of the troparia that are chanted by a reader between the ode and the priest intoning, "Give rest, O Lord,...!" Again, as in all other liturgical matters, the priest (or, main celebrant) makes that decision.

Ode 1 begins with, "When Israel passed on foot, over the sea,...!" If the local practice is to chant the troparia, the reader then does so at this point. In either case, the priest then chants, "Give rest, O Lord,...!", and the people sing the same. The priest chants, "Glory...Spirit!" The people sing, "Now and ever...Amen."

Ode 3 begins with, "There is none so holy as You, O Lord my God,...!" If the local practice is to chant the troparia, the reader then does so at this point. In either case, the priest then chants, "Give rest, O Lord,...!", and the people sing the same. The priest chants, "Glory...Spirit!" The people sing, "Now and ever...Amen."

At this point, the service books call for the singing of Kathisma Hymns, in tone 6 ("Of a truth, all things are vanity,...!", followed by a full "Glory,... now and ever...!", and then the theotokion [in tone 6], "O all-holy Theotokos,...!"). **However**, in **most** parishes, this is **omitted**.

Ode 6 begins with, "Beholding the sea of life, surging with the storm of temptation,...!" If the local practice is to chant the troparia, the reader then does so at this point. In either case, the priest then chants, "Give rest, O Lord,...!", and the people sing the same. The priest chants, "Glory...Spirit!" The people sing, "Now and ever...Amen."

At this point, the Kontakion and Oikos **are** celebrated in most parishes. The Kontakion, in tone 6, begins, "With the saints, give rest, O Christ,...!". This is **immediately** followed, with **no** "Glory,... now and ever...!" at all, with the Oikos, in tone 8, beginning, "You, only, are immortal,...!" There is usually a small censing (sanctuary, iconostasis, people) done during the singing of the Kontakion and the Oikos. If the local practice is to chant the troparia, the reader then does so at this point. In either case, the priest then chants, "Give rest, O Lord,...!", and the people sing the same. The priest chants, "Let us bless the Father, and the Son, and the Holy Spirit, the Lord!" The people sing, "Now and ever...Amen."

Ode 9 begins with, "It is not possible for men to see God,...!" If the local practice is to chant the troparia, the reader then does so at this point.

Little Litany

Following the Kanon, a Little Litany is celebrated.

[Stikhera]

At this point, the service books call for some stikhera to be sung, each in one of the eight tones. **However**, this is usually **omitted** in **most** parishes (**except** the Antiochians).

For those parishes that **do** celebrate these stikhera, they are as follows: in tone 1, beginning, "What earthly sweetness remains unmixed with grief?"; in tone 2, "Woe is me! What manner of ordeal does the soul endure when parted from the body?"; in tone 3, "All mortal things are vanity...!"; in tone 4,

"Where is earthly predilection?"; in tone 5, "I called to mind the prophet,…!"; in tone 6, "Your creating command was my origin and my foundation!"; in tone 7, "When, in the beginning, You had created man,…!"; in tone 8, "I weep and I wail when I think upon death,…!"

The Beatitudes

The main celebrant intones the first four verses of the Beatitudes, then the people respond by singing, "Remember us, O Lord, when You come in Your Kingdom!", and after each set of verses (in the Antiochian tradition, the chanters alternate this with the priest). The celebrant then chants "Glory to the Father, and to the Son, and to the Holy Spirit.", followed by a verse. The people again sing, "Remember us, O Lord, when You come in Your Kingdom!" The celebrant chants, "Now and ever and unto ages of ages. Amen.", followed by a verse. The people sing "Remember us, O Lord, when You come in Your Kingdom!" a final time.

The Prokeimenon

In the Greek practice, the reader and chanters sing the Prokeimenon altogether, as some parishes in the other traditions do when singing the Great Prokeimenon, "Who is so great a God as our God?".

In the other traditions, during the final verses of the Beatitudes, a reader approaches the priest to receive a blessing to celebrate the Prokeimenon, the Epistle reading, and the "Alleluia!" verses (the Antiochians have the reader chant the Prokeimenon *once*, then go immediately to the Epistle). Taking his or her place in the center of the church behind the casket where the newly-departed reposes, the reader chants the Prokeimenon according to the following.

Deacon:	Wisdom! Let us be attentive!
Priest:	Peace be with you all!
Reader:	And with your spirit!
Deacon:	Wisdom!
Reader:	The Prokeimenon is in the 6th tone: Blessed is the way in which you shall walk today, O soul! For, a place of rest is prepared for you!

People:	Blessed is the way in which you shall walk today, O soul! For, a place of rest is prepared for you!
Reader:	To You, O Lord, will I call! O my God, be not silent to me!
People:	Blessed is the way in which you shall walk today, O soul! For, a place of rest is prepared for you!
Reader:	Blessed is the way in which you shall walk today, O soul!
People:	For, a place of rest is prepared for you!

The Epistle

The Epistle reading, 1 Thessalonians 4:13-17, is then celebrated, as follows.

Deacon:	Wisdom!
Reader:	The Reading is from the First Epistle of the holy Apostle Paul to the Thessalonians!
Priest:	Let us be attentive!

The reader then chants, "Brethren!", and then the Epistle reading.

"Alleluia!" Verses

When the Epistle reading is concluded, the priest blesses the reader, saying, "Peace be with you, Reader!" The reader then chants, "And with your spirit! Alleluia! Alleluia! Alleluia!" The people then sing a *triple* "Alleluia!" The reader then chants the verse, "Blessed are they whom You have chosen and taken, O Lord!" The people again sing a *triple* "Alleluia!" The reader then chants the final verse, "Their memory is from generation to generation!" The people then sing a final *triple* "Alleluia!" In the Greek practice, the singing of "Alleluia!" verses is *omitted*.

The Gospel

The Gospel reading, John 5:24-30, is then celebrated. The formula for it is as follows.

Deacon:	Wisdom! Let us be attentive! Let us listen to the Holy Gospel!
Priest:	Peace be with you all!
People:	And with your spirit!
Priest:	The Reading is from the Holy Gospel according to Saint John the Theologian!
People:	Glory to You, O Lord, glory to You!

The priest then chants the Gospel reading. At its conclusion, the people once again sing, "Glory to You, O Lord, glory to You!" In the Greek practice, after the Gospel reading, the service goes ***immediately*** to the Litany for the Departed.

The Sermon

At this point, in ***most*** parishes, the priest preaches the sermon. In the Greek practice, this is usually done ***after*** the Dismissal.

Troparia

Even though the service books do not call for them here, following the sermon in **most** parishes (**except** the Antiochians), the people sing a set of troparia. The first one begins, "With the souls of the righteous departed,....!"; then, "Glory...Spirit!"; then, "You are the God Who descended...!"; then, "Now and ever...Amen."; then, "O Virgin, alone, pure and blameless,....!"

The Litany for the Departed

The Litany for the Departed is then celebrated. It begins with the petition, "Have mercy on us, O Lord,....," which is responded to by the **triple** "Lord, have mercy." This **triple** "Lord, have mercy." is then sung after each subsequent petition. After the petition that begins, "The mercies of God, the Kingdom of Heaven,...!", the people sing, "To You, O Lord." The priest then chants a prayer that begins, "O God of spirits and of all flesh...!" (**except** with the Antiochians, who go **directly** to the exclamation). After the exclamation that begins, "For, You are the Resurrection and the Life and the Repose,....!", the people sing, "Amen."

[*"The Last Kiss"*]

At this point, the service books call for the singing of a series of hymns, beginning with "The Last Kiss" ("Come, let us give the last kiss unto the dead,....!"). ***However***, in ***many*** parishes, this is ***postponed*** until the people come forward to pay their final respects to the newly departed (at this point, the Byzantines do the Prayer of Absolution instead [the Greeks ***only*** if a bishop is present]).

[The Trisagion Prayers and the Lord's Prayer]

The service books then call for the reader to chant the Trisagion Prayers and the Lord's Prayer. Again, in ***most*** parishes, this is ***omitted***.

The Dismissal

The Dismissal then follows, with its exclamations and sung responses: "Wisdom! Most Holy Theotokos, save us!" ("More honorable than the Cherubim,....."), and "Glory to You, O Christ, our God and our Hope, glory to You!" (a full "Glory,...

now and ever...!", a triple "Lord, have mercy.", and "Father [or, "Master"; or, "Most Blessed Master"], bless!"). The dismissal prayer is intoned, concluding with an exclamation, to which the people *usually* respond with a double "Amen." (or, it *could* be a single "Amen."). In the Greek practice, the Dismissal begins with the "Glory to You, O Christ, our God and our Hope, glory to You!".

The Prayer of Absolution

The celebrant reads the Prayer of Absolution over the body of the departed. The usual sung responses of "Lord, have mercy." and "Amen." occur where appropriate. (The Byzantines did this *earlier*.)

"The Last Kiss"

As the people come forward to pay their respects to the departed person, , recessional hymns are sung. These usually consist of "Come, Let Us Give the Last Kiss" (in tone 2) and "The Lord is My Shepherd" (in tone 8). If it is during the Pascha season, "Let God Arise!" may also be added here.

Processional "Holy God!"

As the pallbearers wheel the body of the departed back out to the hearse, the singers again lead the procession, singing the **slow** Processional "Holy God!" ("Holy God! Holy Mighty! Holy Immortal! Have mercy on us!") **repeatedly** until the casket is placed in the hearse. In the Greek practice, this is often done **only** by the priest himself.

The people then proceed to the cemetery for the interment of the newly-departed.[6]

As previously mentioned, the three sections that follow cover the funeral for a priest, the funeral for a child, and the funeral for someone who has died at Pascha or during Bright Week.

---

[6] Cf. below, "E. Interment,", pp. 451-453.

B. FUNERAL FOR A PRIEST

The funeral for a priest is more expanded and elaborate than that for a lay person (**except** in the Greek practice where, except for some additional troparia and inserted petitions in litanies, it is the same as that for a layperson). In **most** parishes, many of these elements may be **omitted**. As always, the main celebrant determines how the service is to be celebrated. The differences from the funeral for a lay person, as called for per the service books, are as follows.[7]

Doxology, the Trisagion Prayers, and the Lord's Prayer

The service begins with the doxology, "Blessed is our God!" !" The **people** respond by **singing**, "Amen.", then sing the Trisagion ("Holy God! Holy Mighty! Holy Immortal! Have mercy on us!") **three** times. A **reader** then reads the Trisagion Prayers ("O Most Holy Trinity, have mercy on us!"; a **triple** "Lord,

---

[7] Hapgood, pp. 394-423.

have mercy."; and a full "Glory,… now and ever…!"), followed by the Lord's Prayer. After the exclamation, "For, Yours are the Kingdom, and the power, and the glory,…!", the reader chants, "Amen.", and then a full "Come, let us worship God, our King!…" (the Antiochians *omit* "Come, let us worship").

Psalm 90

Except for the Antiochians, the reader then *immediately* chants Psalm 90 ("He who dwells in the shelter of the Most High,…!"). At the conclusion of the Psalm, the reader chants a full "Glory,… now and ever…!", and "Alleluia! Alleluia! Alleluia! Glory to You, O God!" *three* times.

1st Stasis

The priest then chants the first verses of the 1st Stasis of Psalm 118 ("Blessed are You, O Lord! Teach me Your statutes! Blessed are those whose way is blameless, who walk in the Law of the Lord! Blessed are those who keep His testimonies, who seek Him with their whole heart!"). **_Note:_** In contrast to the funeral for a lay person, at the funeral for a priest, **all** the verses of Psalm 118 are celebrated in the 1st, 2nd, and 3rd Stases. After each set of verses, the people sing a *single* "Alleluia!" After the priest chants a full "Glory,... now and ever...!", the people sing a *single* "Alleluia!" one final time. (The Antiochians have **two** verses for the 1st Stasis, and **three** verses each for the 2nd and 3rd Stases.)

Little Litany

At this point, a Little Litany *is* celebrated in most parishes (*except* for the Antiochians). The order for a Little Litany is as follows.

Deacon:	Again and again, in peace, let us pray to the Lord.
People:	Lord, have mercy.
Deacon:	Furthermore, we pray for the soul of the servant of God, _____, departed this life, that [he, she] may be pardoned all of [his, her] sins, both voluntary and involuntary.

People:	Lord, have mercy.
Deacon:	That the Lord our God may establish [his, her] soul where the just repose.
People:	Lord, have mercy.
Deacon:	The mercies of God, the Kingdom of Heaven, and the remission of [his, her] sins, let us entreat of Christ, our immortal King and God.
People:	Grant it, O Lord.
Deacon:	Let us pray to the Lord.
People:	Lord, have mercy.

There follows then a prayer chanted by the priest that begins, "O God of spirits and of all flesh,…!", concluding with the exclamation, "For, You are the Resurrection, and the Life, and the Repose of Your servant,…!" The people then respond with "Amen." **<u>Note</u>:** In **many** parishes, the prayer that begins, "O God of spirits and of all flesh,…!" is **omitted**, and **only** the concluding exclamation, "For, You are the Resurrection, and the Life, and the Repose of Your servant,…!" is chanted.

2nd Stasis

The priest then chants the first verses of the 2nd Stasis of Psalm 118 ("Your hands have made and fashioned me! Give me understanding, that I may learn Your commandments! Those who fear You will see me and rejoice, because I have hoped in Your Word! I know, O Lord, that Your judgments are right, and that, in faithfulness, You have afflicted me!"). After each set of verses, the people sing, "Have mercy upon Your servant!" After the priest chants a full "Glory,… now and ever…!", the people sing, "Have mercy upon Your servant!" one final time.

[Little Litany]

Even though the service books call for the celebration of the Little Litany at this point, in **most** parishes it is **omitted**.

3rd Stasis

The priest then chants the first verses of the 1st Stasis of Psalm 118 ("Look on me and be merciful to me, as is Your good pleasure towards those who love Your Name! Order my steps according to Your promise, and let no iniquity have dominion over me! Make Your face to shine on Your servant, and teach me Your statutes!"). After each set of verses, the people sing a **single** "Alleluia!" After the priest chants a full "Glory,... now and ever...!", the people sing a **single** "Alleluia!" one final time.

"Blessed Are You, O Lord" and Stikhera

Following the 3rd Stasis of Psalm 118, the people *immediately* sing the refrain, "Blessed are You, O Lord! Teach me Your statutes!", and the subsequent stikhera. These conclude with the singing of, "Alleluia! Alleluia! Alleluia! Glory to You, O God!" **three** times. Usually, in most parishes, there is a great censing of the church done during the singing of this refrain and these stikhera.

In the Greek practice, there are **two** additional verses inserted between the first and second customary verses: the first begins, "You who have preached the true Lamb of God and, as sheep, were carried off to slaughter...!", and the second starts, "All you who have marched the narrow road of life, that is full of nothing else but sorrow,...!".

[Little Litany]

Even though the service books call for the celebration of the Little Litany at this point, in *most* parishes it is *omitted* (*except* in the Antiochian tradition).

In the Greek practice, *all* Little Litanies for the Funeral for Clergy has the form of the second petition as, "Again, we pray for the repose of the soul of the departed servant of God, ___, [archbishop, bishop, priest, deacon], who was our brother and concelebrant, and for the forgiveness of all his sins, both voluntary and involuntary.". Also, there is an additional petition by the bishop that begins, "We thank You, O Lord our God, for Your Life alone is immortal, and Your glory is incomprehensible...!". The ekphonesis is also expanded: "For, You are the Resurrection, the Life, and the Repose of Your departed servant, ___, a(n) [archbishop, bishop, priest, deacon], and our brother and concelbrant, O Christ our God,...!".

Kathisma Hymns 1 and 2

The people then sing a set of Kathisma Hymns, in tone 5. They are: "Give rest with the just, O our Savior...!"; a full "Glory,... now and ever...!"; and "O Christ our God, from a Virgin, You shone forth to the world,...!"

Antiphon 1

At this point, Antiphon 1 is sung in tone 6, with the sections beginning as follows: "I will lift up my eyes to the Heavens,...!"; "Have mercy upon us who are humble of heart,...!"; "Glory...Spirit!"; "The Holy Spirit is of all things...!"; "Now and ever...Amen."; and, again, "The Holy Spirit is of all things...!". (The Antiochians **omit** this Antiphon.)

Prokeimenon 1

During the final verses of Antiphon 1, a reader approaches the priest to receive a blessing to celebrate Prokeimenon 1, Epistle 1 , and "Alleluia!" Verses 1. Taking his or her place in the center of the church behind the casket where the newly-departed reposes, the reader chants the Prokeimenon according to the following (in the Antiochian tradition, the reader chants it just *once*).

Deacon: Wisdom! Let us be attentive!

Priest: Peace be with you all!

Reader: And with your spirit!

Deacon: Wisdom!

Reader: The Prokeimenon is in the 6th tone: Blessed is the way in which you shall walk today, O soul! For, a place of rest is prepared for you!

People: Blessed is the way in which you shall walk today, O soul! For, a place of rest is prepared for you!

Reader: To You, O Lord, will I call! O my God, be not silent to me!

People:	Blessed is the way in which you shall walk today, O soul! For, a place of rest is prepared for you!
Reader:	Blessed is the way in which you shall walk today, O soul!
People:	For, a place of rest is prepared for you!

Epistle 1

The reading for Epistle 1, 1 Thessalonians 4:13-17, is then celebrated, as follows.

Deacon:	Wisdom!
Reader:	The Reading is from the First Epistle of the holy Apostle Paul to the Thessalonians!
Priest:	Let us be attentive!

The reader then chants, "Brethren!", and then the Epistle reading.

"Alleluia!" Verses 1

When the Epistle reading is concluded, the priest blesses the reader, saying, "Peace be with you, Reader!" The reader then chants, "And with your spirit! Alleluia! Alleluia! Alleluia!" The people then sing a *triple* "Alleluia!" The reader then chants the verse, "Blessed are they whom You have chosen and taken, O Lord!" The people again sing a *triple* "Alleluia!" The reader then chants the final verse, "Their memory is from generation to generation!" The people then sing a final *triple* "Alleluia!"

Gospel 1

The reading for Gospel 1, John 5:24-30, is then celebrated. The formula for it is as follows.

Deacon:	Wisdom! Let us be attentive! Let us listen to the Holy Gospel!
Priest:	Peace be with you all!
People:	And with your spirit!

Priest: The Reading is from the Holy Gospel according to Saint John the Theologian!

People: Glory to You, O Lord, glory to You!

The priest then chants the Gospel reading. At its conclusion, the people once again sing, "Glory to You, O Lord, glory to You!"

Prayer 1

The deacon intones, "Let us pray to the Lord." The people sing, "Lord, have mercy." The main celebrant (the bishop or a presiding priest) then chants a prayer that begins, "O Master, Lord our God, Who alone have immortality,…!". At its conclusion ("through the grace and bounties and love towards mankind of Your only-begotten Son, our Lord, Jesus Christ!"), the people sing, "Amen."

Hymn 1

The people sing, in tone 2: "Today, I part from my kinfolk, and flee to You, the only sinless One! Grant me rest in the mansions of the righteous with Your elect!" (The Antiochians *omit* this hymn.)

Psalm 23 and "Alleluia!"

A reader then chants the verses of Psalm 23 (beginning, "The Lord is my Shepherd I will not want!"), and, interspersed between the verses, the people, each time, sing a *triple* "Alleluia!"

Kathisma Hymn 3

The people now sing a Kathisma Hymn, in tone 6, that begins, "Forasmuch as we are all constrained...!". (The Antiochians *omit* this hymn.)

Prokeimenon 2

A reader then chants Prokeimenon 2, in tone 6, as follows: the reader chants the Prokeimenon, "Blessed is he whom you have chosen and taken, O Lord!"; the people sing this Prokeimenon ("Blessed is he…!"); the reader chants the verse, "To You, O God, belongs a song in Zion!"; the people again sing the full Prokeimenon; the reader chants the ***first half*** of the Prokeimenon "Blessed is he!"; the people sing the ***second half*** of the Prokeimenon ("Whom you have chosen and taken, O Lord!").

Epistle 2

The reader, after the blessing from the main celebrant, chants the reading for Epistle 2, Romans 5:13-22.

"Alleluia!" Verses 2

At the conclusion of the Epistle reading and the blessing from the celebrant, the reader chants, "And with your spirit! Alleluia! Alleluia! Alleluia!"

The people sing a **triple** "Alleluia!", in tone 4. The reader chants the verse, "Blessed is [he, she] whom You have chosen and taken, O Lord!" The people again sing a **triple** "Alleluia!", in tone 4.

Gospel 2

The celebrant then chants the reading for Gospel 2, John 5:17-25. The people sing the usual responses.

Prayer 2

The deacon intones, "Let us pray to the Lord." The people sing, "Lord, have mercy." The main celebrant then chants a prayer that begins, "We give thanks to You, O Lord our God, for You, only, have life immortal,...!". At its conclusion ("now and ever and unto ages of ages!"), the people sing, "Amen."

Antiphon 2

Antiphon 2 is sung in tone 6, beginning as follows: "If the Lord had not been on our side,…!"; "Let not my soul be caught like a bird,…!"; "Glory…Spirit!"; "Adoration comes to all men through the Holy Spirit…!"; "Now and ever…Amen."; and, again, "Adoration comes to all men through the Holy Spirit…!". (The Antiochians **omit** this hymn.)

Psalm 24 and "Alleluia!"

A reader then chants the verses of Psalm 24 (beginning, "The Earth is the Lord's, and the fullness thereof!"), and, interspersed between the verses, the people, each time, sing a **triple** "Alleluia!" (The Antiochians **omit** this section.)

Hymn 2 and Kathisma Hymn 4

The people then sing a hymn, in tone 2, beginning, "In faith, hope, and love,…!", following by the singing of a Kathisma Hymn, in tone 5, beginning, "You know, O our God, that we are born in sin!…!".

Prokeimenon 3

A reader then chants Prokeimenon 3, in tone 6, as follows: the reader chants the Prokeimenon, "Blessed is he whom you have chosen and taken, O Lord!"; the people sing this Prokeimenon ("Blessed is he...!"); the reader chants the verse, "His remembrance is from generation to generation!"; the people again sing the full Prokeimenon; the reader chants the ***first half*** of the Prokeimenon "Blessed is he!"; the people sing the ***second half*** of the Prokeimenon ("Whom you have chosen and taken, O Lord!").

Epistle 3

The reader, after the blessing from the main celebrant, chants the reading for Epistle 3, 1 Corinthians 15:1-12.

"Alleluia!" Verses 3

At the conclusion of the Epistle reading and the blessing from the celebrant, the reader chants,

"And with your spirit! Alleluia! Alleluia! Alleluia!" The people sing a *triple* "Alleluia!", in tone 4. The reader chants the verse, "Blessed is [he, she] whom You have chosen and taken, O Lord!" The people again sing a *triple* "Alleluia!", in tone 4.

Gospel 3

The celebrant then chants the reading for Gospel 3, John 6:35-39. The people sing the usual responses.

Prayer 3

The deacon intones, "Let us pray to the Lord." The people sing, "Lord, have mercy." The main celebrant then chants a prayer that begins, "O Lord of hosts, Who are the Consolation of the afflicted,…!". After the exclamation ("For, You are the Resurrection and the Life and the Repose…!"), the people sing, "Amen."

Antiphon 3

Antiphon 3 is sung in tone 6, with the sections beginning as follows: "Those who put their trust in the Lord...!"; "The assembly of the just,...!"; "Glory...Spirit!"; "The dominion of the Holy Spirit...!"; "Now and ever...Amen."; and, again, "The dominion of the Holy Spirit ...!". (The Antiochians **omit** this.)

Psalm 83 and "Alleluia!"

A reader then chants the verses of Psalm 83 (beginning, "How lovely is Your dwelling place, O Lord of hosts!"), and, interspersed between the verses, the people, each time, sing a ***triple*** "Alleluia!" (The Antiochians **omit** this section.)

Troparia 1 and Hymns 3 – 6

The people then sing a set of troparia, in tone 6, as follows: "My beloved brethren, forget me not when you sing to the Lord,...!"; "Death has suddenly come upon me,...!"; "Have mercy on us, O Lord, have mercy on us!...!"; "Glory...Spirit!"; "Have mercy on us, O Lord, for in You have we put our trust!...!"; "Now and ever...Amen."; "Open to us the door of your loving kindness, O blessed Theotokos,...!".

Prokeimenon 4

A reader then chants Prokeimenon 4, in tone 6, as follows: the reader chants the Prokeimenon, "In the courts of the blessed will his soul be established!"; the people sing this Prokeimenon ("In the courts of the blessed...!"); the reader chants the verse, "Unto You, O Lord, will I cry! Think no scorn of me, O Lord, my Strength!"; the people again sing the full Prokeimenon; the reader chants the ***first half*** of the Prokeimenon "In the courts of the blessed!"; the people sing the ***second half*** of the Prokeimenon ("Will his soul be established!").

Epistle 4

The reader, after the blessing from the main celebrant, chants the reading for Epistle 4, 1 Corinthians 15:20-29.

"Alleluia!" Verses 4

At the conclusion of the Epistle reading and the blessing from the celebrant, the reader chants, "And with your spirit! Alleluia! Alleluia! Alleluia!" The people sing a *triple* "Alleluia!", in tone 4. The reader chants the verse, "Blessed is the man who fears the Lord!" The people again sing a *triple* "Alleluia!", in tone 4. The reader chants the verse, "His seed will be mighty in the land!" The people again sing a *triple* "Alleluia!", in tone 4.

Gospel 4

The celebrant then chants the reading for Gospel 4, John 6:40-44. The people sing the usual responses.

The Beatitudes

The main celebrant intones the first four verses of the Beatitudes, then the people respond by singing, "Remember us, O Lord, when You come in Your Kingdom!", and after each set of verses.

Theotokion

After the final verse from the Beatitudes ("He who is gone from here and lies in the grave,...!"), the people sing a full "Glory,... now and ever...!", and then a theotokion that begins, "In your womb, without seed, you conceived...!"

Prokeimenon 5

A reader then chants Prokeimenon 3, in tone 6, as follows: the reader chants the Prokeimenon, "Blessed is he whom you have chosen and taken, O Lord!"; the people sing this Prokeimenon ("Blessed is he...!"); the reader chants the verse, "Among the blessed will his soul take up its abode!"; the people again sing the full Prokeimenon; the reader chants the ***first half*** of the Prokeimenon "Blessed is he!"; the people sing the ***second half*** of the Prokeimenon ("Whom you have chosen and taken, O Lord!").

Epistle 5

The reader, after the blessing from the main celebrant, chants the reading for Epistle 5, Romans 14:6-9.

"Alleluia!" Verses 5

At the conclusion of the Epistle reading and the blessing from the celebrant, the reader chants, "And with your spirit! Alleluia! Alleluia! Alleluia!" The people sing a *triple* "Alleluia!", in tone 4. The reader chants the verse, "Blessed is he whom you have chosen and taken, O Lord!" The people again sing a *triple* "Alleluia!", in tone 4. The reader chants the verse, "Among the blessed will his soul take up its abode!" The people again sing a *triple* "Alleluia!", in tone 4.

Gospel 5

The celebrant then chants the reading for Gospel 5, John 6:48-54. The people sing the usual responses.

Psalm 50

After the concluding "Glory!" following the Gospel, a reader chants Psalm 50.

The Kanon

The people now sing the Kanon (the Antiochians do an abbreviated version of what follows). After each ode of the Kanon, a refrain, "Give rest, O Lord, to the soul of Your servant who has fallen asleep!", is chanted by a reader in between troparia chanted by another reader. After the troparia, the main celebrant then chants, "Give rest, O Lord, to the soul of Your servant who has fallen asleep!" The people then sing this same petition ("Give rest, O Lord,…!"). The priest then chants, "Glory to the Father, and to the Son, and to the Holy Spirit!" The people then sing, "Now and ever and unto ages of ages! Amen.", followed by the next ode. The only difference is immediately before ode 9, where, instead of chanting, "Glory to the Father,…!", the main celebrant chants, "Let us bless the Father, and the Son, and the Holy Spirit, the Lord!", to which the people respond by singing the "Now and ever…!".

Unlike the funeral for a lay person, at the funeral for a priest, all eight odes (odes 1, and 3-9) of the Kanon are celebrated. After ode 3, the people sing the Kathisma Hymns, in tone 6 ("Of a truth, all things are vanity,...!", followed by a full "Glory,... now and ever...!", and then the theotokion [in tone 6], "O all-holy Theotokos,...!"). After ode 6, the Kontakion, in tone 6, begins, "With the saints, give rest, O Christ,...!". This is *immediately* followed, with *no* "Glory,... now and ever...!" at all, with the Oikos, in tone 8, beginning, "You, only, are immortal,...!" There is usually a small censing (sanctuary, iconostasis, people) done during the singing of the Kontakion and the Oikos.

The Little Litany

At the conclusion of the Kanon, a Little Litany is celebrated. (The Antiochians *omit* this.)

The Exapostilarion

The Exapostilarion is then celebrated, the text of it being, "Now I am at rest and have found great release, in that I have been translated from corruption to life eternal! Glory to You, O Lord!" This is sung a few times by the people (the Antiochians only sing it once), while verses are chanted in between ("Man is like grass! His days are like the flowers of the field!"; "For, his spirit goes forth from him, and he ceases to be!"; "But, the truth of the Lord abides forever!"). After a full "Glory,... now and ever...!" is chanted, a final verse is chanted, "Now I have chosen the Virgin Theotokos! For Christ, the Redeemer of all mankind, was Born of her! Glory to You, O Lord!".

The Praises

The Praises then follow the Exapostilarion. These are sung by the people in tone 6. After singing the initial verses from Psalm 150, stikhera on the Praises are also sung in tone 6: "Your godly minister,...!"; "Strange is the mystery of death,...!"; "He who lived in godliness,...!". Then, the singing of a full "Glory,... now and ever...!"; then, also in tone 6, the theotokion, "We have come to the knowledge of God...!"

The Lesser Doxology

Following the Praises, the main celebrant chants, "Glory to You, Who have shown us the Light!" A reader then chants the Lesser Doxology, beginning, "Glory to God in the highest, and, on Earth, peace, good will towards men!" However, this is an abbreviated form, ending with, "Continue Your loving-kindness to those who know You!"

Oktoechos Hymns

After the Lesser Doxology, the people sing sets of hymns in each of the eight tones (**Oktoechos**) (the Antiochians **omit** this section). The set for tone 1 begins, "What earthly sweetness remains unmixed with grief?"; then, a reader chants the verse, "The Lord is my Shepherd! I will not want!"; then, the people sing the hymn that begins, "Indeed, O my Savior, You show forth…!"; then, the reader chants a full "Glory,… now and ever…!"; then, the people sing the theotokion, "You have manifested yourself a fervent intercessor…!".

The set for tone 2 begins, "Woe is me! What manner of ordeal…!"; then, the verse, "I called upon the Lord when I was in trouble, and He heard me!"; then, the hymn, "Come, let us all gaze...!"; then, the verse, "Deliver my soul, O Lord, from the mouths of the ungodly!"; then, the hymn, "Farewell, life of vanity!"; then, a full "Glory,... now and ever...!"; then, the theotokion, "O gate impassible,...!".

The set for tone 3 begins, "Lo! Here I lie, my beloved brethren,...!"; then, the verse, "I lift up my eyes to the hills, from where my help comes!"; then, the hymn, "All mortal things are vanity...!"; then, the verse, "The Lord will preserve your going out and your coming in, from this time forth and forevermore!"; then, the hymn, "O men, why do we vex ourselves in vain?"; then, a full "Glory,... now and ever...!"; then, the theotokion, "We have you as a haven of salvation,...!".

The set for tone 4 begins, "Where is earthly predilection?"; then, the verse, "I rejoiced when they said to me, 'Let us go to the house of the Lord!'"; then, the hymn, "Death came like a robber!"; then, a full "Glory,... now and ever...!"; then, the theotokion, "O Virgin, alone pure and undefiled,...!".

The set for tone 5 begins, "I called to mind the prophet,...!"; then, the verse, "Our feet have been standing within your gates, O Jerusalem!"; then, the hymn, "You have said, O Christ,...!"; then, a full

"Glory,... now and ever...!"; then, the theotokion, "We entreat you, as the Mother of God,...!".

The set for tone 6 begins, "Your creating command...!"; then, the verse, "To You I lift up my eyes, O You Who dwell in the Heavens!"; then, the hymn, "With Your own image...!"; then, a full "Glory,... now and ever...!"; then, the theotokion, "We have come to the knowledge of God...!".

The set for tone 7 begins, "When, in the beginning, You created man...!"; then, the verse, "How lovely is Your dwelling place, O Lord of hosts!"; then, the hymn, "Death, which loosed every sorrow,...!"; then, a full "Glory,... now and ever...!"; then, the theotokion, "We faithful, O Theotokos, have you...!".

The set for tone 8 begins, "I weep and I wail when I think upon death,...!"; then, a full "Glory,... now and ever...!"; then, the theotokion, "Your protection, O Virgin Theotokos,...!".

Following this is **another** set of hymns in tone 8: "Measureless is the torment...!"; "The trumpet will thunder forth its sound...!"; and, "Lo! The elements and Heaven and Earth will be changed!"; then, a reader chants, "Glory...Spirit!"; then, a hymn in tone 6: "Come, all, and behold a strange and terrible sight!"; then, the reader chants, "Now and ever...Amen."; then, the theotokion, also in tone 6: "By the prayers of her who Bore You, O Christ,...!".

Psalm 91, the Trisagion Prayers, and the Lord's Prayer

These Oktoechos hymns are followed by a reader chanting Psalm 91, which begins, "It is good to give thanks to the Lord, to sing praises to Your Name, O Most High!" The reader, at the conclusion of the Psalm, then ***immediately*** chants the Trisagion Prayers and the Lord's Prayer (the Antiochians **omit** this section).

Troparia

The people then sing a set of troparia: in tone 5, "Give rest, with the just, O our Savior,...!"; in tone 4, "In the place of Your rest, O Lord,...!"; then, this theotokion, in tone 4: "O holy Mother of the Light Ineffable, with angelic songs honoring, devoutly do we magnify you!" (the Antiochians sing **only** the ***first*** one, in tone 5).

Augmented Litany

The Augmented Litany is then celebrated. It begins with the petition, "Have mercy on us, O Lord,…," which is responded to by the **triple** "Lord, have mercy." This **triple** "Lord, have mercy." is then sung after each subsequent petition. After the petition that begins, "The mercies of God, the Kingdom of Heaven,…!", the people sing, "To You, O Lord." The priest then chants a prayer that begins, "O God of spirits and of all flesh,…!" After the exclamation that begins, "For, You are the Resurrection and the Life and the Repose,…!", the people sing, "Amen."

"The Last Kiss"

As the people come forward to pay their respects to the departed priest, recessional hymns are sung (the Antiochians do these *after* the Dismissal). There is a large set in tone 2: "Come, let us give the last kiss unto the dead!; "What is this parting, O brethren?"; "Now is life's artful triumph…!"; "What is our life like unto?"; "A great weeping and wailing…!"; "As we gaze upon the dead…!"; "Draw near, descendents of Adam,…!";

"When the soul from the body...!"; "Come, O brethren, let us gaze...!"; "Vanity and corruption...!"; "Now are all the body's organs...!"; and, the theotokion, "O you, who save those who fix their hope in you,...!".

A reader then chants, "Glory...Spirit!". The people sing, in tone 6, "As you behold me lying before you...!". The reader then chants, "Now and ever...Amen.". The people then sing, again in tone 6, "He who has been translated...!". This is followed by the singing, in tone 4, of "Today is fulfilled the all-praised word of devout David,...!", followed by the singing, in tone 8, of "Give rest, O Lord Almighty,...!", and "I have vanished from among my kin...!".

The Trisagion Prayers and the Lord's Prayer

A reader then chants the Trisagion Prayers and the Lord's Prayer (***except*** in the Antiochian tradition). As always, after the exclamation, the reader chants, "Amen."

The Dismissal

The Dismissal then follows, with its exclamations and sung responses: "Wisdom! Most Holy Theotokos, save us!" ("More honorable than the Cherubim,...."), and "Glory to You, O Christ, our God and our Hope, glory to You!" (a full "Glory,... now and ever...!", a triple "Lord, have mercy.", and "Father [or, "Master"; or, "Most Blessed Master"], bless!"). The dismissal prayer is intoned, concluding with an exclamation, to which the people *usually* respond with a double "Amen." (or, it *could* be a single "Amen.").

"Memory Eternal!"

The celebrant then takes the censer and, standing on the solea and, facing the Altar, intones "Memory Eternal!" for the newly-departed person. The people then sing, "Memory Eternal!" *three* times, followed by "[His, Her] soul will dwell with the blessed!"

The Prayer of Absolution

After this, the celebrant reads the Final Prayer of Absolution over the body of the departed. The usual sung responses of "Lord, have mercy." and "Amen." occur where appropriate.

The Great Kanon of St Andrew of Crete

This concludes the funeral proper for a priest. At the cemetery, as the body of the priest is brought from the hearse to the grave, the priests concelebrating the funeral sing the odes of the Great Kanon of St Andrew of Crete, from Great Lent (*except* in the Antiochian tradition).

Prayers and Hymns

At the gravesite, a reader chants the Trisagion Prayers and the Lord's Prayer. After the exclamation and the "Amen.", the people sing the troparia, "In the place of Your rest, O Lord,…!"; "Glory…Spirit!"; "You are the God Who descended into hell…!"; "Now and ever…Amen."; "O Virgin, alone, pure, and blameless,...!". This is followed by the Augmented Litany, with its petitions, the Dismissal, and the singing of "Memory Eternal!"

• — • — •

As you can see, the funeral for a priest is **much** longer and expanded than that for a lay person. Again, **many** of these elements are shortened or omitted entirely. As always, the main celebrant (whether a bishop or a presiding priest) will determine which liturgical elements of this expanded funeral will or will not be included in the funeral service.

C. FUNERAL FOR A CHILD

The order for the funeral for a child, per the service books, is as follows.[8] Basically, it is the same

---

[8] Hapgood, pp. 424-434.

service as the funeral for an adult lay person,[9] with some slight modifications.

Prayers and Litanies During the Kanon

After the chanting of Psalm 90, when the Kanon is celebrated, instead of chanting, "Give rest, O Lord, to the soul of Your servant who has fallen asleep!", the main celebrant chants, "Give rest to the child, O Lord!" **Therefore**, the people, in response, would sing **this same** replacement phrase, "Give rest to the child, O Lord!".

In the Greek practice, the **only** petition for children two years and younger is, "Let us pray to the Lord!", and the usual petitions for children three to seven years old. Also, instead of the usual prayer, "O God of spirits and all flesh...!", a special prayer is chanted, beginning, "O Lord, Who guard the children in this life and in the life to come...For, the Kingdom of Heaven is Yours alone, and to You we send up glory,...!".

Unlike the funeral for an adult, the priest would most likely chant the Little Litany that is called for between the odes of the Kanon (**except** in the

---

[9] Cf., above, pp. 387-406.

Antiochian tradition). This is because there are specific prayers here dealing with the death of a child. For example, at the Little Litany after Ode 3, the prayer of the priest says, "O Lord, Jesus Christ our God, Who have promised to bestow the Kingdom of Heaven upon them who have been born of water and the Spirit, and, in spotlessness of life, have been translated to You, and have said, 'Let the little children come to Me! For, of such is the Kingdom of Heaven!': We humbly entreat You, that You will give to Your servant, the spotless child, [name], now departed from us, the inheritance of Your Kingdom, according to Your unfailing promise! And grant that we may continue in innocency of living, and make a Christian ending of our life, and attain to an abode in the heavenly mansions, with all Your saints! For, You are the Resurrection, and the Life, and the Repose of all Your servants, and of Your servant, this child, [name], now taken from us, O Christ our God, and to You we ascribe glory, together with Your Father, Who is from everlasting, and Your all-Holy, good, and life-creating Spirit, now and ever and unto ages of ages!"

Furthermore, the troparia chanted for each ode of the Kanon differ from those for the funeral for an adult. At Ode 1, the first troparion begins, "O Word of God, Who humbled Yourself even to the flesh, and were graciously pleased to become a

Babe, yet without change...!" The first troparion of Ode 3 begins, "O Word, all perfect, Who, as Perfect Child, manifested Yourself, You have translated unto Yourself this child, of stature unfulfilled!" Again, subsequent odes also contain troparia dealing with children and childhood, as such. Also, as with the funeral for an adult, all eight odes of the Kanon (odes 1, and 3-9) are called for. Yet, as is the practice in **most** parishes, **only** odes 1, 3, 6, and 9 are **usually** celebrated. As always, check with the main celebrant for the specifics of the local practice.

The Exapostilarion

Once the Kanon is completed and the last Little Litany is celebrated, the people sing the Exapostilarion: "Now, I am at rest, and have found great release! For, I have been translated from corruption, and have passed over into life! Glory to You, O Lord!" This is sung a few times (for the Antiochians, **once**), with a reader chanting the interspersing verses: "Man is as the grass! His days are like the flowers of the field!"; "For, his spirit goes forth from him, and he ceases to be!"; "But, the truth of the Lord endures forever!"; "Glory,... now and ever...!"; "Now, I have chosen the Virgin

Theotokos! For, Christ, the Redeemer of all mankind, was Born of her! Glory to You, O Lord!".

The Trisagion and the Prokeimenon

This is followed by the exclamation that precedes the Trisagion ("For, You are holy, O Lord our God, Who rest in the saints,...!"), and, after singing the "Amen.", the people sing the Trisagion (***except*** in the Antiochian tradition). A reader goes and gets a blessing from the priest to chant the Prokeimenon, the Epistle, and the "Alleluia!" verses.

The Prokeimenon is then chanted in the 6th tone. The reader chants (for the Antiochians, ***once***), "Blessed is the way in which you will walk today, O soul! For, a place of rest is prepared for you!" The people then sing this full Prokeimenon. The reader then chants the verse, "Return to your rest, O my soul! For, the Lord has dealt bountifully with you!" The people then again sing the full Prokeimenon. The reader then chants the ***first half*** of the Prokeimenon, "Blessed is the way in which you will walk today, O soul!", and the people sing the ***second half*** of the Prokeimenon, "For, a place of rest is prepared for you!".

The Epistle and the "Alleluia!" Verses

The Epistle reading is then chanted, which is from 1 Corinthians 15:39-46 (for the **Byzantines**, Romans 6:9-11). At the conclusion of the reading, when the priest blesses the reader and chants, "Peace be with you, Reader!", the reader responds, "And with your spirit! Alleluia! Alleluia! Alleluia!" The people then sing a *triple* "Alleluia!" The reader chants the verse, "Blessed is [he, she] whom you have chosen and taken, O Lord!" The people then again sing a *triple* "Alleluia!" The reader chants the verse, "Among the blessed will [his, her] soul take up its abode!" The people then sing a final *triple* "Alleluia!".

The Gospel

The Gospel reading, from John 6:35-40 (for the **Byzantines**, Luke 19), is then chanted by the main celebrant. The people sing the usual responses.

The Last Kiss Stikhera

The Gospel reading is *immediately* followed by the people giving the last kiss to the departed child. During this time, special stikhera are sung: in tone 8, "Who would not weep, my child,…!" and "Death is a release for babes!"; "Glory…Spirit!"; in tone 6, "Painful to Adam of old in Eden…!"; "Now and ever…Amen."; again, in tone 6, the theotokion, "You, who are the consolation of mourners,…!". (The Antiochians often *omit* this section.).

In the Greek practice, the only two troparia at this point begin as follows: "Who would not lament, O my child,…?" and "Who, then, would not sigh, O my child,…?".

The Trisagion Prayers, the Lord's Prayer, and the Concluding Troparia

A reader then chants the Trisagion Prayers and the Lord's Prayer. After the exclamation and the responding "Amen.", the people sing the concluding troparia: "With the souls of the righteous,…!"; "In the place of Your rest, O Lord,…!"; "Glory…Spirit!"; "You are the God Who descended…!"; "Now and ever...Amen!"; "O Virgin, alone, pure, and blameless,...!". (The Antiochians *omit* this section.)

Litany for the Departed

The Litany for the Departed is then celebrated. For each petition, the people sing a *triple* "Lord, have mercy.". At the petition, "The mercies of God, the Kingdom of Heaven,...!", the people sing, "Grant it, O Lord.". The deacon then chants, "Let us pray to the Lord.", and the people sing a *single* "Lord, have mercy.". The priest then chants a prayer. After the exclamation, the people sing, "Amen.".

The Dismissal and "Memory Eternal!"

This is followed by the Dismissal. At the exclamation, "Wisdom! Most holy Theotokos, save us!", the people sing, "More honorable...!". After the exclamation, "Glory to You, O Christ, our God and our hope, glory to You!", the people sing a full "Glory,...now and ever...!", a *triple* "Lord, have mercy.", and then, "Father, bless!" (or, if a bishop is serving, "Master, bless!"; or, if the Metropolitan is serving, "Most blessed Master, bless!"). The dismissal prayer is chanted, and the people **usually** sing a **double** "Amen." ("Amen. Amen.").

After this, "Memory Eternal!" is intoned for the newly-departed child. The people sing "Memory Eternal!" **three** times, and then conclude with, "[His, Her] soul will dwell with the blessed!".

Concluding Prayer

The deacon then intones, "Let us pray to the Lord.", and the people sing, "Lord, have mercy." The priest then chants a concluding prayer that begins, "O Lord, Who guard little children in this present life,…!". After the exclamation, "For, to You are due all glory, honor, and worship, with the Father and the Holy Spirit, now and ever and unto ages of ages!", the people sing, "Amen." (The Antiochians have **already** done this **earlier**.)

The procession of the child's body from the church to the hearse is accompanied with the usual singing of the processional "Holy God!", as is the procession, at the cemetery, of the casket from the hearse to the grave site. The rite of the interment for the child is the same as that for an adult lay person.[10]

D. FUNERAL FOR BRIGHT WEEK

There are a few specific liturgical elements for a funeral during Bright Week, immediately following Pascha.[11]

Wherever the body of the newly-departed person is before being brought to the church (usually at a funeral home), the priest gives the opening doxology, "Blessed is our God,…!", and the people sing, "Amen." The priest then chants the usual Paschal verses, as he would at any church service during Bright Week: "Let God arise!…"; "As smoke vanishes, so, let them vanish,…!"; "So, the sinners will perish before the Face of God!"; "This is the day that the Lord has made!…"; "Glory…Spirit!"; "Now and ever…Amen!". In between these verses, the people joyously sing the troparion of Pascha: "Christ is Risen from the dead, trampling down death by

---

[10] Cf. "E. Interment", below, pp. 451-453.
[11] Hapgood, pp. 435-436.

death, and, upon those in the tombs, bestowing life!" The deacon, priest, and people then celebrate the customary Litany for the Departed.

In the **Greek** practice, the service is as follows: "Blessed is our God…!"; "Amen."; the Paschal troparion three times (once by the priest, twice by the people); Litany for the Departed; the Paschal Kanon (Katavasia only), each ode followed by the Paschal troparion three times (fast version) and "Jesus, having Arisen from the grave as He foretold,…!" (odes 1, 3-9, with no Hypakoe, Kontakion, Oikos, or litanies); Paschal Exapostilarion twice; Epistle and Gospel for the day (**not** for the departed); Litany for the Departed; Dismissal; "Memory Eternal" three times; Sermon; the Last Kiss (in tone 5: "Glory,…now and ever…!", "This is the day of resurrection! Let us be illumined, O people!"); procession with the casket to the back of the church while singing the Paschal troparion, stopping at the back of the church as the priest intones, "For, You are the Resurrection,…!" and the Paschal troparion once as the casket is placed in the hearse.

Whenever the body of the newly-departed person is being moved, either from the funeral home to the hearse, or from the hearse to the church, instead of singing the usual processional "Holy God!", the odes of the Pascha Kanon are sung

without the accompanying troparia (***instead*** of the Kanon, the Byzantines sing, "Christ is Risen!").

When the body arrives in the center of the church, the priest performs the usual funeral censing with the censer, while the odes of the Paschal Kanon are sung. (The Antiochians begin with a ***triple*** "Christ is Risen!": once by the priest, twice by the people.) Ode 3 is followed by a Little Litany, and then, ***immediately***, the singing of the Hypakoe of Pascha: "Before the dawn, Mary and the women came,…!". Ode 6 is also followed by a Little Litany, and then, ***immediately***, the Kontakion ("With the saints give rest…!") and the Oikos ("You, only, are immortal,…!").

At the time of the celebration of the Trisagion, instead of singing, "Holy God!", the people sing, "As Many As Have Been Baptized!". The Epistle is ***not*** the usual one from 1 Thessalonians 4:13-17 (***except*** for the Antiochians), ***but*** the daily Epistle reading called for in the calendar from the Book of Acts! The "Alleluia!" is sung in tone 2. The Gospel reading is from the Paschal Gospel of St John the Theologian.

Following the Gospel, the people sing the Post-Gospel Stikhera, "Having beheld the Resurrection of Christ,…!" (for the ***Antiochians***, the Gospel is followed by odes 7-9 of the Kanon).

After the entire Kanon element concludes, the Exapostilarion of Pascha is sung ("In the flesh, You fell asleep as a mortal Man,…!"), followed by the tone 5 singing of "Blessed are You, O Lord! Teach me Your statutes!", with the accompanying verses, and then the singing of "Let God Arise!".

The concluding Litany for the Departed is celebrated, as usual, as is the rest of the funeral.

When the celebrant intones the "Memory Eternal!", instead of the people singing "Memory Eternal!", they sing the troparion of Pascha: "Christ is Risen from the dead, trampling down death by death, and, upon those in the tombs, bestowing life!" (***except*** for the Antiochians, who do the Paschal Kanon here).

When the body is processed out of the church to the hearse, as well as, at the cemetery, when the body is processed from the hearse to the grave site, instead of singing the usual processional "Holy God!", the people sing the troparion of Pascha: "Christ is Risen from the dead, trampling down death by death, and, upon those in the tombs, bestowing life!" Again, at the conclusion of the interment, when the celebrant intones the "Memory Eternal!", instead of the people singing "Memory Eternal!", they sing the troparion of Pascha: "Christ is Risen from the dead, trampling down death by death, and, upon those in the tombs, bestowing life!"

E. INTERMENT

The body of the newly-departed is then taken to the cemetery for burial. The order for the interment is as follows.[12]

Processional "Holy God!"

At the cemetery, as the casket containing the body of the newly-departed is brought from the hearse to the grave site, the singers again lead the procession, singing the *slow* Processional "Holy God!" ("Holy God! Holy Mighty! Holy Immortal! Have mercy on us!") **repeatedly** until the casket is placed at the top of the grave. **_Note:_** Even though the service books call for the singing of the full Trisagion Prayers and the Lord's Prayer, this is **_usually_ _not_** done (**except** in the Byzantine tradition).

---

[12] Hapgood, pp. 392-393.

Troparia

At the grave site, with all the people gathered around, the priest intones the doxology, "Blessed is our God, always now and ever and unto ages of ages!" The people sing, "Amen.", and then the series of troparia: "With the souls of the righteous departed,...!"; "In the place of Your rest, O Lord,...!"; "Glory...Spirit!"; "You are the God Who descended...!"; "Now and ever...Amen."; "O Virgin, alone, pure and blameless,...!". All of this is *not* done in the Greek practice.

Augmented Litany

The Augmented Litany is then celebrated. It begins with the petition, "Have mercy on us, O Lord,...," which is responded to by the *triple* "Lord, have mercy." This *triple* "Lord, have mercy." is then sung after each subsequent petition. After the petition that begins, "The mercies of God, the Kingdom of Heaven,...!", the people sing, "To You, O Lord." The priest then chants a prayer that begins, "O God of spirits and of all flesh,...!" After the exclamation that begins, "For, You are the

Resurrection and the Life and the Repose,…!", the people sing, "Amen."

The Dismissal

The Dismissal then follows, with its exclamations and sung responses: "Wisdom! Most Holy Theotokos, save us!" ("More honorable than the Cherubim,…."), and "Glory to You, O Christ, our God and our Hope, glory to You!" (a full "Glory,… now and ever…!", a triple "Lord, have mercy.", and "Father [or, "Master"; or, "Most Blessed Master"], bless!"). The dismissal prayer is intoned, concluding with an exclamation, to which the people **usually** respond with a double "Amen." (or, it **could** be a single "Amen.").

"Memory Eternal!"

The celebrant then takes the censer and, standing on the solea and, standing over the grave, intones "Memory Eternal!" for the newly-departed person. The people then sing, "Memory Eternal!" **three** times, followed by "[His, Her] soul will dwell with the blessed!"

F. MEMORIAL

The service of Memorial is known in the Slavic world as "Panikhida," which literally means, "Little Vigil." Therefore, since it really does **not** have a significant meaning to death, funerals, or memorials, we will refer to it here as the "Memorial" (this service is **not** celebrated by the Byzantines; the Greeks will at times serve a Trisagion service, as done at the cemetery for the interment). The order of the service is as follows.[13]

Doxology, the Trisagion Prayers, and the Lord's Prayer

The service begins with the doxology, "Blessed is our God!" !" The **people** respond by **singing**, "Amen.", then sing the Trisagion ("Holy God! Holy Mighty! Holy Immortal! Have mercy on us!") **three** times. A **reader** then reads the Trisagion Prayers ("O Most Holy Trinity, have mercy on us!"; a **triple** "Lord, have mercy."; and a full "Glory,... now and ever...!"),

---

[13] Hapgood, pp. 437-453.

followed by the Lord's Prayer. After the exclamation, "For, Yours are the Kingdom, and the power, and the glory,...!", the reader chants, "Amen.", and then a full "Come, let us worship God, our King!...".

Psalm 90

The reader then *immediately* chants Psalm 90 ("He who dwells in the shelter of the Most High,...!"). At the conclusion of the Psalm, the reader chants a full "Glory,... now and ever...!", and "Alleluia! Alleluia! Alleluia! Glory to You, O God!" *three* times.

[The Great Litany]

Although the service books call for the Great Litany to be celebrated here, in *most* parishes, this is *omitted*.

"Alleluia!" and Verses and Troparia

The deacon then chants, "Alleluia! Alleluia! Alleluia! Blessed [is he, is she, are they] whom you have chosen and taken, O Lord!" The people then sing a **triple** "Alleluia!" in tone 8. The deacon then chants the verse, "[His, Her, Their] remembrance is from generation to generation!" The people again sing a **triple** "Alleluia!" in tone 8. The deacon then chants the verse, "[His, Her, Their] soul[s] will dwell with the blessed!" The people sing a final **triple** "Alleluia!" in tone 8.

The people then sing the troparia in tone 8: "You, only Creator,…!"; "Glory,… now and ever…!"; "We have you as a wall and a haven…!".

[Psalm 118 and the Litany for the Departed]

At this point, the service books call for the following to be celebrated, even though it is omitted in most parishes, who usually go immediately from "We have you as a wall and a haven…!" to the singing of "Blessed are You, O Lord! Teach me Your statutes!"

Psalm 118 is celebrated in two sections, or stases. The first one goes from verse 1 through verse 93, and the second goes from verse 94 through the end (verse 176). In between these two stases is celebrated a Litany for the Departed.

Again, this entire liturgical element is **usually omitted** in the Memorial in **most** parishes.

"Blessed are You, O Lord!" and Stikhera

After the conclusion of "We have you as a wall and a haven…!", the people **immediately** sing the refrain, "Blessed are You, O Lord! Teach me Your statutes!", and the subsequent stikhera. These conclude with the singing of, "Alleluia! Alleluia! Alleluia! Glory to You, O God!" **three** times. Usually, in **most** parishes, there is a great censing of the church done during the singing of this refrain and these stikhera.

The Little Litany

At this point, a Little Litany *is* celebrated in most parishes. The order for a Little Litany is as follows.

>**Deacon:** Again and again, in peace, let us pray to the Lord.
>
>**People:** Lord, have mercy.
>
>**Deacon:** Furthermore, we pray for the soul of the servant of God, _____, departed this life, that [he, she] may be pardoned all of [his, her] sins, both voluntary and involuntary.
>
>**People:** Lord, have mercy.
>
>**Deacon:** That the Lord our God may establish [his, her] soul where the just repose.
>
>**People:** Lord, have mercy.
>
>**Deacon:** The mercies of God, the Kingdom of Heaven, and the remission of [his, her] sins, let us entreat of Christ, our immortal King and God.
>
>**People:** Grant it, O Lord.

Deacon:	Let us pray to the Lord.
People:	Lord, have mercy.

There follows then a prayer chanted by the priest that begins, "O God of spirits and of all flesh,…!", concluding with the exclamation, "For, You are the Resurrection, and the Life, and the Repose of Your servant,…!" The people then respond with "Amen." **Note**: In **many** parishes, the prayer that begins, "O God of spirits and of all flesh,…!" is **omitted**, and **only** the concluding exclamation, "For, You are the Resurrection, and the Life, and the Repose of Your servant,…!" is chanted.

Kathisma Hymns

The people then sing a set of Kathisma Hymns, in tone 5. They are: "Give rest with the just, O our Savior…!"; a full "Glory,… now and ever…!"; and "O Christ our God, from a Virgin, You shone forth to the world,…!"

[Psalm 50]

At this point, the service books call for a reader to chant Psalm 50 ("Have mercy on me, O God, according to Your steadfast love,...!"). In **many** parishes, however, this is **omitted**. The decision, as always, rests with the main celebrant.

The Kanon

The Kanon is now celebrated. Even though the service books call for the celebration of all of the odes (odes 1, 3-9), in **almost all** parishes only odes 1, 3, 6, and 9 are celebrated. Therefore, that is what is presented here. This Kanon is in tone 6.

Also, in most parishes, the order for celebrating these odes is as follows: the ode is sung, then the priest chants, "Give rest, O Lord, to the soul of Your servant who has fallen asleep!" The people then sing this same petition ("Give rest, O Lord,...!"). The priest then chants, "Glory to the Father, and to the Son, and to the Holy Spirit!" The people then sing, "Now and ever and unto ages of ages! Amen.", followed by the next ode. **However**, **many** parishes are starting to revive the ancient practice of restoring some, if not all, of the troparia that are chanted by a reader between the ode and the priest intoning, "Give rest, O Lord,…!" Again, as in all other liturgical matters, the priest (or, main celebrant) makes that decision.

Ode 1 begins with, "When Israel passed on foot, over the sea,…!" If the local practice is to chant the troparia, the reader then does so at this point. In either case, the priest then chants, "Give rest, O Lord,…!", and the people sing the same. The priest chants, "Glory…Spirit!" The people sing, "Now and ever…Amen."

Ode 3 begins with, "There is none so holy as You, O Lord my God,…!" If the local practice is to chant the troparia, the reader then does so at this point. In either case, the priest then chants, "Give rest, O Lord,…!", and the people sing the same. The priest chants, "Glory…Spirit!" The people sing, "Now and ever…Amen."

At this point, the service books call for the singing of Kathisma Hymns, in tone 6 ("Of a truth, all things are vanity,…!", followed by a full "Glory,… now and ever…!", and then the theotokion [in tone 6], "O all-holy Theotokos,…!"). **However**, in **most** parishes, this is **omitted**.

Ode 6 begins with, "Beholding the sea of life, surging with the storm of temptation,…!" If the local practice is to chant the troparia, the reader then does so at this point. In either case, the priest then chants, "Give rest, O Lord,...!", and the people sing the same. The priest chants, "Glory...Spirit!" The people sing, "Now and ever...Amen."

At this point, the Kontakion and Oikos **are** celebrated in most parishes. The Kontakion, in tone 6, begins, "With the saints, give rest, O Christ,...!". This is **immediately** followed, with **no** "Glory,... now and ever...!" at all, with the Oikos, in tone 8, beginning, "You, only, are immortal,...!" There is usually a small censing (sanctuary, iconostasis, people) done during the singing of the Kontakion and the Oikos. If the local practice is to chant the troparia, the reader then does so at this point. In either case, the priest then chants, "Give rest, O Lord,...!", and the people sing the same. The priest chants, "Let us bless the Father, and the Son, and the Holy Spirit, the Lord!" The people sing, "Now and ever...Amen."

Ode 9 begins with, "It is not possible for men to see God,...!" If the local practice is to chant the troparia, the reader then does so at this point.

For Orthodox Christians slain on the field of battle, the troparia chanted in between the odes are different than for a regular adult lay person.[14]

Little Litany

Following the Kanon, a Little Litany is celebrated.

The Trisagion Prayers and the Lord's Prayer

After the Little Litany, a reader chants the Trisagion Prayers and the Lord's Prayer. After the exclamation ("For, Yours are the Kingdom, and the power, and the glory,…!"), the reader chants the "Amen.".

Troparia for the Departed

Following the Lord's Prayer, the people sing a set of troparia. The first one begins, "With the souls

---

[14] Hapgood, pp. 449-453.

of the righteous departed,…!"; then, "Glory…Spirit!"; then, "You are the God Who descended…!"; then, "Now and ever…Amen."; then, "O Virgin, alone, pure and blameless,…!"

Litany for the Departed

The Litany for the Departed is then celebrated. It begins with the petition, "Have mercy on us, O Lord,…," which is responded to by the triple "Lord, have mercy." This triple "Lord, have mercy." is then sung after each subsequent petition. After the petition that begins, "The mercies of God, the Kingdom of Heaven,…!", the people sing, "To You, O Lord." The priest then chants a prayer that begins, "O God of spirits and of all flesh,…!" After the exclamation that begins, "For, You are the Resurrection and the Life and the Repose,…!", the people sing, "Amen."

The Dismissal

The Dismissal then follows, with its exclamations and sung responses: "Wisdom! Most Holy Theotokos, save us!" ("More honorable than the Cherubim,…."), and "Glory to You, O Christ, our God and our Hope, glory to You!" (a full "Glory,… now and ever…!", a **triple** "Lord, have mercy.", and "Father [or, "Master"; or, "Most Blessed Master"], bless!"). The dismissal prayer is intoned, concluding with an exclamation, to which the people **usually** respond with a double "Amen." (or, it **could** be a single "Amen.").

"Memory Eternal!"

The celebrant then takes the censer and, standing on the solea and, facing the Altar, intones "Memory Eternal!" for the newly-departed person. The people then sing, "Memory Eternal!" **three** times, followed by "[His, Her] soul will dwell with the blessed!"

7
LENTEN SERVICES

A. PRE – LENTEN WEEKS

There is a set of pre-Lenten weeks that prepare us for the upcoming Great Fast. The first of these is the Sunday of Zacchaeus, the only liturgical element being the troparion in tone 8 that begins, "As salvation came to the house of Zacchaeus at Your entrance, O Christ,…!". (In the Greek practice, the *last two* pre-Lenten Sundays are those of Zacchaeus and the Sunday of the Syro-Phoenician Woman.)

The Sunday of the Publican and the Pharisee

The following weekend contains the Sunday of the Publican and the Pharisee. Here, the Church begins the use of the liturgical book known as ***The Lenten Triodion***. The word "triodion" means "three odes," and refers to the fact that, with the Daily Lenten Matins being celebrated during this season, there are only three odes to the Kanon. This book,

The Lenten Triodion, contains the specifics for the Lenten services from the Sunday of the Publican and the Pharisee through the Nocturns of Holy Saturday, celebrated right before midnight on Pascha and immediately preceding the celebration of Paschal Matins.

The Sunday of the Publican and the Pharisee contains the following liturgical elements.[15] At Resurrectional Vespers on Saturday evening, there are 7 stikhera on "Lord, I Call Upon You" sung in the tone of the week, followed by 2 stikhera in tone 1: "Brothers, let us not pray like the Pharisee!...", and "The Pharisee went up to the temple with a proud and empty heart!". (In the Byzantine tradition, there are **10** stikhera, the **first** one being done **twice**.)The "Glory" stikheron is in tone 8 and begins, "I know the value of tears, O almighty Lord!". The "Now and ever" stikheron is the Dogmatikon in the tone of the week. The penitential hymn, "Open the Doors of Repentance!" is sung after the celebration of the Matins Gospel if this is read at Great Vespers in parishes where no Matins is celebrated. This will continue throughout the entire Great Lent. The Apostikha stikhera are taken from the tone of the week, and the special stikheron at the "Glory,... now

---

[15] Mother Mary and Ware, Archimandrite Kallistos, *The Lenten Triodion*, Faber and Faber, London and Boston, 1978 (hereafter referred to as "*Triodion*"), pp. 99-111.

and ever...!", in tone 5, begins, "The weight of my transgressions burdens my eyes!". There is *no* special troparion for this Sunday, but there *is* a special kontakion, in tone 4, that begins, "Let us flee from the pride of the Pharisee!". This kontakion will be sung after Ode 6 of the Kanon at Matins and at its appropriate place in the Divine Liturgy. (In the Greek tradition, the kontakion is chanted by a reader *prior* to the celebration of the odes of the Kanon.)

The Sunday of the Prodigal Son

The following weekend is the Sunday of the Prodigal Son.[16] Once again, at Resurrectional Vespers, there are 7 stikhera in the tone of the week on "Lord, I Call Upon You!", followed by 2 stikhera in tone 1: "Rich and fertile was the Earth allotted to us!", and, "Brothers, our purpose is to know the power of God's goodness!". (Again, in the Byzantine tradition, the *first* stikheron is sung *twice*, making a total of *10* stikhera.) The "Glory" stikheron is in tone 2: "What great blessings have I forsaken, wretch that I am?". The "Now and ever" stikheron is the Dogmatikon in the tone of the week. If Resurrectional Matins *is* celebrated, the people sing

---

[16] Ibid, pp. 112-123.

the special hymn, "By the Waters of Babylon!" after the Polyeleos (**except** in the Greek practice, where this hymn is done **only** in monasteries). If Resurrectional Matins is **not** celebrated, in **most** parishes, during Resurrectional Vespers, after the Evening Prokeimenon, the people sing the special hymn, "By the Waters of Babylon!". This will occur only twice more, on the following two weekends (The Sunday of the Last Judgment and Forgiveness Sunday). Again, the stikhera on the Apostikha are all sung in the tone of the week. The "Glory" stikheron is in tone 6: "I, a wretched man, hide my face in shame!", and this is followed by the Theotokion, **also in tone 6**: "My Maker and Redeemer, Christ the Lord,…!". Once again, there is **no** special troparion for this Sunday, but the special kontakion is in tone 3: "I have recklessly forgotten Your glory, O Father!".

The Saturday for the Departed

On the following weekend, the Saturday is a special Saturday for the Departed.[17] This is **not always** celebrated in the majority of parishes. At Vespers on Friday evening (in the Greek practice,

---

[17] Ibid, pp. 124-141 and pp. 142-149.

Daily Lenten Vespers is celebrated here), at "Lord, I Call!", 6 stikhera are sung, 3 for the martyrs in the tone of the week (therefore, they are varied; cf. ***The Triodion***, pp. 142-149), and 3 for the departed, in tone 8: "O faithful, remembering today, by name,…!", "By Your own Blood, O Savior,…!", and "Through Your Arising from the dead, O Christ,…!". (The Antiochians do **9** stikhera total, ***repeating*** the ***first three*** once each.) The "Glory!" stikheron is in tone 8: "I weep and I wail when I think upon death,…!", and is followed by the Dogmatikon in the tone of the week (***except*** for the Antiochians, who do a straight-through "Glory,…now and ever…!", followed by "I weep and I wail…!"). The special Prokeimenon is in tone 8: "Blessed are they whom You have chosen and taken, O Lord!", with its accompanying verse, "Their remembrance is from generation to generation!". In the Greek practice, this Prokeimenon is replaced with the ***triple*** chanting of "Alleluia!", with two interspersed verses: "Blest are they whom You have chosen and taken, O Lord!" and "Their remembrance is from generation to generation!". At the Apostikha, there is one stikheron for the martyrs and two for the departed, all in the tone of the week (with the interspersed verses, "Blessed are they whom You have chosen and taken, O Lord!" and "Their remembrance is from generation to generation!"). The "Glory!" stikheron is in tone 6: "Your creative ordinance…!", and the theotokion is also in tone 6: "At the intercession of the Mother who bore You, O Christ,…!" (the Antiochians do a straight-through "Glory,…now and ever…!", followed by "Your creative ordinance…!"). In the Greek practice, there are **four** stikhera for the martyrs, followed by a "***split***" "Glory,…now and ever…!" with **two** stikhera. The verses in between the stikhera for the martyrs in this tradition are as follows: "God is wonderful in His saints, the God of Israel!", "The Lord has been marvelous in His saints who are on the Earth! He has worked all His desires in them!", and "The righteous called, and the Lord heard them!". The troparion for the departed is in tone 8: "You, only Creator,…!", followed by "Glory…Spirit!", "For, they have placed their trust in You,…!", "Now and ever…Amen!", and "We have you as a wall and a haven…!", **all** of this in tone 8. In the Greek practice, **Matins** is done **the following morning**, and a full **Memorial service usually follows the evening Vespers**.

At Matins, instead of singing, "God is the Lord!", this is replaced with the Lenten singing of "Alleluia!" in tone 8 and accompanying verses. The singing of "Blessed are You, O Lord! Teach me Your statutes!" in tone 5 is celebrated, just as it is at funerals and memorials. The Kanon is a special one that is specific to the departed.

At Matins in the Greek tradition, the "Alleluia!" and accompanying verses are the same as mentioned; for the Kathisma Hymns, three are done in the tone of the first stikheron, followed by "Glory…Spirit!", a hymn for the departed, "Now and ever…!", and another hymn. The Kathisma Hymns are followed by the singing of "Blessed are You, O Lord! Teach me Your statutes!" in tone 5; another Kathisma Hymn for the departed, "Glory…Spirit!", the repeating of "…and every sin committed in knowledge or in ignorance, O Lover of mankind!", "Now and ever…!", and the Theotokion in the same tone. This is followed by Psalm 50 and the Kontakion and Oikos for the departed, the Synaxarion with special verses added for the departed, special Kanon odes in tone 8, and three Exapostilaria for the departed. On the Praises, there are four stikhera for the departed, followed by "Glory…Spirit!", an idiomelon in tone 2, "As a flower withers…!", "Now and ever…!", and the special Theotokion, "Rejoice, Mary Theotokos, the temple that will never be destroyed!". At the Apostikha, there are three stikhera for the martyrs, "Glory…Spirit!", an idiomelon in tone 2 for the departed, "Now and ever…!", and a special Theotokion in tone 2, "You are the God, Who in wisdom…!". The Apolytikion for the departed follows the Trisagion Prayers.

At the Divine Liturgy, the troparia from Vespers are taken ("You, only Creator,...!", "For, they have placed their trust in You,...!", "We have you as a wall and a haven...!") in tone 8, along with the kontakion, in tone 6, "With the saints give rest,...!". The Prokeimenon is in tone 6: "Their souls will dwell with the blessed!", and its accompanying verse, "To You, O Lord, I lift up my soul! O my God, in You I trust!" The two Epistle readings taken are from 1 Corinthians 10:23-28 and 1 Thessalonians 4:13-17. The "Alleluia!" (the Antiochians **only** take **one** Epistle reading, the one from 1 Thessalonians).

This Divine Liturgy in the **Greek** tradition is as follows: it is celebrated as a daily Divine Liturgy, meaning that the three antiphons are taken from the Psalms that would be used for any weekday Liturgy. The Apolytikion for the departed is used as the Third Antiphon. After "Come, Let Us Worship!", the Apolytikion for the departed is sung a second time, followed by the troparion for the patron saint of the parish where the Liturgy is being celebrated, followed by the Kontakion for the departed. The Epistle for the departed is celebrated, followed by the Gospel reading for the day. The Koinonikon is "Blest are they whom You have chosen and taken, O Lord!". After the Prayer Before the Ambo, a Memorial for the departed is celebrated, with special inserts for a general commemoration of all the departed, with the Liturgy Dismissal following the triple singing of "Memory Eternal!". In the Greek tradition, there are only three Memorial Liturgies served during the Lenten season: the Saturday before Meatfare Sunday, the Saturday before Forgiveness/Cheesefare Sunday, and the Saturday of St. Theodore the Tyro. After that, there are no further Saturday Liturgies until Lazarus Saturday.

The Sunday of the Last Judgment

The next weekend contains the Sunday of the Last Judgment.[18] At "Lord, I Call!" at Vespers, there are 6 stikhera in the tone of the week, followed by 4 stikhera for the Last Judgment, in tone 6: "O righteous Judge of all mankind,…!", "The books will be opened and the works of all men laid bare!", "The trumpets will sound and the graves will be opened!", and "I shudder in terror when I think of that dreadful day!". The "Glory!" stikheron is in tone 8: "When the thrones are set in place and the books are opened,…!", followed by the Dogmatikon in the tone of the week. The Apostikha contains the stikhera in the tone of the week. The "Glory!" stikheron is in tone 8: "Woe to you, O my darkened soul!",

---

[18] Ibid, pp. 150-167.

followed by the theotokion, also in tone 8: "O unwedded Virgin,...!". Once again, there is **no** troparion for this weekend, but the special kontakion is in tone 1: "When You, O God, will come to Earth in glory,...!"

At the Divine Liturgy, there is a special Prokeimenon, in tone 3: "Great is our Lord, and abundant in power! His understanding is beyond measure!", with the accompanying verse, "Praise the Lord! For, it is good to sing praises to our God!" (The **Byzantines** take a Prokeimenon from tone 2, "The Lord is my Strength and my Song!...!"). The Epistle reading is 1 Corinthians 8:8-9:2. The "Alleluia!" verses are as follows: For the Antiochians: in tone 8: "Come, let us sing with joy to the Lord!", and "Let us come before His presence with thanksgiving!"; for the Greeks: in tone 2: "May the Lord hear you on the day of trouble! The Name of the God of Jacob protect you!", and "Save the king, O Lord, and hear us on the day we call!".

The Expulsion of Adam and Eve from Paradise

The last weekend before the beginning of Great Lent includes the Expulsion of Adam and Eve from Paradise.[19] At "Lord, I Call!" at Vespers, there are 6 stikhera taken in the tone of the week, and then 4 stikhera, in tone 6, for the Expulsion of Adam and Eve: "The Lord took a handful of dust from the Earth!", "When the enemy tempted me,...!", "O Paradise, garden of delight and beauty,...!", and "Adam was driven from Paradise through disobedience!". The "Glory!" stikheron is also in tone 6: "Adam sat before the gates of Eden,...!", followed by the Dogmatikon in the tone of the week. The Apostikha contains stikhera in the tone of the week. The "Glory!" stikheron is in tone 6: "Adam ate the forbidden fruit and was driven from Paradise!", and the theotokion is also in tone 6: "My Maker and Redeemer, Christ the Lord,...!". Once again, there is **no** troparion for this Sunday, but the special kontakion is in tone 6: "O Master, Teacher of wisdom,...!".

At the Divine Liturgy, the Prokeimenon is in tone 8: "Pray and make your vows before the Lord our God!", with its accompanying verse, "In Judah, God is known! His Name is great in Israel!" (The **Byzantines** take a Prokeimenon in tone 3, "Sing praises to our God, sing praises!...!"). The "Alleluia!" verses are as follows: For the **Antiochians**: in tone 6: "It is good to give thanks to the Lord, to sing

---

[19] Ibid, pp. 168-180.

praises to Your Name, O Most High!", and "To declare Your steadfast love in the morning, and Your truth by night!". For the **Greeks**: in tone 3: "In You, O Lord, have I hoped! Let me never be put to shame!", and "Be my God and Protector!".

B. FORGIVENESS VESPERS

On this Sunday evening before the beginning of Great Lent, the Forgiveness Vespers is celebrated.[20] **Many** parishes, in order to encourage **all** of the faithful to participate, schedule it right after the Coffee Hour that follows the morning Divine Liturgy. Whenever it takes place, it is an **essential** element of Great Lent!

The Doxology and Psalm 103

The first thing that needs to be said is that this is a form of **_Daily Vespers_**, _not_ Great Vespers. Therefore, after the doxology is chanted, "Blessed is our God,…!", **_a reader_** responds with the "Amen.", the "Come, let us worship…!", and the chanting of

---

[20] Ibid, pp. 180-183.

Psalm 103 ("Bless the Lord, O my soul! O Lord, my God, You are very great! You are clothed with honor and majesty, Who cover Yourself with light as with a garment!..."). At the conclusion of the Psalm, the reader chants a full "Glory,... now and ever...!", and "Alleluia! Alleluia! Alleluia! Glory to You, O God!" **three** times.

The Great Litany

The Psalm is immediately followed by the celebration of the Great Litany. At this point in the service, the Litany can be celebrated with any melody, that is, a **non**-Lenten tone.

"Lord, I Call Upon You"

After the "Amen." at the conclusion of the Great Litany, the people sing "Lord, I Call Upon You!" in tone 2. The service books call for 10 stikhera to be sung: 4 penitential stikhera, 3 stikhera from the Triodion, and 3 stikhera for the saint of the day, followed, after the "Glory,... now and ever...!", by the theotokion from the Menaion. **However**, in **almost all** parishes, this is **greatly reduced** (**except** in the

Greek practice), usually to the singing of **only** the **first 2** stikhera from the Triodion: "Let us humble the flesh by abstinence,...!" and "When I think of my deeds, O Lord,...!". The **third stikhera** from the Triodion in tone 2, "Let us begin the Fast with joy!", is used as the "Glory,... now and ever...!" stikheron. Again, it needs to be stressed: Whatever is decided upon by the main celebrant in that parish is how this liturgical element is to be celebrated.

"Gladsome Light" and the Great Prokeimenon

At the Vesperal Entrance, the people sing "Gladsome Light!" as usual. After the clergy and servers enter the sanctuary, the Great Prokeimenon is celebrated, in tone 8. This is done as follows.

Deacon:	Wisdom! Let us be attentive!
Priest:	Peace be with you all!
Deacon:	And with your spirit!
Priest:	Wisdom!
Deacon:	The Great Prokeimenon is in the 8th tone: Turn not away Your face from Your child, for I am afflicted! Hear me speedily!

Lenten Services

	Draw near to my soul, and deliver it!
People:	Turn not away Your face from Your child, for I am afflicted! Hear me speedily! Draw near to my soul, and deliver it!
Deacon:	O God, O God, Your salvation will encompass me!
People:	Turn not away Your face from Your child, for I am afflicted! Hear me speedily! Draw near to my soul, and deliver it!
Deacon:	Let the poor see, and rejoice!
People:	Turn not away Your face from Your child, for I am afflicted! Hear me speedily! Draw near to my soul, and deliver it!
Deacon:	Seek God, and your soul will live!
People:	Turn not away Your face from Your child, for I am afflicted! Hear me speedily! Draw near to my soul, and deliver it!
Deacon:	Turn not away Your face from Your child, for I am afflicted!
People:	Hear me speedily! Draw near to my soul, and deliver it!

Since this is a Daily Vespers, the **Antiochian** tradition is to chant this Prokeimenon, rather than sing it. In the **Greek** practice, this is celebrated as a Great Vespers and there are only three intoned verses: "Turn not away Your face from Your child, for I am afflicted!", "O God, O God, Your salvation will encompass me!", and "Let the poor see, and rejoice!".

"Vouchsafe, O Lord"

After the Great Prokeimenon comes "Vouchsafe, O Lord!" Again, because this is a **Daily** Vespers, "Vouchsafe, O Lord!" is **chanted** by a **reader**, rather than sung by the people.

Litany of Supplication

Following "Vouchsafe, O Lord!" is the Litany of Supplication. Because this follows the Prokeimenon, which is the liturgical "turning point" in the service from the day just ending to the next day, this Litany is responded to by the people singing in the **_Lenten melody_**.[21]

The Apostikha

After the Litany of Supplication, the Apostikha is celebrated. The stikhera are in tone 4, and the first one begins, "Your grace has shone forth, O Lord,…!". A reader then chants the verse, "To You I lift up my eyes, O You Who are enthroned in the Heavens! Behold! As the eyes of servants look to the hand of their master; as the eyes of a maid to the hand of her mistress; so, our eyes look to the Lord our God, until He has mercy on us!" The people then sing again, in tone 4, "Your grace has shone forth, O Lord,…!". The reader then chants another verse, "Have mercy on us, O Lord, have mercy on us, for we have had more than enough of contempt! Too long our soul has been sated with the scorn of those who are at ease, the contempt of the proud!". Then, the people sing, in tone 4, "You are glorified in the memory of Your saints, O Christ God!". The reader then chants a full "Glory,… now and ever…!",

---

[21] Schmemann, Alexander, *Great Lent: Journey to Pascha*, SVS Press, Crestwood, NY, 1974 (hereafter referred to as, "*Great Lent*"), p. 29. Cf., also, Hapgood, p. 182.

and the people sing, in tone 4, the theotokion, "The angelic hosts glorify you, O Mother of God!'.

St Symeon's Prayer, the Trisagion Prayers, and the Lord's Prayer

Following the theotokion, a reader chants St Symeon's Prayer ("Lord, now let Your servant depart in peace,...!"), the Trisagion Prayers, and the Lord's Prayer. After the exclamation ("For, Yours are the Kingdom, and the power, and the glory,...!"), the reader responds with, "Amen.".

Penitential Troparia

The people then sing a series of penitential troparia, in tone 5, interspersed with prostrations, as follows.

> Rejoice, O Virgin Theotokos, Mary, full of grace, the Lord is with you!
> Blessed are you among women, and blessed is the Fruit of your womb!
> For, You have Borne the Savior of our souls!

[prostration]

Glory to the Father, and to the Son, and to
	the Holy Spirit!
O baptizer of Christ, remember us all,
that we may be delivered from our iniquities!
For, to you is given grace to intercede for us!

[prostration]

Now and ever and unto ages of ages! Amen.
Intercede for us, O holy Apostles and
	all the saints,
that we may be delivered from perils
	and sorrows!
For, we have acquired you as fervent
	intercessors before the Savior!

[prostration]

Beneath your compassion, we take refuge,
	O Theotokos!
Do not despise our supplications in adversity,
but deliver us from perils, O only pure and
	only blessed one!

[metania (bow)]

The **Byzantine** tradition calls for the "Glory" to be sung right before "Intercede for us, O holy Apostles and all the saints...!", and the "Now and ever...!" to be sung right before "Beneath your compassion,...!".

Concluding Petitions

A reader then chants, "Lord, have mercy!" ***forty*** times, followed by a full "Glory,... now and ever...!", "More honorable than the Cherubim,...!", and, "In the Name of the Lord, give the blessing, Father!" (or, if a bishop is serving, "Master!"; or, if the Metropolitan is serving, "Most blessed Master!"). The main celebrant then chants, "Christ our God, the One Who Is, is blessed always, now and ever and unto ages of ages!" The reader chants, "Amen. O Heavenly King, establish the Orthodox Christians! Confirm the Faith! Quiet the heathen! Give peace to the world! Place our departed fathers and brethren in the tabernacles of the righteous, and accept us sorrowers and penitents! For, You are good and the Lover of mankind!" (In the Greek tradition, this is said **only** by the priest or bishop.)

The Prayer of St Ephraim

The penitential Prayer of St Ephraim is then celebrated. The clergy and servers exit the sanctuary. The main celebrant stands before the closed Royal Doors, and intones the Prayer, which is interspersed with prostrations, as follows.

> O Lord and Master of my life, do not give to me the spirit of sloth, despair, lust of power, and idol talk!
>
> *[prostration]*
>
> But, give, rather, the spirit of chastity, humility, patience, and love to your servant!
>
> *[prostration]*
>
> Yes, O Lord and King, grant me to see my own sins, and not to judge my brother or sister, for

You are blessed unto ages of ages! Amen!

[prostration]

Then, the people, led by the clergy and servers, all make **twelve** metania (bows) (except in the Greek practice), saying silently to themselves each time, "God, cleanse me a sinner, and have mercy on me!" After this, the main celebrant says the full Prayer of St Ephraim, followed by one final prostration.

> O Lord and Master of my life, do not give to me the spirit of sloth, despair, lust of power, and idol talk!
> But, give, rather, the spirit of chastity, humility, patience, and love to your servant!

> Yes, O Lord and King, grant me to see my own sins, and not to judge my brother or sister, for You are blessed unto ages of ages! Amen!

[prostration]

The Dismissal

The main celebrant then chants, "Glory to You, O Christ, our God and our Hope, glory to You!" The people then sing a full "Glory,... now and ever...!", a *triple* "Lord, have mercy.", and, then, "Father (or, if a bishop is serving, "Master!"; or, if the Metropolitan is serving, "Most blessed Master!"), bless!" The main celebrant then intones the Dismissal Prayer, and the people *usually* sing a *double* "Amen." ("Amen. Amen."). **All** of these responses are sung in the Lenten melody.

[The Sermon]

If a sermon is to be given, it is usually at this point that this is done.

The Rite of Forgiveness and the Paschal Stikhera

There then follows the Rite of Forgiveness. Each person comes up, venerates the icons, and then greets each person (starting with the parish priest) by bowing in front of them, and saying, "Forgive me, a sinner!" The person they are in front of does the same. They then exchange a *triple* kiss of peace, responding to each other with, "God forgives!" When the person has greeted everyone who is already in the line, he or she then takes their own place at the end of the line, so that, as subsequent people come through the line, they, also, ask forgiveness of the person. By this method, **every person present** has asked forgiveness of **every other person present**.

During the Rite of Forgiveness, the people sing the Paschal stikhera, beginning with, "Let God arise! Let His enemies be scattered! Let those who hate Him flee from before His Face!". (The **Antiochian** tradition is to, instead, sing the Odes of the Paschal Kanon. In the **Greek** practice, the Theotokion, "You shelter all those, O good one!", is sung.) At the end of these stikhera is sung, *just as it will be on Pascha*, "Christ is Risen from the dead, trampling down death by death, and, upon those in the tombs, bestowing life!" **three** times, manifesting Pascha as the goal of Great Lent! This is an **official** and **essential** liturgical element of this service, and should **not** be eliminated![22]

---

[22] *Great Lent*, p. 30. Hapgood, p. 183.

C. KANON OF ST ANDREW OF CRETE

Since the particulars of Daily Lenten Vespers[23] and Daily Lenten Matins[24] were enumerated elsewhere, that information will not be repeated here.

A unique feature of Great Lent is the celebration of Grand Compline, with the Kanon of St Andrew of Crete, celebrated on the first four weeknights (Monday through Thursday) of the first week of Great Lent,[25] as well as Thursday of the fifth week of Great Lent.[26] Here, in the fifth week, the service books call for the Kanon of St Andrew of Crete to be celebrated during the Daily Lenten Matins for Thursday, along with contemplating the life of St Mary of Egypt, who will be commemorated on the following weekend, on the fifth Sunday of Great Lent. *However*, in *most* parishes, since people are working and cannot attend this service in the morning, it is again celebrated as during the first week, as part of Grand Compline. In *many* parishes, because the Liturgy of the Pre-Sanctified Gifts is celebrated on Wednesday evenings during Great

---

[23] Cf. above, *Volume 1*, pp. 56-70.
[24] Cf. above, *Volume 1*, pp. 148-168.
[25] *Triodion*, pp. 198-209, 218-228, 237-247, and 255-266.
[26] Ibid, pp. 378-415.

Lent, Grand Compline with the Kanon of St Andrew of Crete is **omitted** on the first Wednesday of Great Lent (this is **definitely** the case in the **Greek** practice). As always, the choir director and singers should follow the local custom.

The Doxology, the Trisagion Prayers, and the Lord's Prayer

The service begins with the usual doxology, "Blessed is our God,…!". The reader chants the response, "Amen.", then "Glory to You, our God, glory to You!", then "O Heavenly King!", the Trisagion Prayers, and the Lord's Prayer. After the exclamation ("For, Yours are the Kingdom, and the power, and the glory,…!"), the reader responds, "Amen.", then "Lord, have mercy." **twelve** times, then a full "Glory,… now and ever…!", then "Come, let us worship God, our King!…".

Psalm 12

The reader then chants Psalm 12, which begins, "How long, O Lord? Will You forget me forever?"[27] After the Psalm, the reader chants a full

---

[27] The Psalms are numbered here according to the Septuagint (LXX).

"Glory,... now and ever...!", and then "Alleluia! Alleluia! Alleluia! Glory to You, O God!" *three* times. (In the **Byzantine** tradition, Psalm 12 is preceded by Psalms 4 and 6.)

Kanon of St Andrew of Crete

In the **Byzantine** tradition, Psalm 12 is followed by Psalms 24, 30, and 90; then, "God is With Us!"; then, other hymns in tone 6; then, the Trisagion Prayers; then, Psalms 50 and 101; then, the Prayer of Manasseh; then, the Trisagion Prayers again and other prayers; then, Psalms 69 and 142; then, the Little Litany; then, the Kanon of St Andrew of Crete. In all other traditions, following Psalm 12 and its concluding elements, the Kanon of St Andrew of Crete is celebrated. Unlike the rest of the liturgical year, when the Kanon consists of odes 1 and 3-9, during Great Lent, ode 2 is celebrated. Ode 2 consists of the Song of Moses in Deuteronomy (Deuteronomy 32: 1-43), and is, therefore, a penitential ode.

The celebration of the Kanon is as follows. Each ode is sung by the people. Then, the clergy (bishop, priest, and/or deacon) chant the penitential troparia that are the hallmark of this Kanon. After each troparion, a refrain is sung by the people. For most of the troparia, the refrain is, "Have mercy on me, O God! Have mercy on me!" Before the troparion that focuses on the Holy Trinity, the refrain is, "Glory to the Father, and to the Son, and to the Holy Spirit!". Then, before the troparion that focuses on the Theotokos, the refrain is, "Now and ever and unto ages of ages! Amen.". In some of the odes, there are troparia addressed to St Mary of Egypt. Before those troparia, the refrain is, "O holy mother Mary, pray to God for us!" Finally, some of the odes have troparia addressed to St Andrew of Crete. Before those troparia, the refrain is, "O holy father Andrew, pray to God for us!"

The Kanon is sung in tone 6. The singing of ode 1 begins, "A Helper and a Protector has become Salvation to me!" Ode 2 begins, "Attend, O Heaven, and I will speak and will sing of Christ,...!". Ode 3 states, "Establish Your Church on the unshakable rock of Your commandments, O Christ!", and is followed by a Kathisma Hymn in tone 8.

Ode 4 begins, "The prophet heard of Your coming, O Lord, and was afraid...!". Ode 5 starts, "Out of the night, watching early for You,...!". Ode 6 leads off with, "I cried with my whole heart to the merciful God,...!".

After ode 6, the people sing, in tone 6, the Kontakion that begins, "My soul! My soul! Arise! Why are you sleeping?". This is *immediately* followed an Oikos and (in the *Antiochian* tradition) the Beatitudes, and then by the singing of ode 7, which starts, "We have sinned, transgressed, done wrong before You!" Ode 8 begins, "Him, Whom the heavenly hosts glorify,…!". In the Antiochian tradition, this is followed by "More honorable…!" and "It is Truly Meet…!" and then Ode 9. In all other traditions, Ode 9 follows with, "Ineffable is the Childbearing of a seedless Conception!" In *most* parishes, after the accompanying troparia for ode 9 are concluded, the people *again* sing ode 9 as the katavasia to the Kanon.

The Little Litany

After the Kanon comes the Little Litany, the responses to which are sung in the Lenten melody.

Psalm 90

Following the Little Litany (*except* in the Antiochian tradition, where all of these elements, as previously stated, were done *earlier*), a reader chants Psalm 90 ("He who dwells in the shelter of the Most High,…!"). At the conclusion of the Psalm, the reader chants a full "Glory,… now and ever…!", and then, "Alleluia! Alleluia! Alleluia! Glory to You, O God!" *three* times.

"God is With Us"

Following this, "God is With Us!" is celebrated. The deacon chants the full exclamation: "God is with us! Understand, all you nations, and submit yourselves! For, God is with us!" The people then sing this entire exclamation, in tone 4, in full voice. The deacon then chants the prayer that begins, "Hear this, all you ends of the Earth! Submit yourselves, you mighty ones! Even if your strength returns, you will be overthrown once more!..." The people then repeatedly sing an abbreviated ending of the exclamation: "For, God is with us!" In **some** parishes, this is done **very** quietly during the entire chanting of the prayer by the deacon, which, in effect, ends up **covering over** the prayer itself. For this reason, in **other** parishes, after the deacon chants each paragraph of the prayer, the people then sing the abbreviated ending, with the deacon **waiting** until the singing is concluded before going on with the prayer. That way, everyone in church gets to hear and meditate on the entire prayer. Obviously, this second method of celebrating the prayer is the preferred one. However, as always, the decision remains with the main celebrant of the service. After completing the prayer with a full "Glory,... now and ever...!", the deacon full proclaims the entire exclamation again: "God is with us!

Understand, all you nations, and submit yourselves! For, God is with us!" The people then sing this entire exclamation fully, one last time.

Hymns of Praise

After "God is with us!", a reader chants hymns of praise. They begin as follows.

> The day is past! I thank you, O Lord! Grant me, I entreat You, that this evening and this night I fall into no sin, and save me, O my Savior!
>
> Glory to the Father, and to the Son, and to the Holy Spirit!
>
> The day is past! I sing praises to You, O Master! Grant me, I entreat You, that this evening and this night I may be without guile, and save me, O my Savior!
> Now and ever and unto ages of ages. Amen.
>
> The day is past! I hymn You, O Holy One! Grant me, I entreat You, that this evening and

this night I may be assailed by no temptation, and save me, O my Savior!

Then, the reader chants a hymn that begins, "With unceasing hymns, the bodiless powers of the Cherubim glorify You!". This is followed by the reader chanting a hymn to the Theotokos and the saints that begins, "O most-holy Virgin Theotokos, and you eye-witnesses and servants of the Word,…!".

The Creed

Then, the reader (or, most likely, another reader) chants the Nicean-Constantinopolitan Creed ("I believe in God, the Father Almighty, Maker of Heaven and Earth, and of all things visible and invisible;…!").

Lenten Services

Verses of Supplication

The main celebrant then exits the sanctuary and stands on the solea before the Royal Doors, chanting a series of petitions. After **each** petition, the people sing this **same** petition. The petitions are as follows:

- All-holy sovereign Lady Theotokos, pray for us sinners!

- All you heavenly hosts of angels and archangels, pray for us sinners!

- Holy John, the prophet and Forerunner and Baptist of our Lord Jesus Christ, pray for us sinners!

- Holy glorious Apostles, prophets, martyrs, and all the saints, pray for us sinners!

- Our reverent and God-bearing fathers, pastors, and ecumenical teachers, pray for us sinners!

- Saint(s) [name of the saint(s) of the parish church], pray for us sinners!

- Invincible, ineffable, and divine power of the honorable and life-giving Cross, forsake not us sinners!

- God, cleanse us sinners!

- God, cleanse us sinners!

- God, cleanse us sinners, and have mercy on us!

With this last petition, the people sing it in a musical manner (final musical chord, etc.) to show that this is the end of this liturgical element.

Penitential Petitions

At this point, a reader chants a series of penitential petitions. On **Monday** and **Wednesday** evenings, the petitions begin as follows: "Enlighten my eyes, O Christ God, that I not sleep the sleep of death;…!"; "Glory…Spirit!"; "Be the Defender of my soul, O God;…!"; "Now and ever…Amen."; "And since, through the multitude of our iniquities,…!".

On **Tuesday** and **Thursday** evenings, the penitential petitions begin as follows: "You know, O Lord, my Creator, the sleepless vigilance of my invisible enemies,…!"; "Look on me and give ear to me, O my God!"; "How terrible is Your judgment, O Lord,…!"; "Glory…Spirit!"; "Grant me tears, O God, as You did to the sinning woman of old;…!"; "Now and ever…Amen."; "In that I have in you, O Virgin Theotokos, that hope that makes me not ashamed,…!".

Psalm 50

Following the penitential petitions, a reader (usually a different one) chants Psalm 50 (beginning, "Have mercy on me, O God,…!"). When the Psalm is concluded, the reader chants a full "Glory,… now and ever…!", and then, "Alleluia! Alleluia! Alleluia! Glory to You, O God!" **three** times.

The Prayer of Manasseh

The reader (or, another reader) then chants the Prayer of Manasseh (beginning, "O Lord Almighty, God of our fathers, of Abraham and Isaac and Jacob and of their posterity,…!").

Penitential Hymns

Following the Prayer of Manasseh, the people sing a set of penitential hymns, in tone 6: "Have mercy on us, O God, have mercy on us!…!"; "Glory…Spirit!"; "Have mercy on us, O Lord! For, we have put our trust in You!…!"; "Now and ever…Amen."; "Open to us the door of your loving-kindness, O blessed Theotokos!…!".

The Lesser Doxology

The celebrant intones, "Glory to You, Who have shone us the Light!" A reader then chants the Lesser Doxology ("Glory to God in the highest,…!").

"Remain With Us, O Lord of Hosts!"

The people then sing a refrain, "Remain with us, O Lord of hosts! In affliction, we have no other Helper but You! O Lord of hosts, have mercy on us!" After this, select verses from the Praises (Psalms 148, 149, and 150) are sung in couplets (*except* in the Byzantine tradition), each couplet followed again by the singing of the refrain, "Remain with us, O Lord of hosts!" (In the Greek practice, **only** the **six** verses of Psalm 150 are celebrated.)

When all of the couplets have been sung, then the people sing, "Glory...Spirit!", followed by the singing of a petition that begins, "O Lord, if we did not have Your saints as intercessors,...!". Then, the people sing, "Now and ever...Amen.", followed by another petition that begins, "Great is the multitude of my transgressions, O Theotokos!". Two more petitions follow, the first one beginning, "Do not forsake me throughout all the days of my life,...!", and the second one beginning, "All of my hope have I placed in you,...!".

Concluding Petitions

A reader then chants "Lord, have mercy." **forty** times, followed by the petitions that begin, "You, Who at every season and every hour, in Heaven and on Earth, are worshipped and glorified, O Christ our God;...!". The reader then chants a **triple** "Lord, have mercy.", followed by a full "Glory,... now and ever...!", "More honorable than the Cherubim,...!", and, then, "In the Name of the Lord, give the blessing, Father!" (or, if a bishop is serving, "Master!"; or, if the Metropolitan is serving, "Most blessed Master!"). The main celebrant then chants, "God be bountiful to us, and bless us, and show the light of His countenance on us, and have mercy on us!" The reader then responds, "Amen."

The Prayer of St Ephraim

The Prayer of St. Ephraim, with interspersed prostrations and metania, is then chanted.

Prayers of Supplication

The main celebrant then comes out and stands on the solea before the Royal Doors. Turning to the icon of the Theotokos on the iconostasis, he chants a prayer that begins, "O Virgin, pure, spotless, incorrupt, undefiled, all-pure;...!". He then turns to the icon of Christ on the iconostasis and chants a prayer that begins, "And, grant us, O Master, as we lay down to sleep, repose both of body and of soul,...!". He then again turns to the icon of the Theotokos on the iconostasis and chants a prayer that begins, "O exceedingly glorious, ever-Virgin Mother of Christ our God,...!". In the Greek tradition, this is done by lay people: a woman stands in front of the icon of the Theotokos and chants her prayer, while a man stands in front of the icon of Christ and chants His prayer.

    The celebrant then turns and faces directly forward to the Royal Doors and chants the Prayer of St Ioannikios: "The Father is my Hope! The Son is my Refuge! The Holy Spirit is my Protection! O Holy Trinity, glory to You!" After this is intoned, a reader **immediately** chants a full "Glory,… now and ever…!", a **triple** "Lord, have mercy.", and, then, "Father (or, "Master;" or, "Most blessed Master"), bless!" (**except** in the Antiochian tradition, where this is **omitted** and the service **immediately** goes to the prayer that begins, "O Master, great in mercy, Lord Jesus Christ our God, through the intercessions…!"). The celebrant then turns and faces the people from the ambo and chants a prayer that begins, "O greatly-merciful Master, Lord, Jesus Christ, our God…!". **The people** then **sing** an "Amen." in the Lenten tone. The celebrant then prostrates on the ambo before the people, chanting, "Forgive me, my brothers and sisters!" The people respond with, "May our Lord God forgive you, and forgive us!"

Closing Litany

The celebrant then chants a series of remembrance petitions in the Closing Litany ("Remember, O Lord, Your holy Church and our parish community...!"; "Remember, O Lord, and have mercy on the bishops, priests, deacons, the monks and the nuns,...!"; etc.). Depending on the local custom, the people may either sing "Lord, have mercy." in the Lenten melody after each petition, or may sing "Lord, have mercy." in the Lenten melody continuously while the celebrant intones the petitions. As always, the choir director and singers should follow the local custom.

For the final petition, the celebrant usually raises his voice louder and chants, "And, remember us, O Lord, who offer You these petitions, and have mercy on us!", to which the people respond by singing a **triple** "Lord, have mercy.". The celebrant then gives the final exclamation, "Through the prayers of our holy fathers and mothers, and of all the saints, have mercy on us, O Lord, and save us!" (**except** in the Byzantine tradition, where the celebrant exclaims, "Forgive, O Lord, those who hate us and those who oppress us!"). The people respond with either a **single** "Amen.", or, usually, a **double** "Amen." ("Amen. Amen.").

Recessional Hymns

At this point, the main celebrant usually gives some words of exhortation about repentance, etc. As everyone comes forward to venerate the icons and the Holy Cross, the people ***may*** sing some recessional hymns (many times, the odes of the Kanon of St Andrew of Crete). In the Antiochian tradition, on Mondays and Wednesdays, the people sing, "O Good One, defend us by Your mighty hand!" in tone 2; on Tuesdays, Thursdays, and on Holy Monday, the people sing, "As she beheld You unjustly slain, O Christ, the Virgin…!" in tone 1. In some parishes, the people come forward to venerate the icons and the Holy Cross quietly. As always, the local custom should be followed.

D. THE LITURGY OF THE PRESANCTIFIED GIFTS

On Wednesday evenings of Great Lent (and, in some parishes, on Friday evenings of Great Lent, as well), the Liturgy of the Pre-Sanctified Gifts is celebrated.[28] In many parishes of the various traditions, this Liturgy is preceded by the celebration of the 9th Hour and Typika.

The Doxology and Psalm 103

Since this service is basically a Vespers with Holy Communion, the doxology at the beginning of the service is eucharistic: "Blessed is the Kingdom of the Father, and of the Son, and of the Holy Spirit, now and ever and unto ages of ages!" The people then *sing* the "Amen." in the Lenten melody. In the Greek tradition, there is no special Lenten melody used. Instead, a simple melody in tone 5 or tone 6 may be used, or "Lord, have mercy!" may be sung on

---

[28] *Triodion*, pp. 93-97.

a single note with a half-step movement for the cadence syllable.

Then, a reader chants the "Come, let us worship...!", followed by the Vesperal Psalm 103, "Bless the Lord, O my soul! O Lord, my God, You are very great! You are clothed with honor and majesty, Who cover Yourself with light as with a garment;...!". At the conclusion of the Psalm, the reader chants a full "Glory,... now and ever...!", and then, "Alleluia! Alleluia! Alleluia! Glory to You, O God!" **three** times.

The Great Litany

The Great Litany is then celebrated, with the responses sung by the people in the Lenten melody.

The First Antiphon and the Little Litany

Following the Great Litany is the celebration of Kathisma 18 from the Psalter.[29] This is comprised of Psalms 119-133, sung in three stases or antiphons:[30] The First Antiphon contains Psalms 119-123, the

---

[29] Ibid, p. 93.
[30] The Psalm numbering here is according to the Septuagint.

Second Antiphon comprises Psalms 124-128, and the Third Antiphon has Psalms 129-133. (On Wednesday of the 5th week of Great Lent, Kathisma 7 [Psalms 46-54] is celebrated, and, on Thursday of the 5th week of Great Lent, Kathisma 12 [Psalms 85-90] is celebrated, **except** in the Greek tradition.)[31]

Even though the service books call for these antiphons to be chanted by a reader,[32] in **most** parishes, they are **sung** by the people in a special melody. At the conclusion of the First Antiphon (Psalm 123) is sung a full "Glory,… now and ever…!", and then, "Alleluia! Alleluia! Alleluia! Glory to You, O God!" **three** times.

However, there is an **additional** liturgical element in the Byzantine tradition. In the singing of Stasis 1 and Stasis 2, following the triple singing of the "Alleluia!" element, a reader chants a triple "Lord, have mercy." and "Glory…Spirit!", **then** the Little Litany is celebrated, **then** the reader chants "Now and ever…Amen.", and **then** the next stasis is sung. Again, this is **only** done in the Byzantine tradition.

Then, a Little Litany is celebrated, with the responses sung in the Lenten melody.

---

[31] *Triodion*, p. 93, footnote 38.
[32] Ibid, p. 93.

The Second Antiphon and the Little Litany

The Second Antiphon (Psalms 124-128) is then sung by the people. Again, at its conclusion (Psalm 128) is sung a full "Glory,... now and ever...!", and then, "Alleluia! Alleluia! Alleluia! Glory to You, O God!" **three** times.

Then, a Little Litany is celebrated, with the responses sung in the Lenten melody.

The Third Antiphon and the Little Litany

The Third Antiphon (Psalms 129-133) is then sung by the people. Again, at its conclusion (Psalm 133) is sung a full "Glory,... now and ever...!", and then, "Alleluia! Alleluia! Alleluia! Glory to You, O God!" **three** times. (In the **Antiochian** tradition, at the point of the verse, "Arise, O Lord, and go to Your resting place, You and the ark of Your might!", the reader stops and the priest reverently carries the diskos and the chalice to the Table of Oblation, as everyone kneels. Then, the reader continues with, "Your priests will be clothed...!".)

Then, a Little Litany is celebrated, with the responses sung in the Lenten melody.

"Lord, I Call Upon You" and Stikhera

Following the Third Antiphon and the Little Litany, "Lord, I Call Upon You", with its accompanying stikhera, is sung. **Usually, "Lord, I Call Upon You"** *is sung in the tone of the <u>first</u> <u>stikheron</u> that follows*. So, for example, on the first Wednesday of Great Lent, the first stikheron ("Come, O faithful! Let us perform the works of God in the light!…!") is sung in tone 5 (except in the Byzantine tradition, where, in tone 8, the people sing, "While fasting physically, brethren,…!"). **Therefore**, the singing of "Lord, I Call Upon You" before this first stikheron will **also** be sung in tone 5.

After the prescribed stikhera for the particular week are sung, then, **usually**, the theotokion **is sung in the particular <u>tone</u> <u>of</u> <u>the</u> <u>week</u> from the Oktoechos**. So, again, for example, on the first Wednesday of Great Lent, if the tone of that particular week happens to be tone 3, the theotokion from tone 3 ("By your great might, O most pure one,…!") is sung; if the tone of that particular week happens to be tone 7, the theotokion from tone 7 ("We acknowledge you to be a Virgin after Childbearing!…!") is sung; etc. In any case, during the singing of the theotokion, the clergy and servers exit the sanctuary for the Vesperal

Entrance. (In the **Byzantine** tradition, the last four stikhera and the "Glory" verse are from the Menaion.)

The Vesperal Entrance and "Gladsome Light"

When the clergy and servers are in the center of the church, at the conclusion of the singing of the theotokion, the deacon intones, "Let us pray to the Lord!". The people then respond with "Lord, have mercy." in the Lenten melody. The main celebrant then chants the Prayer of the Vesperal Entrance ("In the evening and in the morning and at noonday,…!"). After the exclamation ("For, to You are due all glory, honor, and worship,…!"), the people sing the "Amen." in the Lenten melody. (This is all done **silently** in the Byzantine tradition.)

After the deacon intones, "Wisdom! Let us be attentive!", the people sing "Gladsome Light!" (**except** in the Greek practice, where **only** the main celebrant intones the hymn), while the clergy and servers enter the sanctuary.

The 1ˢᵗ Prokeimenon and the Reading from Genesis

Following "Gladsome Light!", a reader will intone the 1ˢᵗ Prokeimenon. This is different for each service of each week of Great Lent. So, for example, on the first Wednesday of Great Lent, the 1ˢᵗ Prokeimenon, in tone 5, is "You, O Lord, will protect us and preserve us from this generation forever!", with its accompanying verse, "Save me, O Lord! For, there are no longer any who are godly!"; on the second Wednesday of Great Lent, the 1ˢᵗ Prokeimenon, in tone 6, is "Be glad and rejoice in the Lord, O you righteous!", with its accompanying verse, "Blessed are they whose transgressions are forgiven, and whose sins are covered!"; etc. for the other services.

After the 1ˢᵗ Prokeimenon, the reader chants the prescribed reading from Genesis.[33] For the first Wednesday of Great Lent, the reading is from Genesis 1:24-2:3; for the second Wednesday of Great Lent, the reading is from Genesis 4:16-26; etc.

---

[33] During Holy Week, the reading is from Exodus. Cf. *Triodion*, p. 94, footnote 39.

The 2nd Prokeimenon, "The Light of Christ!", and the Reading from Proverbs

At this point, a reader (usually, a different reader) then chants the 2nd Prokeimenon, which, as with the 1st Prokeimenon, is different for each service of each week of Great Lent. So, for example, on the first Wednesday of Great Lent, the 2nd Prokeimenon, in tone 6, is "Consider and answer me, O Lord my God!", with its accompanying verse, "How long, O Lord? Will You forget me forever? How long will You hide Your Face from me?"; on the second Wednesday of Great Lent, the 2nd Prokeimenon, in tone 1, is "Let Your steadfast love, O Lord, be upon us as we have set our hope in You!", with its accompanying verse, "Rejoice in the Lord, O you righteous! Praise befits the just!"; etc. for the other services.

Now, **_before_** the chanting of the reading from Proverbs, the main celebrant comes out from the sanctuary with a lit candle on top of the Gospel Book, and intones, "The light of Christ illumines all!". When the deacon then intones "Wisdom!", the reader then proceeds to chant the reading from

Proverbs.[34] (In the **Byzantine** tradition, this is preceded by the reader chanting, "Command!".)

"Let My Prayer Arise"

After the second reading from the Old Testament (whether from Proverbs or from Job), "Let My Prayer Arise" is celebrated. Even though the service books call for the priest or a reader to chant the verses from this (which is *still* done this way in the Antiochian tradition),[35] in *most* parishes, it is customary for these verses to be *sung*, either by a single chanter, a trio, or all the singers (in the **Greek** practice, the priest chants "Let my prayer arise", then comes out and faces and censes the icon of Christ on the iconostasis while chanting, "in Your sight as incense"; after this, the chanters conclude with, "and let the lifting up of my hands be an evening sacrifice!", whereby the priest censes the entire congregation from the solea). There are four sets of verses that are sung: "Let my prayer arise…!", "Lord, I have cried to You!…!", "Set a watch, O Lord,…!", and "Incline not my heart…!".

---

[34] During Holy Week, the reading is from the Book of Job. Cf. *Triodion*, p. 94, footnote 40.
[35] *Triodion*, p. 94.

After the singing of each of these verses, **all** the people sing the refrain, "Let my prayer arise in Your sight as incense, and let the lifting up of my hands be an evening sacrifice!", in the Lenten melody. After the refrain following the fourth verse ("Incline not my heart…!"), the single chanter, trio, or people sing "Let my prayer arise…!" (the first verse) one last time, with **no** singing of the refrain afterwards.

The Prayer of St Ephraim (Short Version)

When the singing of "Let My Prayer Arise" is concluded, the main celebrant comes out to the solea and chants a short version of the Prayer of St Ephraim. This consists of the three sections of the prayer being chanted, with a prostration after each section, as follows.

> O Lord and Master of my life, do not give to me the spirit of sloth, despair, lust of power, and idol talk!

[prostration]

But, give, rather, the spirit of chastity,
humility, patience, and love to your servant!

[prostration]

Yes, O Lord and King, grant me to see my own sins, and not to judge my brother or sister, for You are blessed unto ages of ages! Amen!

[prostration]

Unlike the longer version of the Prayer of St Ephraim, the third prostration is **_not_** followed by everyone bowing three times and silently praying, "God be merciful to me, a sinner!" and the final chanting of the prayer. In other words, once the third prostration is made, this shorter version of the Prayer of St Ephraim is concluded.

The Augmented Litany

In the **Antiochian** tradition, for the first Wednesday of Lent **only**, the Augmented Litany is preceded by a Gospel Reading. In all other traditions, the Augmented Litany is then celebrated. **All** of the responses are sung by the people in the Lenten melody. The first two petitions ("Let us say, with all our soul and all our mind, let us say:" and "O Lord Almighty, the God of our fathers…!") are followed by a **single** "Lord, have mercy.". Starting with the **third** petition ("Have mercy on us, O God, according to Your great goodness,…!"), the people respond by singing a **triple** "Lord, have mercy.". Following the final petition ("Again, we pray for those who bring offerings and do good works in this holy and all-venerable house,…!") and its triple "Lord, have mercy.", the main celebrant intones a prayer that begins, "O Lord our God, accept this fervent supplication of Your servants,…!". Following the exclamation ("For, You are a merciful God Who love mankind,…!"), the people sing the "Amen." in the Lenten melody.

The Litany of the Catechumens

The Litany of the Catechumens is then celebrated. Again, **_all_** the responses by the people are sung in the Lenten melody. After the final petition ("Bow your heads to the Lord, you catechumens!") and its response ("To You, O Lord!"), the main celebrant chants a prayer that begins, "O God our God, the Creator and Maker of all things,…!". After the exclamation ("that, with us, they may glorify Your all-honorable and majestic Name,…!"), the people sing the "Amen." in the Lenten melody. In the **Greek** tradition, this litany is followed by a dismissal for the catechumens.

[The Litany for Those Preparing for Illumination]

Starting with the second half of Great Lent, on the fourth Wednesday, the Litany of the Catechumens is followed by a Litany for Those Preparing for Illumination (that is, Baptism). This manifests the original function of Great Lent as preparation for Baptism on the feast of the Lord's Pascha.[36] Again, this occurs **_only_** in the second half

---

[36] *Great Lent*, p. 58. *Triodion*, p. 95.

of Great Lent. During the first three weeks of Great Lent, the Litany of the Catechumens is *immediately* followed by the Litanies for the Faithful. Starting with the fourth week of Great Lent, the Litany of the Catechumens is followed by the Litany of Those Preparing for Illumination, which is *then* followed by the Litanies for the Faithful.

The Litanies for the Faithful

At this point, two Litanies for the Faithful are celebrated. In *most* parishes, after the prayer for the second of these litanies (beginning, "O Master, holy and exceedingly good,…!") and its exclamation ("through the gift of Your Christ, with Whom You are blessed,…!"), the people sing a *double* "Amen." ("Amen. Amen."), *except* in the Greek practice, which virtually *never* uses a double "Amen.".

"Now the Powers of Heaven"

Following the last Litany for the Faithful, the people sing the Entrance hymn, "Now the Powers of Heaven!". As with the singing of the Cherubic Hymn at a regular Divine Liturgy, this hymn is sung in two sections. The first consists of the text, "Now the Powers of Heaven do serve invisibly with us! Lo! The King of glory enters! Lo! The mystical Sacrifice is upborne, fulfilled!" After this is sung through **only once**, the people then prostrate fully on the floor as the clergy and servers exit the sanctuary with the Holy Gifts. Unlike a regular Divine Liturgy, there are **no** commemorations made during this Entrance. It is done in silence. Therefore, as will also be the case at the Entrance at the Vesperal Liturgy of Holy Saturday, there is **no** "Amen." sung before the second portion of the hymn continues. Instead, when the main celebrant quietly intones, "Let us draw near…!", the people sing, "Let us draw near in faith and love, and become communicants of life eternal! Alleluia! Alleluia! Alleluia!".

The Prayer of St Ephraim (Short Version)

When the singing of the Entrance hymn is concluded, the main celebrant comes out to the solea and chants a short version of the Prayer of St Ephraim, in three sections, each with a full prostration, as was done after the singing of "Let My Prayer Arise" (in the Greek tradition, this celebration of the Prayer of St Ephraim after the Entrance is usually **omitted**). Since the Holy Gifts were presanctified at the previous Sunday Divine Liturgy (from where this service gets its name), there is **no** Anaphora celebrated at this service.

The Litany Before the Lord's Prayer

Then, the Litany Before the Lord's Prayer is celebrated, again, with the responses sung in the Lenten melody.

The Lord's Prayer

The Lord's Prayer is then sung by the people, **<u>also</u>** in the Lenten melody (**except** in the Byzantine tradition, where it is chanted by a reader).

"One is Holy!" and the Communion Hymn

After the exclamation and the "Amen." following the Lord's Prayer, the celebrant raises the Holy Gifts (**except** in the Greek practice, where the Gifts are **only** raised at the previous Sunday's Liturgy) and intones, "The Pre-Sanctified Holy Things for the holy!" The people then sing, ***in the Lenten melody***, "One is holy!". This is ***immediately*** followed by the singing of the Communion Hymn: "O taste and see that the Lord is good! Alleluia! Alleluia! Alleluia!" This is ***not*** sung in the Lenten melody, but in a separate melody. (In the ***Antiochian*** tradition, "One is holy!" is followed immediately by the Prayer of Communion, "I believe, O Lord, and I confess...!". In the ***Greek*** practice, if there are very few lay communicants, the Prayer of Communion is ***not*** celebrated.)

The Prayer of Communion and the Communion of the Clergy

The people, led by the clergy, then chant the Prayer of Communion, "I believe, O Lord, and I confess,...!".

After this, the clergy partake of Holy Communion. During this time, the people again sing (often, repeatedly, if necessary) the Communion Hymn: "O taste and see that the Lord is good!" When the clergy emerge from the sanctuary with the Holy Gifts, the people conclude the singing with "Alleluia! Alleluia! Alleluia!"

The Communion of the Faithful

When the deacon intones, "In the fear of God, and with faith and love, draw near!", the people respond by singing, "I will bless the Lord at all times! His praise will always be on my lips!" (*except* in the Byzantine tradition, where the usual response from the Sunday Liturgy, "Blessed is He Who comes in the Name of the Lord!" is sung).

Then, the faithful partake of Holy Communion. During this time, the people repeatedly sing, "O taste and see that the Lord is good!" (this is **omitted** in the Greek practice). When all the people have received the Eucharist, and after (as it is done in many parishes) the celebrant chants, "Lo! This has touched your lips, has taken away all your iniquities, and cleansed you of all your sins!", the people then conclude by singing, "Alleluia! Alleluia! Alleluia!"

Liturgy Ending

For the Liturgy Ending, when the celebrant intones, "O God, save Your people and bless Your inheritance!", instead of singing "We have seen the true Light!" (as is done at a regular Divine Liturgy), the people sing, "Taste the heavenly Bread and the Cup of life! And see how good the Lord is! Alleluia! Alleluia! Alleluia!" (in the **Byzantine** tradition, "Taste the heavenly Bread is preceded by "I will bless the Lord at all times!" [sung earlier in other traditions].)

When the celebrant intones, "Blessed is our God, always now and ever and unto ages of ages!", the people then sing, *as is done at a regular Divine Liturgy*, "Amen.", followed by "Let our mouths be filled with Your praise, O Lord!...!".

The Litany of Thanksgiving

The Litany of Thanksgiving then follows, beginning with the petition, "Let us be attentive! Having partaken of the divine, holy, most-pure,...!". *At this point*, the people *once again* sing the responses in the Lenten melody. **All** of the responses done here ("Lord, have mercy.", "To You, O Lord.", "Amen.", "In the Name of the Lord.", and, again, "Lord, have mercy.") are sung in this same Lenten melody.

The Prayer Before the Ambo and "Blessed be the Name of the Lord"

The celebrant, having exited the sanctuary, chants the Prayer Before the Ambo that begins, "O Almighty Master, Who, in wisdom, have fashioned all creation;...!". After the exclamation ("For, blessed and glorified is Your all-honorable and majestic Name,...!"), the people sing an "Amen." and, then, "Blessed be the Name of the Lord, henceforth and forevermore!" ***three*** times, **both elements** (the "Amen." and the "Blessed be the Name") sung in the Lenten melody (in the **Byzantine** tradition, "Blessed be the Name" is sometimes chanted by a reader). The celebrant then comes out to the ambo and, blessing the people, chants, "The blessing of the Lord be upon you, through His grace and love for mankind, always now and ever and unto ages of ages!". The people sing, in the Lenten melody, "Amen.".

The Dismissal

The Dismissal is then celebrated. The celebrant chants, "Glory to You, O Christ, our God and our Hope, glory to You!" The people then sing _all_ of the following in the Lenten melody: A full "Glory,... now and ever...!", a **triple** "Lord, have mercy.", and "Father (or, if there is a bishop, "Master"; or, if there is the Metropolitan, "Most blessed Master"), bless!" The celebrant then chants the Dismissal Prayer, and the people respond, in the Lenten melody, **usually** with a **double** "Amen." ("Amen. Amen."). In the **Greek** practice, the Dismissal Prayer is followed by a reader chanting Psalms 33 ("I will bless the Lord at all times!") and 144 ("I will exalt You, O God my King!") before the exclamation, "Through the prayers of our holy fathers...!".

Recessional Hymns

Depending on the local custom, as everyone comes forward to venerate the icons and the Holy Cross, the people **may** sing some penitential hymns from the service, or other penitential hymns ("Open the Doors of Repentance," for example). In other parishes, the veneration of the icons and the Holy Cross is done in silence. In other places, the Prayers of Thanksgiving After Holy Communion may be chanted by a reader. As always, whatever the local custom is should be followed.

E. AKATHIST TO THE THEOTOKOS

The Akathist to the Theotokos is celebrated on the fifth Saturday of Great Lent.[37] The word "akathist" comes from the Greek word, "***akathistos***" ("'ακάθιστος"), meaning, "unseated." This is because, during this entire service, everyone present is to remain standing and not sit down.[38] Although this Akathist can be celebrated either as part of Little Compline on Friday evening or as part of Matins on Saturday morning, in **many** parishes, it is celebrated as a service by itself, that is, as an Akathist service alone. As always, the choir director and singers should confer with the main celebrant as to how this will be celebrated liturgically. Here, in this book, since many parishes celebrate the Akathist independently of Little Compline or Matins (in the Byzantine tradition, it is ***still*** done as part of Little Compline), the Akathist service will be presented as it is celebrated as a separate service on its own.

Also, it is the custom in the **Byzantine** practice to celebrate this Akathist in sections on the first five Fridays of Great Lent. However, the service books

---

[37] *Triodion*, pp. 422-445. Nassar, pp. 702-719.
[38] The Internet website, Wikipedia, under "Akathist".

do not call for that, and the **Russian** practice of celebrating it once, in its entirety, on the fifth Saturday of Great Lent, is what is called for. In the Byzantine tradition, it is done in four sections on the first four Fridays of Great Lent, and in its entirety on the fifth Friday of Great Lent.

If there are more than one clergy person concelebrating (two or more priests, or a priest and a deacon, etc.), the various clergy may share the chanting of each set of Kontakion and Oikos. In the **Greek** practice all the Oikos are chanted by the priests. The people only respond with the refrains, "Rejoice, O unwedded Bride!" or "Alleluia!".

The Doxology, the Trisagion Prayers, and the Lord's Prayer

The celebrant chants the doxology, "Blessed is our God, always now and ever and unto ages of ages!" A reader chants, "Amen.", "Glory to You, our God, glory to You!", "O Heavenly King!", and then the Trisagion Prayers and the Lord's Prayer. After the exclamation ("For, Yours are the Kingdom, and the power, and the glory,...!"), the reader responds with "Amen.".

Troparion 1

The people then sing, slowly and repeatedly while a great censing is done of the entire church, Troparion 1, in tone 8: "When the archangel understood the mysterious command, he came to the house of Joseph, with haste, and proclaimed to the unwedded Lady: 'The One Who bowed the Heavens by His condescension is taking abode in you! As I behold Him in your womb, taking the form of a Slave, I am frightened, but cry: "Rejoice, unwedded Bride"!'".

Kontakion 1 and Oikos 1

When the censing is completed and the clergy have returned to the center of the church, the people sing Kontakion 1, once, in tone 8: "Victorious leader of triumphant hosts! We, your servants, delivered from evil, sing our grateful thanks to you, Theotokos! As you possess invincible might, set us free from every calamity, so that we may sing: 'Rejoice, unwedded Bride!'".

The celebrant then chants Oikos 1, which says, "The first of the angels was sent from Heaven to greet the Theotokos: 'Rejoice!' Upon seeing You, Lord, becoming incarnate as his bodiless Word, he stood in awe, and cried:". Then, the people take up the singing of the refrains, the first word of each being, "Rejoice!": "Rejoice, by whom joy will be enkindled! Rejoice, by whom the curse will be quenched! Rejoice, recall of fallen Adam! Rejoice, deliverance of weeping Eve!...!". As with each Oikos that follows, the last "Rejoice!" of this Oikos is, "Rejoice, unwedded Bride!"

Kontakion 2 and Oikos 2

The celebrant then chants Kontakion 2: "Seeing herself in purity, the holy Lady cried to Gabriel, with boldness: 'The mystery of your words seems very hard to my soul! For, you foretell a Childbirth of seedless conception, crying: "Alleluia!"'". At this and each subsequent kontakion, the chanting by the celebrant concludes with this "Alleluia!", and is responded to by the people singing a **triple** "Alleluia!" ("Alleluia! Alleluia! Alleluia!"). (In the **Antiochian** tradition, what are called "kontakia" in other traditions are called "oikoi".)

Oikos 2 has the celebrant chant, "Desiring to know the unknowable, the Virgin cried to the ministering angel: "Tell me how a Child can be Born of my virginal womb!" He answered in fear, crying:". Again, the people respond with a set of refrains, each beginning with the word, "Rejoice!": "Rejoice, initiate of the ineffable counsel! Rejoice, belief of what must stay silent! Rejoice, first of Christ's miracles!…!". Again, the final refrain is, "Rejoice, unwedded Bride!"

Kontakion 3 and Oikos 3

Kontakion 3 has the celebrant chanting, "The power of the Most High overshadowed the handmaiden, so that she might conceive, transforming her womb into a blossoming meadow for all who seek the harvest of salvation by crying: 'Alleluia!'". The people then respond by singing a **triple** "Alleluia!".

Oikos 3 chants, "Having begotten God in her womb, the Virgin hastened to Elizabeth, whose unborn child understood the greeting and rejoiced, leaping as if in song, crying to the Theotokos:". The people respond with a set of refrains, each beginning with the word, "Rejoice!": "Rejoice, flower of an unwithering Stem! Rejoice, gift of an incorruptible Fruit! Rejoice, fountain of the Source of Life, the

Lover of man!...!". The final refrain is, "Rejoice, unwedded Bride!"

Kontakion 4 and Oikos 4

Kontakion 4 states, "The sober Joseph was tossed by a storm of doubts in his mind: Knowing you to be unwedded, blameless one, he feared a stolen union! But, learning that the Conception was of the Holy Spirit, he cried aloud: 'Alleluia!'". The people then respond by singing a *triple* "Alleluia!".

Oikos 4 states, "The shepherds heard the angels glorifying Christ's Coming in the flesh! Hastening to the Shepherd, they saw Him as a blameless Lamb, grazing at His Mother's breast, and they sang praises to her, crying out:". The people respond with a set of refrains, each beginning with the word, "Rejoice!": "Rejoice, Mother of the Lamb and Shepherd! Rejoice, pasture of spiritual sheep! Rejoice, defender against unseen enemies!...!". The final refrain is, "Rejoice, unwedded Bride!"

Kontakion 5 and Oikos 5

Kontakion 5 chants, "Seeing the star pointing to God, the Magi followed its radiance! Keeping it before them as a beacon, with its help, they sought out the Mighty King, and, attaining the Unattainable, they rejoiced in Him, and cried: 'Alleluia!'". The people then respond by singing a **triple** "Alleluia!".

Oikos 5 chants, "The children of the Chaldeans saw, in the Virgin's hands, Him Who, with His hands, had fashioned mankind! Though He had taken the form of a Slave, yet they knew Him as their Master! With haste, they knelt before Him with their gifts, and cried to the blessed Virgin:". The people respond with a set of refrains, each beginning with the word, "Rejoice!": "Rejoice, Mother of the ever-shining Star! Rejoice, bright dawn of the mystical Day! Rejoice, dispeller of deceit!...!". The final refrain is, "Rejoice, unwedded Bride!"

Kontakion 6 and Oikos 6

Kontakion 6 states, "Becoming God's messengers, the Magi returned to Babylon! Having fulfilled the prophecy concerning You, and preaching

You to all as the Christ, they left Herod to his raving! For, he knew not how to sing: 'Alleluia!'". The people then respond by singing a *triple* "Alleluia!".

Oikos 6 states, "Shining upon Egypt with the light of truth, You dispelled the darkness of falsehood! For, the idols of that land fell down, unable to withstand Your power, O Savior! And, all who were delivered from them cried to the Theotokos:". The people respond with a set of refrains, each beginning with the word, "Rejoice!": "Rejoice, restoration of men! Rejoice, despoiler of demons! Rejoice, for you trampled on evil's deceits!…!". The final refrain is, "Rejoice, unwedded Bride!"

Kontakion 7

Kontakion 7 chants, "As Symeon drew near to the time of his departure from this deceitful age, he received You as an Infant in his arms! But, he knew You to be perfect God! And, amazed at Your ineffable wisdom, He cried out: 'Alleluia!'". The people then respond by singing a *triple* "Alleluia!".

Troparion 2, Troparion 3, and Kontakion 1

Then, the people sing, in tone 4, Troparion 2: "I will open my mouth, inspired by the Spirit! I will sing a song to the Queen and Mother! And I will come, rejoicing in the feast, and I will extol her wonders in gladness!".

Then, a first reader chants, "O pure Virgin, living book of Christ, sealed by the Spirit: Seeing you, the great archangel cried: 'Rejoice, vessel of joy! Through you, we will be freed from the curse of our first mother, Eve!'". A second reader chants the verse, "Most holy Theotokos, save us!" The first reader then chants, "Rejoice, Virgin Bride of God, restoration of Adam, and death of hell! Rejoice, all-pure pavilion of the King of all! Rejoice, fiery throne of the Almighty!" The second reader again chants the verse, "Most holy Theotokos, save us!" The first reader then chants, "Rejoice, Lady, treasury of purity, raising us from our fall! Rejoice, lily whose sweet scent is known to all the faithful! Rejoice, fragrant incense and precious oil of myrrh!".

The people then sing Troparion 3, in tone 4: "In your divine glory, Theotokos, living and inexhaustible fountain: Give strength to everyone who sings hymns of praise to you, making them worthy of crowns of glory!".

Then, a reader chants, "Rejoice, Mother who has Borne for the faithful the sacrificial Victim without blemish! Rejoice, Ewe who have brought forth the Lamb of God, Who takes away the sins of all the world! Rejoice, mercy-seat, our fervent intercessor!". Another reader chants the verse, "Most holy Theotokos, save us!" The first reader then chants, "Rejoice, radiant dawn, who alone Bore Christ the Sun! Rejoice, dwelling-place of the Light! You dispersed the gloom and utterly destroyed the demon's darkness!". The second reader then again chants, "Most holy Theotokos, save us!" The first reader then chants, "Rejoice, only gate through whom the Word, alone, has passed! By your Birthgiving, you have broken the bars and gates of hell! Rejoice, Bride of God, and divine entry of the saved!".

The people then sing Kontakion 1, in tone 8: "Victorious leader of triumphant hosts! We, your servants, delivered from evil, sing our grateful thanks to you, Theotokos! As you possess invincible might, set us free from every calamity, so that we may sing: 'Rejoice, unwedded Bride!'".

(In the **Antiochian** tradition, the ordo for Little Compline here is: 1) Little Compline, up to the Creed and "It is Truly Meet"; 2) "With mystical apprehension…!", in tone 8; 3) Oikoi 1-6; 4) Odes 1-3, with their troparia and verses; 5) "O Victorious

Leader", in tone 8; 6) Oikoi 7-12; 7) Odes 4-6, with their troparia and verses; 8) "O Victorious Leader", in tone 8; 9) Oikoi 13-18; 10) Odes 7-9, with their troparia and verses; 11) "O Victorious Leader", in tone 8; 12) Oikoi 19-24, followed by Oikos 1; 13) "O Victorious Leader", in tone 8; 14) "Holy God!", and the rest of Little Compline.)

Oikos 7

The celebrant then chants Oikos 7: "The Creator has revealed a new creation, manifesting Himself to us, His creatures! From a Virgin's womb, He came, preserving it inviolate, as it was before, so that, seeing this miracle, we might extol her, crying out:". The people respond with a set of refrains, each beginning with the word, "Rejoice!": "Rejoice, flower of incorruption! Rejoice, crown of chastity! Rejoice, bright image of the Resurrection!…!". The final refrain is, "Rejoice, unwedded Bride!"

Kontakion 8 and Oikos 8

Kontakion 8 states, "Seeing this strange Birth, let us become strangers to the world, fixing our minds on Heaven! To this end, the Most High God has appeared on Earth as a lowly Man, in order to raise up all who cry aloud to Him: 'Alleluia!'". The people then respond by singing a ***triple*** "Alleluia!".

Oikos 8 states, "The Word, uncircumscribed, was wholly present here below, yet in no way absent from the Realm on high! God descended to Earth, yet underwent no change of place! He was Born of a Virgin, overshadowed by divine power! And, to her, we sing:". The people respond with a set of refrains, each beginning with the word, "Rejoice!": "Rejoice, boundary of the boundless God! Rejoice, gate of the precious mystery! Rejoice, sorrow of unbelievers!…!". The final refrain is, "Rejoice, unwedded Bride!"

Kontakion 9 and Oikos 9

Kontakion 9 chants, "All the ranks of angels marveled at the great work of Your Incarnation! For, they saw God, Whom none can approach, as a Man approachable by all, dwelling in our midst, and hearing, from our lips: 'Alleluia!'". The people then respond by singing a ***triple*** "Alleluia!".

Oikos 9 chants, "Eloquent orators we see dumb as the fishes in your presence, Theotokos!

For, they are at a loss to see how you Bear a Child, yet remain a Virgin! But, we, marveling at the Mystery, cry aloud with faith:". The people respond with a set of refrains, each beginning with the word, "Rejoice!": "Rejoice, receiver of the wisdom of God! Rejoice, treasury of His dispensation! Rejoice, by whom philosophers are foiled!...!". The final refrain is, "Rejoice, unwedded Bride!"

Kontakion 10 and Oikos 10

Kontakion 10 states, "Desiring to save the world, the Maker of all came on His own to His own! As God, He is our Shepherd, yet He appeared among us as a Sheep! Having called like to like, as God, He hears our cry: 'Alleluia!'". The people then respond by singing a *triple* "Alleluia!".

Oikos 10 states, "For virgins and for all who flee to you, you are a wall, Virgin Theotokos undefiled! For, the Creator of Heaven and Earth has made you ready, and adorned you, dwelling in your womb, and teaching all to sing:". The people respond with a set of refrains, each beginning with the word, "Rejoice!": "Rejoice, pillar of virginity! Rejoice, gate of salvation! Rejoice, first fruits of spiritual re-creation!...!". The final refrain is, "Rejoice, unwedded Bride!"

Kontakion 11 and Oikos 11

Kontakion 11 chants, "Every song is inadequate to tell the greatness of Your mercies! Were we to offer You as many odes as the sands of the sea, Holy King, we could not be worthy of the blessings You have given us, who sing: 'Alleluia!'". The people then respond by singing a **triple** "Alleluia!".

Oikos 11 chants, "We see the holy Virgin as a lamp of living light, shining on those in darkness! Kindling the immaterial Light, she guides all to the knowledge of God! She, the radiance who enlightens every mind, we praise with this song:". The people respond with a set of refrains, each beginning with the word, "Rejoice!": "Rejoice, ray of the spiritual Sun! Rejoice, radiance of the unwaning Light! Rejoice, splendor illumining our souls!...!". The final refrain is, "Rejoice, unwedded Bride!"

Kontakion 12 and Oikos 12

Kontakion 12 states, "Desiring to grant release from ancient debts, the Redeemer of all came to those who were exiled from His grace! Tearing up the record of our sins, He hears this song from all: 'Alleluia!'". The people then respond by singing a **triple** "Alleluia!".

Oikos 12 states, "Extolling your Birthgiving, we glorify you as a living temple, O Theotokos! For, the Lord, Who holds all things in His hand, made His dwelling in your womb! He sanctified and glorified you, teaching all to sing:". The people respond with a set of refrains, each beginning with the word, "Rejoice!": "Rejoice, tabernacle of the Word of God! Rejoice, greater Holy of Holies! Rejoice, ark guided by the Spirit!...!". The final refrain is, "Rejoice, unwedded Bride!"

Kontakion 13 and Oikos 13

Kontakion 13 chants, "Mother, worthy of all praise, who have Borne the Word, Holiest of all Holies: Accept this, our offering, delivering from every ill and the condemnation to come, all those who sing: 'Alleluia!'". The people then respond by singing a **triple** "Alleluia!".

Oikos 13 chants, "The first of the angels was sent from Heaven to greet the Theotokos with this salutation: 'Rejoice!' (this is repeated **three** times in the Antiochian tradition). Upon seeing You, O Lord, becoming Incarnate at his bodiless word, he stood in awe, and cried out:". The people respond with a set of refrains, each beginning with the word, "Rejoice!": "Rejoice, by whom joy will be enkindled! Rejoice, by whom the curse will be quenched! Rejoice, recall of fallen Adam!...!". (**_Note:_** The "Rejoice!" refrains for this Oikos 13 are the same as the "Rejoice!" refrains for Oikos 1.) The final refrain is, "Rejoice, unwedded Bride!"

Kontakion 1

The people then sing Kontakion 1, in tone 8: "Victorious leader of triumphant hosts! We, your servants, delivered from evil, sing our grateful thanks to you, Theotokos! As you possess invincible might, set us free from every calamity, so that we may sing: 'Rejoice, unwedded Bride!'".

The Augmented Litany

The Augmented Litany is then celebrated, beginning with the petition, "Have mercy on us, O God, according to Your great goodness, we pray You: Hear us and have mercy!". The people then respond, **from this <u>first</u> petition**, a **triple** "Lord, have mercy.". **<u>Note:</u>** Because this is a service for a Saturday during Great Lent, which is a eucharistic day, the melody used for the responses to this litany is **<u>non</u>**-Lenten! After the exclamation ("For, You are a merciful God Who love mankind,…!"), the people sing, "Amen.". The deacon then intones, "Again and again, on bended knees, let us pray to the Lord.". The people again sing a **triple** "Lord, have mercy.". The celebrant then chants a prayer that begins, "Virgin, pure, spotless, incorrupt, undefiled, all-pure!…!". After the exclamation, which ends, ", through the mercy and love for mankind of your only-begotten Son, our Lord, God, and Savior, Jesus Christ, to Whom are due all glory, honor, and worship, together with His Father, Who is from everlasting, and His all-Holy, good, and life-creating Spirit, now and ever and unto ages of ages!", the people sing, "Amen.".

The Dismissal

The Dismissal is then celebrated. **Note:** Again, because this is a service for a Saturday during Great Lent, which is a eucharistic day, the melody used for the responses to the Dismissal is **non**-Lenten! The celebrant intones, "Most holy Theotokos, save us!". The people sing, "More honorable than the Cherubim,…!". The celebrant then intones, "Glory to You, O Christ, our God and our Hope, glory to You!". The people then sing a full "Glory,… now and ever…!", a *triple* "Lord, have mercy.", and then, "Father (or, if it is a bishop, "Master"; or, if it is the Metropolitan, "Most blessed Master"), bless!". The celebrant then chants the Dismissal Prayer. After this, the people *usually* respond by singing a *double* "Amen." ("Amen. Amen."). In the **Greek** practice, the final hymn of the service, in tone 3, is, "Awed by the beauty of your virginity,…!", after which the priest concludes, "Through the prayers of our holy fathers,…!".

"Beneath Your Compassion"

In *many* parishes, it is customary, at this point, for the people to sing the following penitential hymn to the Theotokos. The triple singing of "Most holy Theotokos, save us!" at the end is accompanied, each time, by the people doing a full prostration. The text of this hymn is: "Beneath your compassion, we take refuge, Virgin Theotokos! Despise not our prayers in our necessities, but deliver us from harm, only pure, only blessed one! Most holy Theotokos, save us! Most holy Theotokos, save us! Most holy Theotokos, save us!".

Recessional Hymns

There are various practices in different parishes as to what is done while everyone comes forward to venerate the icons and the Holy Cross. In some parishes, Troparion 1 and/or Kontakion 1 may be sung. In other parishes, the venerations are done in silence. As always, the local custom as prescribed by the main celebrant should be observed.

F. LITTLE COMPLINE

Though it is not often done in many parishes, some communities *do* celebrate the service of Little Compline on the weeknights of Great Lent. In the Greek practice, the chanting of "It is truly meet" precedes the rest of the service. The order of the service is as follows.[39]

The Doxology, the Trisagion Prayers, and the Lord's Prayer

The celebrant chants the doxology, "Blessed is our God, always now and ever and unto ages of ages!" A reader (or, in the Antiochian tradition, the priest) chants, "Amen.", "Glory to You, our God, glory to You!", "O Heavenly King!", and then the Trisagion Prayers and the Lord's Prayer. After the exclamation ("For, Yours are the Kingdom, and the power, and the glory,…!"), the reader responds with "Amen.", "Lord, have mercy." *twelve* times, a full "Glory,… now and ever…!", and "Come, let us

---

[39] Nassar, pp. 82-90.

worship God, our King!...!". In the Greek practice, however, "Lord, have mercy." is chanted **forty** times, and then followed by the Prayer of the Hours.

Psalms 50, 69, and 142

The reader then chants Psalm 50 ("Having mercy on me, O God, according to Your steadfast love! According to Your abundant mercy, blot out my transgressions!").[40]

After this is the chanting of Psalm 69 ("Be pleased, O God, to deliver me! O Lord, make haste to help me!"). This can either be done by the same reader, or different readers can participate in the chanting of the Psalms. The latter would be the preferred practice, as it would give many people a chance to actively participate in the service. However, whatever the local practice is should be observed.

Following this is the chanting of Psalm 142 ("Hear my prayer, O Lord! Give ear to my supplications! In Your faithfulness, answer me, in Your righteousness! Enter not into judgment with Your servant! For, no man living is righteous before

---

[40] The Psalm numbering is according to the Septuagint.

You!"), one of the Six Psalms celebrated at the beginning of Matins.

The Creed

After the completion of Psalm 142, a Little Doxology is done, and then the Nicean-Constantinopolitan Creed is chanted ("I believe in one God, the Father Almighty, Maker of Heaven and Earth, and of all things visible and invisible;…!"). If three separate readers had chanted the previous three Psalms, a fourth reader should chant the Creed. If, however, one reader chanted all three Psalms, a second reader should chant the Creed. This will liturgically manifest that the Psalms constitute one liturgical element, while the Creed constitutes another. In any case, the local custom should be observed.

Hymn to the Theotokos

Once the Creed has been chanted, the Hymn to the Theotokos is celebrated: "It is truly meet to bless you, O Theotokos, ever-blessed and most-pure and the Mother of our God! More honorable than the Cherubim, and more glorious beyond compare than the Seraphim! Without defilement, you gave Birth to the Word of God! True Theotokos, we magnify you!" (If a kanon is to be celebrated, it is done **before** the Hymn to the Theotokos.) The service books do not specify whether this hymn should be sung by the people or chanted by a reader. However, being that this is a penitential service celebrated on the weeknights of Great Lent, the chanting of it by a reader seems more liturgically appropriate.

The Trisagion Prayers and the Lord's Prayer

A reader will then chant the Trisagion Prayers and the Lord's Prayer. After the exclamation ("For, Yours are the Kingdom, and the power, and the glory,…!"), the reader chants "Amen.".

Penitential Hymns

Following the Trisagion Prayers and the Lord's Prayer, the people sing a set of penitential hymns, in tone 6: "Have mercy on us, O God, have mercy on us!…!"; "Glory…Spirit!"; "Have mercy on us, O Lord!

For, we have put our trust in You!...!"; "Now and ever...Amen."; "Open to us the door of your loving-kindness, O blessed Theotokos!...!". Being penitential in nature, and having been sung at Grand Compline with the Kanon of St Andrew of Crete during Great Lent,[41] they are sung here, as well. (In the **Antiochian** tradition, these penitential hymns are **preceded** by the kontakion. These penitential petitions are **not** done in the **Greek** tradition.)

Concluding Petitions

A reader then chants "Lord, have mercy." **forty** times, followed by the petitions that begin, "You, Who at every season and every hour, in Heaven and on Earth, are worshipped and glorified, O Christ our God;...!". The reader then chants a **triple** "Lord, have mercy.", followed by a full "Glory,... now and ever...!", "More honorable than the Cherubim,...!", and, then, "In the Name of the Lord, give the blessing, Father!" (or, if a bishop is serving, "Master!"; or, if the Metropolitan is serving, "Most blessed Master!"). The main celebrant then chants, "God be bountiful to us, and bless us, and show the light of His countenance on us, and have

---

[41] Cf. above, p. 495.

mercy on us!" The reader then responds, "Amen." (In the **Antiochian** tradition, the Prayer of St Ephraim is then done here. In the **Greek** practice, a reader chants "Lord, have mercy." **twelve** times, followed by "Most holy Theotokos, save us!".)

Prayers of Supplication

The main celebrant then comes out and stands on the solea before the Royal Doors. (Being a non-sacramental service, it is not necessary to have an ordained celebrant present. However, in most parishes, the pastor is usually concelebrating the service. When this is the case, he would chant these prayers of supplication.) Turning to the icon of the Theotokos on the iconostasis, he chants a prayer that begins, "O Virgin, pure, spotless, incorrupt, undefiled, all-pure;…!". He then turns to the icon of Christ on the iconostasis and chants a prayer that begins, "And, grant us, O Master, as we lay down to sleep, repose both of body and of soul,…!". He then again turns to the icon of the Theotokos on the iconostasis and chants a prayer that begins, "O exceedingly glorious, ever-Virgin Mother of Christ our God,…!". (In the **Byzantine** tradition, many times a laywoman will chant the prayer to the

Theotokos, and a layman will chant the prayer to Christ.)

The celebrant then turns and faces directly forward to the Royal Doors and chants the Prayer of St Ioannikios: "The Father is my Hope! The Son is my Refuge! The Holy Spirit is my Protection! O Holy Trinity, glory to You!" After this is intoned, a reader ***immediately*** chants a full "Glory,… now and ever…!", a ***triple*** "Lord, have mercy.", and, then, "Father (or, "Master;" or, "Most blessed Master"), bless!" (In the **Antiochian** tradition, after the Prayer of St Ioannikios, there is a prayer to the Theotokos and then a prayer to the guardian angel.) The celebrant then turns and faces the people from the ambo and chants a prayer that begins, "O greatly-merciful Master, Lord, Jesus Christ, our God…!". **The people** then ***sing*** an "Amen." in the Lenten tone. (In the **Greek** practice, both the Prayer of St Ioannikios and the prayer, "O greatly-merciful Master, Lord, Jesus Christ, our God…!" are **omitted**.) The celebrant then prostrates on the ambo before the people, chanting, "Forgive me, my brothers and sisters!" The people respond with, "May our Lord God forgive you, and forgive us!"

"All of My Hope Have I Placed in You"

The people then sing the following in tone 6, which are the final verses from "O Lord of Hosts" celebrated at the Grand Compline with the Kanon of St Andrew of Crete:[42] "All of my hope have I placed in you, O Mother of God! Protect me beneath your veil!" (This is **omitted** in the Byzantine tradition.)

[Prayer to the Guardian Angel]

The service books then call for the chanting of a prayer to the guardian angel that begins, "O holy angel, who accompany my wretched soul and my lowly life,...!". Depending on the local custom, this liturgical element may be either celebrated or omitted. (This **is** usually done in the Greek practice.)

[The Prayer of St Ephraim]

Although the service books do not specifically call for this, in **many** parishes, at this point, the full

---

[42] Cf. above, p. 497.

Prayer of St Ephraim is celebrated in its ***full*** form: The main celebrant, standing on the solea, chants the prayer in three sections ("O Lord and Master of my life,...!", "But, give, rather, the spirit of chastity,...!", and "Yes, O Lord and King, grant me to see my own transgressions...!"), each section concluding with a full prostration by all of the people. Then, everyone makes a metania (bow) ***twelve*** times, while saying silently to themselves, "God, cleanse me a sinner and have mercy on me!". Finally, the celebrant chants the entire prayer as a full unit, one last time, and everyone makes a final prostration. This celebration of the Prayer of St Ephraim is ***usually omitted*** in the Greek practice.

The Dismissal

The main celebrant then chants, "Glory to You, O Christ, our God and our Hope, glory to You!" The people then sing a full "Glory,... now and ever...!", a ***triple*** "Lord, have mercy.", and, then, "Father (or, if a bishop is serving, "Master!"; or, if the Metropolitan is serving, "Most blessed Master!"), bless!" The main celebrant then intones the Dismissal Prayer, and the people ***usually*** sing a ***double*** "Amen." ("Amen. Amen."). ***All*** of these responses are sung in the Lenten melody.

8
HOLY WEEK, PASCHA, AND BRIGHT WEEK

Great Lent officially ends on the sixth Friday, the day before Lazarus Saturday. Therefore, Lazarus Saturday and Palm Sunday are beyond Lent and constitute the preparation and beginning of Holy Week.[43]

A. LAZARUS SATURDAY AND PALM SUNDAY

The service books call for the Liturgy of the Presanctified Gifts to be celebrated for Lazarus Saturday on Friday evening. Then, after the celebration of Grand Compline and Nocturns (the Midnight Office), Matins is celebrated on Saturday morning, followed by the Divine Liturgy of St John

---

[43] *Great Lent*, p. 83.

Chrysostom.[44] However, **some** parishes celebrate a more standard Vigil service, combining either the Vespers or the Grand Compline with the Matins. What is present here, though, is according to the regular practice of the service books.

Lazarus Saturday: The Liturgy of the Presanctified Gifts

At "Lord, I Call Upon You!", there are 10 stikhera called for. Since the first one ("We have completed the forty days that profit our souls!...!") is in tone 8, the singing of "Lord, I Call" that precedes it is also in tone 8. The service books call for this stikheron to be sung twice, as are the third and fourth stikhera (hence, the total of 10 stikhera). However, **many** parishes only sing them **once** (in which case, only 7 stikhera total are sung). The second stikheron, in the same tone, is to the martyrs: "O martyrs of the Lord, we beseech you, offer intercession to our God...!". Then follows a set of 5 stikhera for St Lazarus, all in tone 6: "Wishing to see the tomb of Lazarus, O Lord,...!", "You came to

---

[44] *Triodion*, pp. 464-488.

the place of burial of Lazarus, O Lord,…!", "Your voice destroyed the kingdom of hell, O Lord,…!", "You came to the tomb of Lazarus, O Lord,…!", and "You came to Bethany to awaken Lazarus, O Lord,…!". Then, after a reader chants "Glory…Spirit!", the people sing, in tone 8, "Standing before the tomb of Lazarus, O Savior,…!". After the reader chants "Now and ever…Amen.", the people sing, again in tone 8, "We have completed the forty days that profit our souls!…!".

After the Vesperal Entrance and the singing of "Gladsome Light", the First Prokeimenon is chanted in the 6th tone: "Our help is in the Name of the Lord, Who made Heaven and Earth!", with its accompanying verse, "If it had not been the Lord Who was on our side when men rose up against us, then they would have swallowed us alive!". The first Old Testament reading is Genesis 49:33-50:26. The Second Prokeimenon is in tone 4: "Those who trust in the Lord are like Mount Zion, which cannot be moved, but abides forever!", with its accompanying verse, "For, the scepter of wickedness will not rest upon the land allotted to the righteous!". The second Old Testament reading is Proverbs 31:8-31.

The rest of the Liturgy of the Presanctified Gifts is celebrated as usual.

Lazarus Saturday: Grand Compline

Grand Compline for Lazarus Saturday contains the odes and troparia of the Kanon of St Andrew of Crete. The rest of the service is celebrated as usual.

Lazarus Saturday: Nocturns

In the rare instances in which Nocturns for Lazarus Saturday is celebrated in a parish, the main liturgical elements specific for the day are the Troparion, in tone 1 ("By raising Lazarus from the dead before Your Passion,….!"), and the Kontakion, in tone 2 ("Christ, the Joy, the Truth, and the Light of all,….!").

Lazarus Saturday: Matins

At Matins, following the usual opening and the chanting of the 6 Psalms, "God is the Lord!" is sung in tone 1, as is the Troparion for the feast ("By raising Lazarus from the dead before Your

Passion,…!"). Following this is the chanting of the 16th Kathisma of the Psalter (Psalms 109-117), a Kathisma Hymn in tone 1, then the 17th Kathisma of the Psalter, the entire Psalm 118, all 176 verses (***except*** in the Greek practice, where the 16th and 17th Kathismata are ***omitted***; only the Kathisma Hymns are chanted). This is followed by the Troparia of the Resurrection, in tone 5: "Blessed are You, O Lord! Teach me Your statutes!", and the accompanying stikhera. The service books then call for the celebration of a Little Litany, but this ***may*** be ***omitted***, depending on the instructions of the main celebrant. Then, a Kathisma Hymn, in tone 5, begins, "O Lord, the Giver of Life,…!"

There is ***no*** Gospel reading at this Matins. However, the usual Post-Gospel Stikhera, in tone 6, are then sung by the people: "Having beheld the Resurrection of Christ…!", concluding with "He has destroyed death by death!" Psalm 50 then may either be chanted or eliminated, depending on the discretion of the main celebrant.

The Kanon is in tone 8, and each ode is accompanied by troparia, the refrain to each being, "Glory, O Lord, to Your holy Resurrection!" The service books call for two Kanons through Ode 5, and then, beginning with Ode 6, two four-canticled

Kanons are celebrated. However, in **most** parishes, only **<u>one</u> Kanon** is celebrated (**except** in the Byzantine tradition, which **only** sings the Katavasia of the Kanon), as follows. Ode 1 begins, "Let us sing a song of victory to the Lord,…!". Since Great Lent has now been completed, there is <u>**no**</u> Ode 2. Ode 3 chants, "You are the confirmation of those who run to You,…!". This ode is followed by two Kathisma Hymns: the first one, in tone 4, begins, "The sisters of Lazarus stood at Jesus' side!". A reader then chants a full "Glory,… now and ever…!", and then the people sing, in tone 8, "O Creator, all things are known to You!"

    Ode 4 states, "I have heard, O Lord, the mystery of Your dispensation!". Ode 5 chants, "Why have you cast me away from Your Face, O never-setting Light?". Ode 6 states, "O Lord, Jonah was saved from the whale!". After this, the Kontakion, in tone 2, is sung: "Christ, the Joy, the Truth, and the Light of all,…!". A reader chants the Oikos, which begins, "The Creator of all foretold to His Apostles…!", and the people complete it by singing the cadence phrase of the Kontakion: "Granting divine forgiveness to all!"

    Ode 7 chants, "The Hebrew youths braved the flaming furnace!". Ode 8 states, "When the people worshipped the king's image,...!". Ode 9 chants, "Let us honor the pure Theotokos!". Though the service books call for the katavasia to be taken from Ode 9 of the second Kanon ("Saved through you, pure Virgin,...!"), where most parishes celebrated just the **one** Kanon, the katavasia repeats the ode that begins, "Let us honor the pure Theotokos!". In the Greek practice, four verses from the 9th ode are chanted. A Little Litany follows the singing of the katavasia.

      The usual **triple** singing of "Holy is the Lord our God!" then occurs. Following this is the Exapostilarion, in tone 3, each line of which is first chanted by a reader and then sung by the people (**except** in the Byzantine tradition): "By Your Word, O Word of God!", "Lazarus leaps up, restored to life!", "The people honor you with palms, O almighty Lord!", and "For, hell will be utterly destroyed by Your death!". The reader then chants a full "Glory,... now and ever...!", and then again alternates the chanting with the singing, again in tone 3: "Through Lazarus, Christ is already despoiling you, O death!", "The weeping of Bethany is bequeathed to you!", and "Let us raise victory branches to honor the Lord!".

The Praises are then celebrated in tone 1, with the following stikhera: "O Christ, Who are the Resurrection and the Life of man,…!", "By raising Lazarus from hell, O Christ,…!", "Martha and Mary said to the Savior:…!", and "O Lord, You gave Your disciples signs of Your divinity,…!". The following two stikhera are in tone 4: "By raising Your friend, Lazarus, who had been dead for four days,…!", and "Martha cried to Mary: 'The Teacher is here!'". Then, the next two stikhera are again in tone 8: "O great and mighty wonder!", and "As You told Martha, O Lord,…!". The reader then chants, "Glory…Spirit!", and the people sing, in tone 2, "A great and strange wonder is performed today!". Then, after the reader chants, "Now and ever…Amen.", the people sing, again in tone 2, "You are most blessed, O Virgin Theotokos!".

The main celebrant intones, "Glory to You, Who have shone us the Light!" (***except*** in the Greek practice, where the singers chant this exclamation). The people then sing the Great Doxology, which begins, "Glory to God in the highest, and, on Earth, peace, good will to men!". As always, the Great Doxology concludes with the singing of a ***triple*** "Holy God!", a full "Glory,… now and ever…!", "Holy Immortal!", and then a final "Holy God!".

Two litanies then follow (*except* in the Greek practice). The Augmented Litany begins with the petition, "Have mercy on us, O God,...!" and a *triple* "Lord, have mercy.". The Morning Litany follows the usual form of a Litany of Supplication, complete with a closing prayer that begins, "O Lord our God, Who bowed the Heavens and came down for the salvation of the human race...!". After the exclamation ("Blessed and glorified be the majesty of Your Kingdom,...!"), the people sing, "Amen.". The Dismissal is celebrated in the usual manner, followed, most of the time, by the singing of the Troparion, in tone 1: "By raising Lazarus from the dead before Your Passion,...!" (or, in the *Byzantine* tradition, "Today, salvation has come...!").

Lazarus Saturday: The Divine Liturgy

The Divine Liturgy of St John Chrysostom for Lazarus Saturday begins in the usual manner. At the singing of "O Come, Let Us Worship", we sing, as on Sundays, "Who Arose from the dead", since this service celebrates the raising of Lazarus. After the Gospel Entrance, the Troparion, in tone 1 ("By raising Lazarus from the dead before Your

Passion,…!"), is sung, followed by a full "Glory,… now and ever…!", and then the Kontakion, in tone 2 (Christ, the Joy, the Truth, and the Light of all,…!"). Instead of singing the regular Trisagion ("Holy God!"), "As many as have been baptized into Christ!" is sung (**except** in the Greek practice). The Prokeimenon for the feast is in tone 3: "The Lord is my Light and my Salvation! Whom should I fear?", with its accompanying verse, "The Lord is the Defender of my life! Of whom should I be afraid?". The Epistle reading is Hebrews 12:28-13:8. The "Alleluia!" verses are in tone 5: "The Lord is King! He is robed in majesty!", and "For, He has established the world, so that it will never be moved!" The Gospel reading is John 11:1-45.

The Hymn to the Theotokos is Ode 9 of the Matins Kanon, in tone 8: "Let us honor the pure Theotokos!". After the singing of "One is holy!", the people do **not** sing, "Praise the Lord from the Heavens!" as the Communion Hymn, but, instead, sing, "Out of the mouths of babes and infants You have fashioned perfect praise! Alleluia! Alleluia! Alleluia!" The rest of the Divine Liturgy concludes as usual. (**Note:** In the Byzantine tradition, instead of singing, "We have seen the true Light!", the people sing the troparion for Lazarus in tone 1.)

Palm Sunday: Vespers and Matins

In many parishes of the Byzantine tradition, Vespers and Matins for Palm Sunday are celebrated separately (Vespers on Saturday evening, Matins on Sunday morning before the Divine Liturgy). In most parishes of the Slavic tradition, Vespers and Matins are celebrated together as a Vigil service on Saturday evening.

At "Lord, I Call Upon You!", sung in tone 6, there are 10 stikhera called for. This is because there are actually 5 different stikhera, each of which is called for to be sung twice. In **many** parishes, however, the local practice is to sing each stikheron once. Therefore, with **that** practice, there are only 5 stikhera (**except** in the Greek practice, where there are **six** because the **first** stikheron is sung **twice**). The 5 different stikhera begin as follows: "Today, the grace of the Holy Spirit has assembled us!", "Today, the Word of God the Father, the co-eternal Son,...!", "Let us, the new Israel, the Church of the Gentiles,...!", "Prefiguring for us Your holy Resurrection, loving Lord,...!", and "Six days before the feast of Passover,...!". The service books call for a "split 'Glory!'" ("Glory...Spirit!", then "Now and ever…Amen." [*except* in the Byzantine tradition]) and, after each half of the split, to sing, again, "Today, the grace of the Holy Spirit has assembled us!". Again, however, in **many** parishes, the reader chants a full "Glory,… now and ever…!", and then the people sing "Today, the grace of the Holy Spirit has assembled us!" *only once*.

After the Vesperal Entrance, the singing of "Gladsome Light," and the Evening Prokeimenon ("The Lord is King! He is robed in majesty!"), there are 3 Old Testament readings called for. Usually, three different readers take part, each one chanting one of the readings, which are as follows: Genesis 49:1-2, 8-12; Zephaniah 3:14-20 (some service books say verses 14-19, which the **Greeks** follow); and Zechariah 9:9-17 (some service books say verses 9-15, which the **Greeks** follow). After the singing of "Vouchsafe, O Lord!," the people sing the stikhera of the Litya as the clergy and servers exit the sanctuary and go to the back of the nave. Not all parishes sing all of the stikhera for the Litya (the Greeks usually **omit** this Litya altogether), but only enough to enable the clergy and servers to process to the back of the church. The stikhera, however, are as follows: in tone 1, "The all-Holy Spirit, Who taught the Apostles…!"; in tone 1, "The Son and Word of the

Father,…!"; in tone 1, "Six days before the Passover, O Lord,…!"; in tone 2, "Entering, O Lord, into the holy city,…!"; and, in tone 2, "Glory to You, O Christ, Who are enthroned on high!". After a reader chants a full "Glory,… now and ever…!", the people sing, in tone 3, "Six days before the Passover, Jesus came to Bethany,…!". The Litya Prayers are then chanted, with "Lord, have mercy." as the response to be sung. This is done differently in different parishes. The **full** practice called for in the service books has **five petitions**: after the **first three** petitions, the people sing "Lord, have mercy." **twelve** times each; after the **last two** petitions, the people sing "Lord, have mercy." **three** times each. **Some** parishes only chant **four petitions**, and the people sing the response **twelve** times after the **first two** petitions and **three** times after the **last two** petitions. In the Antiochian tradition, after the first five petitions, the people sing "Lord, have mercy." **three** times (and the same after the 7th petition); after the 6th petition, the people sing "Lord, have mercy." **forty** times. As always, the choir director and singers should follow the local custom.

The Apostikha stikhera are in tone 8. First, there is, "Rejoice and be glad, O city of Zion!". Then, a reader chants the verse, "Out of the mouths of babes and infants, You have fashioned perfect praise!". Then, the next stikheron begins, "Today, the Savior comes to Jerusalem,...!". The reader then chants, "O Lord, our Lord, how glorious is Your Name in all the Earth!". The third stikheron says, "O gracious Lord, Who ride on the Cherubim,...!". As with "Lord, I Call Upon You!", the service books then call for a "split 'Glory!'" (**except** in the Byzantine tradition), with "Today, the grace of the Holy Spirit has assembled us!", being sung in tone 6 after each half of that doxology. Again, in **many** parishes, the reader chants a full "Glory,... now and ever...!" straight through, and "Today, the grace of the Holy Spirit has assembled us!" being sung **only once**.

St Symeon's Prayer, the Trisagion Prayers, and the Lord's Prayer then follow. After this, the people sing two troparia for the feast: in tone 1, "By raising Lazarus from the dead before Your Passion,...!" is **sung twice**, and, in tone 4, "When we were buried with You in Baptism, O Christ God,...!" is **sung once**. This is followed, in most parishes, with the blessing of the loaves, wheat, wine, and oil, with the usual responses ("Lord, have mercy." and "Amen.") sung by the people. (In the **Antiochian** tradition, the blessing of the loaves, wheat, wine, and oil is done **before** the Apostikha.)

At Matins, after the opening doxology, the 6 Psalms, and the Great Litany, "God is the Lord!" is chanted by the deacon and responded to (sung by) the people, in tone 1. After the final singing of "God is the Lord!", the people sing the two troparia for the feast, as it was done at the end of Vespers: in tone 1, "By raising Lazarus from the dead before Your Passion,…!" is **sung twice**, and, in tone 4, "When we were buried with You in Baptism, O Christ God,…!" is **sung once**.

At this point, the first reading from the Psalter, Kathisma 2 (Psalms 9-16[45]) is prescribed to be chanted by a reader (as before, **only** the Kathisma Hymns are celebrated in the **Greek** tradition). However, in **many** parishes, this is **omitted**. Then, two Kathisma Hymns, sung in tone 4, are called for: "Let us join the children in spirit,…!", followed by a full "Glory,… now and ever…!" by a reader, and then the second Kathisma Hymn, "Lazarus has been dead for four days,…!". Then, the service books call for the second reading from the Psalter, Kathisma 3 (Psalms 17-23), which, again, in **many** parishes, is **omitted**. Then, two more Kathisma Hymns are called for: in tone 4, "O Christ, You have mystically shed tears over Your friend,…!", followed by a full

---

[45] The Psalm numbering is according to the Septuagint.

"Glory,... now and ever...!" by a reader, and then the second Kathisma Hymn, in tone 1, "Praise the Lord, all peoples and nations!".

The Polyeleon is then sung. This is followed, in the Slavic practice *only*, of the singing of the Magnification: "We magnify You, O Life-Giver Christ! Hosanna in the highest! And we cry unto You: 'Blessed is He Who comes in the Name of the Lord!'." The people then sing the verse, "O Lord, our Lord, how glorious is Your Name in all the Earth!". The Magnification is then sung again. The people then sing a full "Glory,... now and ever...!" (the service books then call for the singing of "Alleluia! Alleluia! Alleluia! Glory to You, O God!" *three* times, but, in *many* parishes, this is *omitted*), and then sing the Magnification one final time. Even though it is not called for in the service books, in *many* parishes, a Little Litany is celebrated at this point.

After this, the service books call for the singing, in tone 8, of a Kathisma Hymn, "He Who sits upon the throne of the Cherubim,...!", *twice*, with a full "Glory,... now and ever...!" interspersed between the two singings of the Kathisma Hymn. Again, in *many* parishes, this Kathisma Hymn is sung *only once*, with *no* "Glory,... now and ever...!" sung (all of this is *not* done in the *Antiochian* tradition). After the Kathisma Hymn, "From My Youth!" is sung in tone 4.

Then, the Matins Prokeimenon, in tone 4, is celebrated: "Out of the mouths of babes and infants, You have fashioned perfect praise!", with its accompanying verse, "O Lord, our Lord, how glorious is Your Name in all the Earth!". There is an intercessory petition and "Lord, have mercy.", an exclamation and an "Amen.", and then "Let every breath!" is sung in the same tone 4. The Matins Gospel, Matthew 21:1-11, 15-17, is then chanted. This is followed by the blessing of the palms. Following this is the singing of the Post-Gospel Stikhera, in tone 6 (tone 2 in the **Byzantine** tradition): "Glory…Spirit", "Today, Christ enters the holy city,…!", "Now and ever…Amen.", "Today, Christ enters the holy city,…!", "Have mercy on me, O God,…!", and, finally, "Today, the grace of the Holy Spirit has assembled us!". In the **Antiochian** tradition, the blessing of the palms is done either after Psalm 50 (which follows the Gospel) or after the Exapostilarion. In the **Greek** practice, the blessing of the palms is done near the end of the Divine Liturgy.

The Kanon is then celebrated in tone 4. Even though the service books call for the odes to be sung twice and the troparia to be repeated four to six times, in **most** parishes, both the ode and the troparia are celebrated **only once**. One reader chants the troparia after the singing of the ode, with another reader chanting the refrain, "Glory to You, our God, glory to You!" until the final refrain, which is a full "Glory,... now and ever...!". In the **Greek** practice, a reader chants the Hypakoe, Kontakion, Oikos, and Synaxarion; also, only the Katavasia are celebrated; at Ode 9, the Irmos ("God is the Lord") is sung, followed by three troparia, and then the Katavasia again.

Ode 1 begins, "The springs of the deep appeared as dry land!". Ode 3 chants, "The Israelites drank from a hard and barren rock,...!". After the final troparion of Ode 3, the people singing the Hypakoe in tone 6, "First, the multitude praised Christ our God with palms!".

Then, Ode 4 begins, "Christ, our God, is coming and will not tarry!". Ode 5 chants, "O you, who tell good tidings to Zion,...!". Ode 6 begins, "The souls of the righteous cry aloud, saying,...!". After the final troparion of Ode 6, the people singing the Kontakion in tone 6, "Sitting on Your throne in Heaven!". A reader then chants the Oikos, "You have bound hell, slain death, and raised the world!".

When the reader finishes chanting, "We cry aloud in great exultation:", the people then sing the cadence phrase of the Kontakion, "Blessed is He Who comes to recall Adam!".

Ode 7 chants, "You have saved the children of Abraham from the fire!". Ode 8 begins, "Rejoice, O Jerusalem!". Ode 9 chants, "God is the Lord and has revealed Himself to us!". After the final troparion, Ode 9, "God is the Lord and has revealed Himself to us!", is again sung, as the katavasia.

There is **no** Exapostilarion sung. Instead, after the katavasia of Ode 9 of the Kanon, "Holy is the Lord our God!" is celebrated in tone 4 (tone 2 in the **Antiochian** tradition, where the blessing of the palms follows). This is followed by the Praises, in tone 4. There are 6 stikhera called for on the Praises. However, the first two stikhera are each called to be sung twice. In **many** parishes, each of these stikhera is sung **only once**, making a total of 4 stikhera (which the **Greeks** follow). The stikhera are: "A great multitude spread their garments...!", "When You were about to enter the holy city, O Lord,...!", "Come forth, all you nations!", and "Before Your voluntary Passion, O Lord,...!". A reader then chants a full "Glory,... now and ever...!", and then the people sing, in tone 6, "Six days before the feast of Passover,…!".

The Great Doxology is then sung, followed by the singing, once in tone 4, of the troparion, "When we were buried with You in Baptism, O Christ God,…!". After this is the Augmented Litany (beginning with the petition, "Have mercy on us, O God,…!", and the singing of a *triple* "Lord, have mercy." from the beginning), followed by the Morning Litany, with its prayer ("O Lord our God, Who bowed the Heavens…!") at the bowing of the heads. Then, the Dismissal is celebrated. As everyone comes forward to venerate the icons and the Holy Cross, *many* parishes have the people sing the two troparia for the feast ("By raising Lazarus from the dead before Your Passion,…!" and "When we were buried with You in Baptism, O Christ God,…!"), along with the Kontakion of the feast ("Sitting on Your throne in Heaven!").

Palm Sunday: The Divine Liturgy

After the Great Litany, special antiphons are sung for Palm Sunday. The 1st Antiphon is from

Psalm 115:[46] "I love the Lord because He has heard the voice of my supplication!", "Because He inclined His ear to me, therefore I will call on Him as long as I live!", "The snares of death encompassed me! The pangs of hell laid hold on me!", "I suffered distress and anguish, then I called upon the Name of the Lord!", and, a full "Glory,… now and ever…!". After each verse of the Psalm is sung the refrain, "Through the prayers of the Theotokos, O Savior, save us!"

The 2nd Antiphon is also from Psalm 115: "I kept my faith even when I said: 'I am greatly afflicted!'", "What should I render to the Lord for all the things He has given me?", "I will receive the cup of salvation and call on the Name of the Lord!", and, "I will pay my vows to the Lord in the presence of all His people!". After each verse of the Psalm is sung the refrain, "O Son of God, Who sat upon the foal, save us who sing to You: 'Alleluia!'". This is followed by a full "Glory,… now and ever…!" and then "Only-Begotten Son".

For the 3rd Antiphon, the first Troparion of the feast, in tone 1, is sung: "By raising Lazarus from the dead before Your Passion,…!". Before each singing of this Troparion, a reader chants the following

---

[46] The Psalms are numbered according to the Septuagint.

verses for the 3rd Antiphon: "O give thanks to the Lord, for He is good! For, His steadfast love endures forever!", "Let the house of Israel say: 'For, He is good! For, His steadfast love endures forever!'", "Let the house of Aaron say: 'For, He is good! For, His steadfast love endures forever!'", and "Let all those who fear the Lord say: 'For, He is good! For, His steadfast love endures forever!'" Then, after the Gospel Entrance is made, the deacon, raising up the Gospel Book, intones the Introit for the Entrance: "Wisdom! Let us be attentive! Blessed is He Who comes in the Name of the Lord! We bless you from the house of the Lord! God is the Lord and has revealed Himself to us!". The people then sing this first Troparion, in tone 1, once more.

In the **Byzantine** practice, the Entrance Hymn is sung as follows: "O Son of God, Who sat upon the foal, save us who sing to You: 'Alleluia!'". This is omitted in the Slavic practice. The singing of the festal hymns continues, as follows: "Glory...Spirit!", the Troparion, in tone 4, "When we were buried with You in Baptism, O Christ God,...!", "Now and ever...Amen.", and the Kontakion, in tone 6, "Sitting on Your throne in Heaven!".

After the Trisagion, the Prokeimenon is celebrated in tone 4: "Blessed is He Who comes in the Name of the Lord! God is the Lord and has revealed Himself to us!", with its accompanying verse, "O give thanks to the Lord, for He is good! For, His steadfast love endures forever!". The Epistle reading is Philippians 4:4-9. The "Alleluia!" verses are in tone 1: "O sing to the Lord a new song! For, the Lord has done marvelous things!" and "All the ends of the Earth have seen the salvation of our God!" The Gospel reading is John 12:1-18.

      The Hymn to the Theotokos is from Ode 9 of the Matins Kanon, in tone 4: "God is the Lord and has revealed Himself to us!". After "Praise the Lord from the Heavens!", the Communion Hymn of the feast is sung: "Blessed is He Who comes in the Name of the Lord! God is the Lord and has revealed Himself to us!", followed by a *triple* "Alleluia!" (in the *Greek* practice, "Praise the Lord from the Heavens!" is *omitted*, and the Communion Hymn begins with "Blessed is He Who comes in the Name of the Lord!"). The rest of the Divine Liturgy concludes as usual.

B. BRIDEGROOM MATINS

Since the celebration of Vespers, the Hours, the Liturgy of the Presanctified Gifts, and Grand and Little Compline, celebrated on the first three days of Holy Week, do not differ radically from their celebration elsewhere, it will not be necessary to cover them here in detail.

The celebration of the Bridegroom Matins takes place on the first three days of Holy Week: Holy Monday (usually celebrated Sunday evening),[47] Holy Tuesday (usually celebrated Monday evening),[48] and Holy Wednesday (usually celebrated Tuesday evening).[49]

The First Doxology, "O Heavenly King!", the Trisagion Prayers, the Second Doxology

The service begins with the celebrant intoning the first doxology, "Blessed is our God, always now and ever and unto ages of ages!" A reader then chants, "Amen.", "Glory to You, our God, glory to

---
[47] *Triodion*, pp. 511-516.
[48] Ibid, pp. 524-528.
[49] Ibid, pp. 535-541.

You!", "O Heavenly King!" (all of this is done by the **priest** in the **Antiochian** tradition), the Trisagion Prayers, and the Lord's Prayer. After the exclamation ("For, Yours are the Kingdom, and the power, and the glory…!"), the reader chants, "Amen." (In the **Antiochian** tradition, this is followed by "Lord, have mercy." **twelve** times, a full "Glory,…now and ever…!", "Come, let us worship…!", Psalms 19 and 20, the Trisagion Prayers again, "O Lord, save Your people!", "Glory…!", "Do You, of Your own good will…!", "Now and ever…!", "O dread champion…!", and petitions with a **triple** "Lord, have mercy.".) Then, in **all** the traditions, the reader chants, "In the Name of the Lord, Father (or, if it be a bishop, "Master"; or, if it be the Metropolitan, "Most blessed Master"), bless!" The celebrant then intones the second doxology, "Glory to the Holy, consubstantial, life-creating, and undivided Trinity, always now and ever and unto ages of ages!" The reader then chants "Amen.", then "Glory to God in the highest and, on Earth, peace, good will towards men!" **three** times, and "O Lord, open my lips, and my mouth will show forth your praise!" **two** times.

The 6 Psalms

The 6 Psalms of Matins are then chanted: Psalms 3, 37, 62, 87, 102, and 142.[50] It is customary to have two readers chant these Psalms, as follows: the first reader, who has done all the introductory chanting up to now, chants Psalms 3, 37, and 62. He or she then chants a full "Glory,… now and ever…!", "Alleluia! Alleluia! Alleluia! Glory to You, O God!" ***three*** times, a ***triple*** "Lord, have mercy.", and, then, the ***first half*** of a "***split*** 'Glory!'": "Glory to the Father, and to the Son, and to the Holy Spirit!". The second reader then takes up the chanting at this point with the ***second half*** of the "***split*** 'Glory!'": "Now and ever and unto ages of ages! Amen.", and, then, ***immediately*** chants the remaining three Psalms, Psalms 87, 102, and 142. After the conclusion of the final Psalm, this second reader then chants a full "Glory,… now and ever…!", and "Alleluia! Alleluia! Alleluia! Glory to You, O God!" ***three*** times.

---

[50] The Psalms are numbered according to the Septuagint.

The Great Litany

The Great Litany is then celebrated, with **_all_** of its responses sung in the Lenten melody.

"Alleluia!" and Troparion

The deacon then chants a set of Matinal "Alleluia!" petitions, each one followed by the singing by the people of a **_triple_** "Alleluia!", in tone 8. The "Alleluia!" petitions are: "Alleluia! Alleluia! Alleluia! In the night, my soul rises early for You, O God; for, Your commandments are a light on the Earth!", "Learn righteousness, O inhabitants of the Earth!", "Jealousy will grasp an untaught people!", and "Bring more evils on them, O Lord! Bring more evils on those who are glorious on the Earth!".

Following the singing of the last **_triple_** "Alleluia!", the people sing, in tone 8, the Troparion: "Behold! The Bridegroom comes at midnight, and blessed is the servant whom He shall find watching, and again, unworthy is the servant whom He shall find heedless. Beware, therefore, O my soul, do not be weighed down with sleep, lest you be given up to death and lest you be shut out of the Kingdom! But, rouse yourself, crying, 'Holy! Holy! Holy! are You, O God!' Through the Theotokos, have mercy on us!" (in the **Byzantine** tradition, the ending is different each day: for Monday, it is "Through the intercessions of the bodiless hosts, have mercy on us!"; for Tuesday, it is "Through the intercessions of the Forerunner, have mercy on us!"; for Wednesday, it is "By the power of Your Cross, have mercy on us!". After the second singing, the ending is "Through the prayers of [the patron saint of the church], have mercy on us!". After the third singing it is "Through the Theotokos, have mercy on us!".). Then, the people sing, "Glory...Spirit!", then the full Troparion ("Behold! The Bridegroom...!") again, then "Now and ever...Amen.", then the full Troparion ("Behold! The Bridegroom...!") one final time. All of this is sung in tone 8. A great censing is done during this singing.

Kathisma Readings from the Psalter and Kathisma Hymns

At this point, the service books call for the first Kathisma reading from the Psalter (**except** in the Antiochian tradition, where **only** the Kathisma Hymns are sung): for Monday, it is Kathisma 4 (Psalms 24-31); for Tuesday, it is Kathisma 9 (Psalms

64-69); and, for Wednesday, it is Kathisma 14 (Psalms 101-104). Then, Kathisma Hymns are then sung. For Monday, in tone 8, the people sing, "Today, Christ's holy Passion dawns…!"; for Tuesday, in tone 4, the people sing, "Let us love the Bridegroom, O brethren!"; and, for Wednesday, in tone 3, the people sing, "The harlot came to You, O Lover of mankind,…!". The service books call for a reader to chant a full "Glory,… now and ever…!", and then repeat this first Kathisma Hymn.

Then, the second Kathisma reading from the Psalter is called for: for Monday, it is Kathisma 5 (Psalms 32-36); for Tuesday, it is Kathisma 10 (Psalms 70-76); and, for Wednesday, it is Kathisma 15 (Psalms 105-108). Another set of Kathisma Hymns are then sung: for Monday, in tone 1, the people sing, "O invisible Judge,…!"; for Tuesday, in tone 4, the people sing, "In envy, the priests and scribes…!"; and, for Wednesday, in tone 4, the people sing, "Deceitful Judas,…!". The service books call for a reader to chant a full "Glory,… now and ever…!", and then repeat this second Kathisma Hymn.

Then, the third Kathisma reading from the Psalter is called for: for Monday, it is Kathisma 6 (Psalms 37-45); for Tuesday, it is Kathisma 11 (Psalms 77-84); and, for Wednesday, it is Kathisma 16 (Psalms 109-117). Another set of Kathisma

Hymns are then sung: for Monday, in tone 8, the people sing, "Today shines as the first-fruits...!"; for Tuesday, in tone 8, the people sing, "Judas loves money with his mind!"; and, for Wednesday, in tone 1, the people sing, "In tears, the harlot cried out,...!". The service books call for a reader to chant a full "Glory,... now and ever...!", and then repeat this third Kathisma Hymn.

<u>However</u>, in **many** parishes, this liturgical unit is **<u>greatly diminished!</u>** In these parishes, the Kathisma readings from the Psalter are altogether omitted! What happens, then, is that the **<u>first</u> Kathisma Hymn** is sung, followed by a reader chanting "Glory...Spirit!", with the people then singing the **<u>second</u> Kathisma Hymn**, then the reader chanting "Now and ever...Amen.", then the people singing the **<u>third</u> and final Kathisma Hymn**. As always, however, the choir director and singers should follow the local practice as prescribed by the main celebrant.

The Matins Gospel

The Matins Gospel is then celebrated: for Monday, it is Matthew 21:18-46; for Tuesday, it is Matthew 22:15-23:39; and, for Wednesday, it is John

12:17-50. **_Note_:** In **some** parishes that do **_not_** celebrate the Liturgy of the Presanctified Gifts during Holy Week, the main celebrant will **_add_ _on_** the Gospel reading from the Liturgy of the Presanctified Gifts to the Matins Gospel. So, for Monday, after chanting Matthew 21:18-46, the celebrant will chant Matthew 24:3-35; for Tuesday, after chanting Matthew 22:15-23:39, the celebrant will chant Matthew 24:36-26:2; and, for Wednesday, after chanting John 12:17-50, the celebrant will chant Matthew 26:6-16. Again, this added Gospel reading from Liturgy of the Presanctified Gifts is **_not_** called for at the Bridegroom Matins. As always, however, the choir director and singers should follow the local practice as prescribed by the main celebrant.

Psalm 50 and the Prayer of Intercession

The Matins Gospel is then followed by a reader chanting Psalm 50: "Have mercy on me, O God, according to Your steadfast love. According to Your abundant mercy, blot out my transgressions!...!". Then, a prayer of intercession is intoned (**except** in the Byzantine tradition) that begins, "O God, save Your people and bless Your inheritance! Visit Your world in mercy and compassion! Exalt the estate of Orthodox Christians, and send down upon us Your rich mercies…!". The people respond by singing "Lord, have mercy." **twelve** times, in the Lenten melody. The celebrant then intones the exclamation, "Through the mercy and compassion and love for mankind of Your only-begotten Son, with Whom You are blest, together with Your all-Holy, good, and life-creating Spirit, now and ever and unto ages of ages!" The people then sing "Amen." in the Lenten melody.

The Kanon

The Kanon follows the Prayer of Intercession. It is different for each of the first three days of Holy Week.

For Monday, the Kanon is in tone 2, and Ode 1 begins, "Let us sing to the Lord! By His divine command, He dried up the raging and impassible sea,…!". Two readers then interchange, one chanting the troparia, the other chanting the refrain, "Glory to You, our God, glory to You!" and, after the last troparion, a full "Glory,… now and ever…!". Then, the Kontakion, in tone 8, begins, "Jacob lamented the loss of Joseph,…!". This is followed by a reader chanting the Oikos, "Today, let us add lamentation to lamentation!". The people end the

Oikos by singing, again in tone 8, the cadence phrase, "For, God prepares for His servants an incorruptible crown!". Returning to the Kanon in tone 2, Ode 8 begins, "The relentless fire was fed by fuel in endless supply!". After the final troparion, the reader chants, "Let us bless the Father, and the Son, and the Holy Spirit, the Lord, now and ever and unto ages of ages! Amen.", and the people sing, "We praise, bless, and worship the Lord, singing and exalting Him throughout all ages!" (*except* in the Antiochian tradition, which *repeats*, "The relentless fire was fed by fuel in endless supply!", and the deacon intoning, "The Theotokos and the Mother of the Light!"). This is followed by Ode 9, which begins, "You have magnified the Theotokos who Bore You, O Christ!". After the final troparion, this same Ode 9, "You have magnified the Theotokos who Bore You, O Christ!", is sung again in many parishes as the katavasia.

For Tuesday, since there is no Ode 1 through 7, this liturgical section begins with the Kontakion in tone 2, "You know that this is the last hour, O wretched soul,…!". A reader then chants the Oikos, which begins, "Why are you slothful, O wretched soul?", which is concluded by the people singing the cadence phrase of the Kontakion, "Let us not remain outside the bridal chamber of Christ!". Ode 8 follows, in tone 2, "The three holy youths would not obey the decree of the tyrant!". Troparia and refrain ("Glory to You, our God, glory to You!" and, after the last troparion, a full "Glory,… now and ever…!") follow. Again, after the final troparion, the reader chants, "Let us bless the Father, and the Son, and the Holy Spirit, the Lord, now and ever and unto ages of ages! Amen.", and the people sing, "We praise, bless, and worship the Lord, singing and exalting Him throughout all ages!" (**except** in the Antiochian tradition, which **repeats**, "The three holy youths would not obey the decree of the tyrant!", and the deacon intoning, "The Theotokos and the Mother of the Light!"), and then Ode 9 chants, "In your womb, you contained God Who cannot be contained!". Again, after the final troparion, this same Ode 9, "In your womb, you contained God Who cannot be contained!", is sung again in many parishes as the katavasia.

    For Wednesday, the Kanon, in tone 2, has Ode 3 beginning, "You have established me on the rock of faith!". Troparia and refrain ("Glory to You, our God, glory to You!" and, after the last troparion, a full "Glory,… now and ever…!") follow, and then the Kontakion, in tone 4, is sung: "Though I have transgressed more than the harlot, O Good One,…!". A reader then chants the Oikos, which begins, "The woman who was once a profligate suddenly is wise!", which is concluded by the people singing the cadence phrase of the Kontakion, "Deliver me from the filth of my evil deeds!". Ode 8 begins, "The command of the tyrant prevailed!". Again, after the final troparion, the reader chants, "Let us bless the Father, and the Son, and the Holy Spirit, the Lord, now and ever and unto ages of ages! Amen.", and the people sing, "We praise, bless, and worship the Lord, singing and exalting Him throughout all ages!" (**except** in the Antiochian tradition, which **repeats**, "You have established me on the rock of faith!", and the deacon intoning, "The Theotokos and the Mother of the Light!"), and Ode 9 starts, "With pure souls and blameless lips,…!". Again, after the final troparion, this same Ode 9, "With pure souls and blameless lips,…!", is sung again in many parishes as the katavasia.

The Little Litany

At the conclusion of the Kanon, a Little Litany is celebrated, with **_all_** of the responses sung by the people in the Lenten melody. (In the **Greek** practice, the Little Litany is **only** celebrated when the Kontakion is immediately preceded by an ode [as on Sunday and Tuesday evenings].)

The Exapostilarion

The Exapostilarion is then sung in tone 8 (or, in some traditions, tone 3): "Your bridal chamber I see adorned, O my Savior, and I have no wedding garment that I may enter! O Giver of light, enlighten the vesture of my soul and save me!" A reader then chants, "Glory…Spirit!" and the full Exapostilarion ("Your bridal chamber I, see adorned,…!") is sung again. After the reader chants, "Now and ever…Amen!", the full Exapostilarion ("Your bridal chamber I see adorned,…!") is sung a third and final time. (In the **Byzantine** tradition, the three singings of the Exapostilarion is **not** separated by a "Glory,…!" or a "Now and ever…!".) **Note:** It is the custom, in **many** parishes, for the Exapostilaria of Holy Week to be sung by either a single chanter, or, more commonly, by a trio. Again, the local parish practice should be followed.

The Praises

Following the Exapostilarion, the Praises are celebrated. A reader chants the Psalms of Praise (Psalms 148, 149, and 150 [the Greeks **only** chant the **first two** verses of Psalm 148, **then** go to "Praise

Him for His mighty deeds!"]), until he or she intones, "Praise Him according to His exceeding greatness!" Then, the people sing the stikhera on the Praises, which are different for each day.

For Monday, the first stikheron, in tone 1, begins, "As the Lord was going to His voluntary Passion,…!". The service books call for this stikheron to be sung **twice**. However, in **many** parishes, it is sung **only once**. (As always, the local practice should be followed.) After this, a stikheron in tone 5 begins, "We have reached the saving Passion of Christ our God!" Following a full "Glory,… now and ever…!" chanted by the reader, the people sing another stikheron, again in tone 5, that begins, "Going to Your Passion, O Lord,…!".

For Tuesday, the first stikheron, in tone 1, begins, "How should I, the unworthy one,…?". Again, the service books call for this stikheron to be sung **twice**. However, in **many** parishes, it is sung **only once**. (As always, the local practice should be followed.) After this, a stikheron in tone 2 begins, "Christ, the Bridegroom,…!". Following a full "Glory,… now and ever…!" chanted by the reader, the people sing another stikheron, in tone 4, that begins, "You have heard the condemnation, O soul,…!".

For Wednesday, the first stikheron, in tone 1, begins, "A harlot recognized You as God,…!". This time, the service books do ***not*** call for this first stikheron to be repeated. After this, another stikheron in tone 1 begins, "The harlot mingled precious myrrh with her tears!". The third stikheron, also in tone 1, starts, "As the sinful woman was bringing her offering of myrrh,…!". A fourth stikheron, again in tone 1, begins, "O, the wretchedness of Judas!". Following the ***<u>first</u> half*** of a ***split*** "Glory!" ("Glory… Spirit!") that is chanted by the reader, the people sing another stikheron, in tone 2, that begins, "The sinful woman ran to buy the precious myrrh,…!". The reader then chants the ***<u>second</u> half*** of the ***split*** "Glory!" ("Now and ever…Amen."), after which the people sing, in tone 6, "The woman who was engulfed in sin…!".

For ***<u>all</u>*** of these days (Monday, Tuesday, and Wednesday), after the final stikheron, the reader chants, "To You, O Lord our God, belongs glory, and to You we send up glory: to the Father, and to the Son, and to the Holy Spirit, now and ever and unto ages of ages! Amen.".

The Lesser Doxology and the Little Litany

Following the Praises, the celebrant intones, "Glory to You, Who have shown us the Light!" (***except*** in the Byzantine tradition). A reader then chants the Lesser Doxology, which begins, "Glory to God in the highest and, on Earth, peace, good will towards men! We praise You! We bless You! We worship You! We glorify You! We give thanks to You for Your great glory!".

After the Lesser Doxology is concluded, a Little Litany is celebrated (***except*** in the Greek practice, where a ***full Litany of Supplication*** is celebrated). Again, ***all*** of the responses to this Little Litany are sung in the Lenten melody.

The Apostikha

The Apostikha is then celebrated. It differs on each of the three days.

For Monday, the first stikheron, in tone 5, begins, "The mother of Zebedee's children, O Lord,…!". A reader then reads the verse, "Satisfy us in the morning with Your steadfast love, that we may be glad all our days! Make us glad as many days as

You have afflicted us, and as many years as we have seen evil! Let Your work be manifest to Your servants, and Your glorious power to their children!" The second stikheron, also in tone 5, starts, "You taught Your disciples, O Lord,…!". The reader then chants, "Let the favor of the Lord our God be upon us, and establish the work of our hands upon us! Yes, the work of our hands, establish it!" The people then sing, in tone 8, "The fig tree was withered up because it was unfruitful!". After a full "Glory,… now and ever…!" by the reader, the people sing, still in tone 8, "The serpent found a second Eve…!".

For Tuesday, the first stikheron, in tone 6, begins, "Come, O faithful! Let us work zealously for the Master!". A reader then chants the verse that begins, "Satisfy us in the morning with Your steadfast love,…!". The second stikheron, also in tone 6, starts, "When You will come in glory, O Jesus,…!". The reader then chants the verse that begins, "Let the favor of the Lord our God be upon us,…!". The third stikheron, still in tone 6, begins, "You are more beautiful than all men, O Bridegroom!". After a full "Glory,… now and ever…!" by the reader, the people sing, in tone 7, "Behold! The Master has entrusted you with a talent, O my soul!".

For Wednesday, the first stikheron, in tone 6, begins, "Today, Christ comes to the house of the

Pharisee!". A reader then chants the verse that begins, "Satisfy us in the morning with Your steadfast love,…!" (for the **Greeks**, the verse is, "We were filled in the morning with Your mercy, O Lord, and we rejoiced and were glad all our days!"). The second stikheron, also in tone 6, starts, "The harlot spread out her hair to You, O Master!". The reader then chants the verse that begins, "Let the favor of the Lord our God be upon us,…!" (for the **Greeks**, the verse is, "Let us be glad for the days when You humbled us…!"). The third stikheron, still in tone 6, begins, "The corrupt and filthy woman…!". The reader then chants the verse, "I will thank You, O Lord, with my whole heart! I will tell of all Your wondrous works!" (for the **Greeks**, the verse is, "And let the brightness of the Lord our God be upon us…!"). The fourth stikheron, staying in tone 6, starts, "Despairing for her life, and despaired of for her deeds,…!". The reader then chants a full "Glory,… now and ever…!". Then, the Hymn of Cassia, sung in tone 8, begins, "The woman had fallen into many sins, O Lord!". In **many** parishes, this is sung to a special melody in tone 8, and is also sung by either a single chanter, or, more commonly, as a trio.

Prayer, the Trisagion Prayers, the Lord's Prayer, and Concluding Prayers

Following the Apostikha, a reader (in the **Greek** practice, the priest) chants the prayer, "It is good to give thanks to the Lord, to sing praises to Your Name, O Most–High, to declare Your steadfast love in the morning, and Your truth by night!". The reader then chants the Trisagion Prayers and the Lord's Prayer. After the exclamation ("For, Yours are the Kingdom, and the power, and the glory,…!"), the reader chants an "Amen.", and then, "Standing in the temple of your glory, we think that we are in Heaven, O Theotokos, gate of Heaven! Open to us the gates of your mercy!". (In the **Byzantine** tradition, instead of "Standing in the temple of your glory!", the reader chants the kontakion.) The reader then chants "Lord, have mercy." **forty** times (**twelve** times in the **Antiochian** tradition), then a full "Glory,… now and ever…!", then "More honorable than the Cherubim,…!", (then, in the **Antiochian** tradition, "O Heavenly King, strengthen our civil authorities,) then, "In the Name of the Lord, Father (or, if a bishop is serving, "Master!"; or, if the Metropolitan is serving, "Most blessed Master!"), bless!" The celebrant chants, "Christ our God, the One Who Is, is blest always, now and ever and unto ages of ages!". The reader then chants, "Amen.", followed by "O Heavenly King, establish the Orthodox Christians! Confirm the Faith! Quiet the heathen! Give peace to the world! Place our departed fathers and brethren in the tabernacles of the righteous, and accept us sorrowers and penitents! For, You are good and the Lover of mankind!".

The Prayer of St Ephraim

The full Prayer of St Ephraim is then celebrated in its full form: The main celebrant, standing on the solea, chants the prayer in three sections ("O Lord and Master of my life,…!", "But, give, rather, the spirit of chastity,…!", and "Yes, O Lord and King, grant me to see my own transgressions…!"), each section concluding with a full prostration by all of the people. Then, everyone makes a metania (bow) **twelve** times, while saying silently to themselves, "God, cleanse me a sinner and have mercy on me!". Finally, the celebrant chants the entire prayer as a full unit, one last time, and everyone makes a final prostration. (In the **Greek** tradition, only the **one** chanting of the Prayer of St. Ephraim, with the three full prostrations, is practiced.)

The Dismissal

The celebrant then chants, "Glory to You, O Christ, our God and our Hope, glory to You!". The people then sing, **_all_** of it in the Lenten melody, a full "Glory,… now and ever…!", a **_triple_** "Lord, have mercy.", and then "Father (or, if a bishop is serving, "Master!"; or, if the Metropolitan is serving, "Most blessed Master!"), bless!" The celebrant chants the Dismissal Prayer, and the people **_usually_** sing a **_double_** "Amen." ("Amen. Amen." [**_except_** in the **_Greek_** practice]), in the Lenten melody.

Recessional Hymns

As everyone comes up to venerate the icons and the Holy Cross, this venerating may be done in silence, or some appropriate hymn from the service (such as the Troparion ["Behold! The Bridegroom comes at midnight,…!"] or the Exapostilarion ["Your bridal chamber I see adorned, O my Savior,…!"]) may be sung. As always, the local practice should be observed.

C. MATINS OF HOLY THURSDAY

Although the service books call for it to be celebrated at the 7th hour of the night (at approximately 1 o'clock in the morning), the Matins of Holy Thursday is *usually* celebrated in parishes on Wednesday evening of Holy Week.[51] Again, parishes of the **Byzantine** tradition may celebrate the Sacrament of Holy Unction on Wednesday evening, rather than the Matins of Holy Thursday. In any case, the order of the service for the Matins of Holy Thursday is as follows.[52]

The First Doxology, "O Heavenly King!", the Trisagion Prayers, the Second Doxology

The service begins with the celebrant intoning the first doxology, "Blessed is our God, always now and ever and unto ages of ages!" A reader then chants, "Amen.", "Glory to You, our God, glory to You!", "O Heavenly King!" (in the **Antiochian** tradition, this is all done by the ***priest***), the Trisagion

---

[51] *Triodion*, p. 548.
[52] Ibid, pp. 548-557.

Prayers, and the Lord's Prayer. After the exclamation ("For, Yours are the Kingdom, and the power, and the glory...!"), the reader chants, "Amen." (In the **Antiochian** tradition, this is followed by "Lord, have mercy." **twelve** times, a full "Glory,...now and ever...!", "Come, let us worship...!", Psalms 19 and 20, the Trisagion Prayers again, "O Lord, save Your people!", "Glory...!", "Do You, of Your own good will...!", "Now and ever...!", "O dread champion...!", and petitions with a **triple** "Lord, have mercy.".) Then, in **all** the traditions, the reader chants, "In the Name of the Lord, Father (or, if it be a bishop, "Master"; or, if it be the Metropolitan, "Most blessed Master"), bless!" The celebrant then intones the second doxology, "Glory to the Holy, consubstantial, life-creating, and undivided Trinity, always now and ever and unto ages of ages!" The reader then chants "Amen.", then "Glory to God in the highest and, on Earth, peace, good will towards men!" **three** times, and "O Lord, open my lips, and my mouth will show forth your praise!" **two** times.

The 6 Psalms

The 6 Psalms of Matins are then chanted: Psalms 3, 37, 62, 87, 102, and 142.[53] It is customary to have two readers chant these Psalms, as follows: the first reader, who has done all the introductory chanting up to now, chants Psalms 3, 37, and 62. He or she then chants a full "Glory,… now and ever…!", "Alleluia! Alleluia! Alleluia! Glory to You, O God!" ***three*** times, a ***triple*** "Lord, have mercy.", and, then, the <u>***first half***</u> of a ***"split*** 'Glory!'": "Glory to the Father, and to the Son, and to the Holy Spirit!". The second reader then takes up the chanting at this point with the <u>***second half***</u> of the *"**split** 'Glory!'"*: "Now and ever and unto ages of ages! Amen.", and, then, <u>***immediately***</u> chants the remaining three Psalms, Psalms 87, 102, and 142. After the conclusion of the final Psalm, this second reader then chants a full "Glory,… now and ever…!", and "Alleluia! Alleluia! Alleluia! Glory to You, O God!" ***three*** times.

---

[53] The Psalms are numbered according to the Septuagint.

The Great Litany

The Great Litany is then celebrated, in a **_regular_ melody**. The singing of the responses sung in the Lenten melody is thus discontinued until Great Lent of the following year.

"Alleluia!" and Troparion

The deacon (or, in the **Antiochian** tradition, a **reader**) then chants a set of Matinal "Alleluia!" petitions, each one followed by the singing by the people of a **triple** "Alleluia!", in tone 8. The "Alleluia!" petitions are: "Alleluia! Alleluia! Alleluia! In the night, my soul rises early for You, O God; for, Your commandments are a light on the Earth!", "Learn righteousness, O inhabitants of the Earth!", "Jealousy will grasp an untaught people!", and "Bring more evils on them, O Lord! Bring more evils on those who are glorious on the Earth!".

Following the singing of the last **triple** "Alleluia!", the people sing, in tone 8, the Troparion: "When the glorious disciples were enlightened at the washing of their feet before the Supper, then the impious Judas was darkened, ailing with avarice;

and, to the lawless judges, he betrays You, the righteous Judge! Behold! O lover of money, this man who, because of money, hanged himself! Flee from the greedy soul who dared such things against the Master! O Lord, Who are good towards all mankind, glory to You!". Then, the people sing, "Glory…Spirit!", then the full Troparion ("When the glorious disciples …!") again, then "Now and ever…Amen.", then the full Troparion ("When the glorious disciples …!") one final time. All of this is sung in tone 8. A great censing is done during this singing. (The "***split***" "Glory…Spirit!" and "Now and ever…Amen." is ***omitted*** in the **Greek** practice).

The Gospel

The Gospel reading, Luke 22:1-39, is then celebrated. ***Note:*** In **some** parishes that do ***not*** celebrate the Liturgy of the Presanctified Gifts during Holy Week, the main celebrant will ***add on*** the Gospel reading from the Liturgy of the Presanctified Gifts to the Matins Gospel. So, for Thursday, before chanting Luke 22:1-39, the celebrant will chant Matthew 26:6-16. Again, this added Gospel reading from Liturgy of the Presanctified Gifts is ***not*** called for at the Matins of Holy Thursday. As always, however, the choir director and singers should follow the local practice as prescribed by the main celebrant.

[The Blessing of Oil]

In *some* parishes, the blessing of oil by the celebrant *may* take place at this point (the *Greeks* do *not* practice this here). Local parish practice should be observed.

Psalm 50

A reader then chants Psalm 50: "Have mercy on me, O God, according to Your steadfast love. According to Your abundant mercy, blot out my transgressions!...!". The prayer of intercession that begins, "O God, save Your people and bless Your inheritance!...!" is **<u>not</u>** celebrated, but is ***omitted***.

The Kanon

Following the chanting of Psalm 50, the Kanon is celebrated, in tone 6 (usually a special melody).

Again, it is customary to have two different readers chanting after the singing of the odes, one chanting the troparia, the other chanting the refrain, "Glory to You, our God, glory to You!" until the final refrain, a full "Glory,… now and ever…!".

Ode 1 begins, "At a stroke, the Red Sea was parted in two!". Again, because the penitential season of Great Lent has concluded, there is **not** a singing of Ode 2. Ode 3 begins, "The Lord and Creator of all, the changeless God,…!". After the final portion of Ode 3, Kathisma Hymns are sung: the first one, in tone 1, begins, "The Lord, Who alone loves mankind,…!"; a reader then chants, "Glory…Spirit!"; the second hymn, in tone 3, starts, "In Your goodness, You humbled Yourself,…!"; the reader then chants, "Now and ever…Amen."; the third hymn, in tone 4, begins, "Eating with Your disciples, O Master,…!".

Ode 4 starts, "Foreseeing Your ineffable mystery,…!". Ode 5 begins, "The Apostles were united by a bond of love,…!". Ode 6 starts, "The final abyss of sins has encompassed me!". After Ode 6, **some** parishes celebrate a Little Litany, while others omit it (it is **not** called for in the service books). In any case, the Kontakion, in tone 2, follows: "With his hands, the betrayer receives the bread!". A reader then chants the Oikos ("Let us all approach the mystical Table in fear…!"). After chanting, "For,

Christ Himself thus commanded His disciples!", the people sing, in the same tone 2 of the Kontakion, the cadence phrase, "But, the servant and deceiver, Judas, did not take heed!". The **Greeks** then take the **Synaxaria** for the day.

Ode 7 begins, "The youths in Babylon were not afraid of the flaming furnace!". Ode 8 starts, "The blessed youths in Babylon braved dangers for their fathers' laws!". After the last troparion, instead of chanting a full "Glory,... now and ever...!", the reader chanting refrains intones, "Let us bless the Father, and the Son, and the Holy Spirit, the Lord, now and ever and unto ages of ages! Amen." The people then sing, in the same tone 6 special melody of the Kanon, "We praise, bless, and worship the Lord, singing and exalting Him throughout all ages!". Then, the people ***immediately*** sing Ode 9, which begins, "Come, O faithful! Let us enjoy the Master's hospitality,...!". After the full "Glory,... now and ever...!" is chanted following the last troparion, this same Ode 9, "Come, O faithful! Let us enjoy the Master's hospitality,...!", is sung again as the katavasia. In the **Greek** practice, there are **Little Litanies** after odes 3, 6, and 9.

[The Little Litany]

Even though it is **_not_** called for in the service books, **many** parishes, at this point, celebrate a Little Litany, in a **_non_**-Lenten melody. As always, the local custom should be observed.

The Exapostilarion

The Exapostilarion is then celebrated: "Your bridal chamber I see adorned, O my Savior, and I have no wedding garment that I may enter! O Giver of Light, enlighten the vesture of my soul and save me!". In **many** parishes, this is sung by a single chanter, or, more likely, a trio. A reader then chants, "Glory...Spirit!". The full Exapostilarion, "Your bridal chamber...!", is then sung again. The reader intones, "Now and ever...Amen.", and the full Exapostilarion, "Your bridal chamber...!", is sung again a third and final time. (The "**split**" "Glory...Spirit!" and "Now and ever...Amen." is **omitted** in the **Greek** practice).

The Praises

The Praises (Psalms 148, 149, and 150) are then chanted by a reader. After the phrase, "Praise Him according to His exceeding greatness!", the people sing, in tone 2, "The assembly of the Jews gathers together...!". The next stikheron, also in tone 2, starts, "The transgressor, Judas, O Lord,...!". The third stikheron in tone 2 begins, "Judas, the treacherous deceiver,...!". The fourth stikheron in tone 2 starts, "Servant and deceiver, disciple and betrayer, friend and devil,...!". Then, the reader chants a full "Glory,... now and ever...!", and the people sing, again in tone 2, "The Lamb, Whom Isaiah proclaimed, goes willingly to the slaughter!". The reader then chants, "To You, O Lord our God, belongs glory, and to You we send up glory: to the Father, and to the Son, and to the Holy Spirit, now and ever and unto ages of ages! Amen.".

The Lesser Doxology and the Litany of Matins

The celebrant intones, "Glory to You, Who have shown us the Light!" (*except* in the Byzantine tradition). A reader then chants the Lesser Doxology ("Glory to God in the highest and, on Earth, peace, good will towards men! We praise You! We bless You! We worship You! We glorify You! We give thanks to You for Your great glory!").

After the Lesser Doxology, the Litany of Matins is celebrated, in a **non**-Lenten melody, with the usual responses ("Lord, have mercy.", "Grant it, O Lord.", "To You, O Lord.", "Amen.", "And with your spirit.", "To You, O Lord.", and "Amen.").

The Apostikha

The Apostikha starts in tone 8, with a stikheron that begins, "Today, the evil assembly gathers against the Christ…!". A reader then chants the verse, "He who ate of My Bread has lifted his heel against Me!". The people then sing, again in tone 8, "Today, Judas abandons all pretense of love for the poor!". The reader then chants the verse, "When he goes out, he tells it abroad!". The people then sing, still in tone 8, "Your life, O lawless Judas, is filled with deceit!". The reader then chants the verse, "He utters lawless words against Me!". Remaining in tone 8, the people sing, "Let no one be ignorant of the Lord's Supper, O believers!".

At **this** point, the service books call for the reader to chant, "Glory…Spirit!", the people to then *repeat* the singing of the stikheron, ""Your life, O lawless Judas, is filled with deceit!", the reader to chant, "Now and ever...Amen.", and then for the people to sing, in tone 5, the stikheron, "Instructing Your disciples in the mystery, O Lord,...!". **However**, in **many** parishes, the **repeating** of the singing of the stikheron, ""Your life, O lawless Judas, is filled with deceit!" *is **omitted**! **Instead**,* the reader chants a *full* "Glory,... now and ever...!", and **then** the people sing, in tone 5, the stikheron, "Instructing Your disciples in the mystery, O Lord,...!". As always, the local parish practice should be followed.

Prayer, the Trisagion Prayers, and the Lord's Prayer

Following the Apostikha, a reader (in the **Greek** practice, the **priest**) chants the prayer, "It is good to give thanks to the Lord, to sing praises to Your Name, O Most High, to declare Your steadfast love in the morning, and Your truth by night!". The reader then chants the Trisagion Prayers and the Lord's Prayer. After the exclamation ("For, Yours are the Kingdom, and the power, and the glory,...!"), the reader chants an "Amen.".

The Troparion

The people then sing the Troparion, "When the glorious disciples…!", in tone 8, **once**!

[The Divine Washing of the Feet]

Though the service books do **not** call for this, **many** parishes, more and more, are beginning to insert the Divine Washing of the Feet at the end of Matins for Holy Thursday (in the **Antiochian** tradition, this is done **after** the Vesperal Liturgy for Holy Thursday; current, the **Greek** practice does **not** include the Divine Washing of the Feet). (At this point, parishes that do **not** celebrate this rite go directly from the singing of the Troparion to the Augmented Litany.) Even though the service books do **not** call for this, the following is a standard and commonly celebrated order of this rite.

Twelve chairs are placed in the middle of the church, in two rows of six, facing each other, for the twelve men of the parish who will have their feet washed during this rite. Therefore, one row of six men will have their backs to the north (left wall) of the church, facing south, and the other row of six men will have their backs to the south (right wall) of the church, facing north. A wide path between these two rows is left (usually the width of the runner rug leading up to the analoi holding the central icon). As the men gather for this rite, the people sing the following stikhera: in tone 1, "O Lord God, Who girded Yourself with a towel and washed the feet of Your disciples, wash clean the thoughts of our souls and gird us together with a spiritual bond, enabling us to do the commandments of Your goodness!"; in tone 2, "O faithful, who desire to witness a great and wondrous deed, come to the precious washing, not for the cleansing of physical impurity, but for the mystical sanctification of the soul! Christ is our Savior! He Who glances at the Earth and causes it to tremble, humbles Himself! Let us sing to Him with thanksgiving! To those worthy of being uplifted, He has shown the way of humility! Save us, O Good One, Who love mankind!"; in tone 3, "Peter desired to have his feet washed by the pure hand that created Adam! He heard: 'If I do not wash you, you will not have a portion with Me!' Filled with great trembling, he cried to You, O Lord: 'Not only will You wash my feet, but also my hands and my head!' O great gift of the Master! He makes His disciples partakers of His grace! He makes them to share in His unspeakable glory at the time of the mystical Cup! He promised to drink with them of the new Cup in the Kingdom of Heaven! Make us worthy of the same! For, You are the merciful Lover of man!". A reader then chants a full "Glory,… now and ever…!", and the people sing, in tone 8, "Judas was captured by the dream of the devil! He fell asleep even unto death! But, it is time for us to be bold! It is time for us to hold firm! Let our hearts groan! Let our tears fall! And let the psalm be sung! Great is the power of the Cross! Christ is at the door! The paschal Sacrifice is come! Glory to You, O Lord, glory to You!".

The deacon intones, "Let us pray to the Lord.", and the people sing, "Lord, have mercy.". The celebrant then chants the prayer, "O most gracious God, unapproachable in Your divinity: In the image of a servant, You have become the Image of service! And, in the likeness of saving humility, You have washed the feet of Your disciples with Your pure hands, and wiped them with a towel! Look on us, Your unworthy servants, who likewise emulate Your glorious condescension! Grant us to be washed of the evils of our flesh and the impurities of our souls! Grant us the descent of the most Holy Spirit! Strengthen us to withstand the assaults of the crafty serpent who leads astray; so that, being purified, we may worthily serve You, Who overcame the serpent and every power of the enemy! For, to You are due all glory, honor, and worship: to the Father, and to the Son, and to the Holy Spirit, now and ever and unto ages of ages!" The people sing, "Amen.". The celebrant turns, blesses the people, and intones, "Peace be with you all!", and the people sing, "And with your spirit!". The deacon intones, "Let us bow our heads to the Lord.". The people sing, "To You, O Lord.". The celebrant then chants the prayer, "O Lord our God, Who have shown us the image of humility in Your most sublime condescension, and Who have called the last to be the first: Sanctify us in the service of one another! Raise us up by divine humility! Keep us from all evil, always cleansed by tears and by the illumination of Your holy grace! In truth, we bow down before You, imploring Your mercy and goodness at Your awesome Judgment! For, You are our God, merciful and the Lover of all, and to You we ascribe glory, with Your Father Who has no beginning, and Your all-Holy, good, and life-creating Spirit, now and ever and unto ages of ages!". The people sing, "Amen."

Then, the deacon intones, "And, that we may be accounted worthy to listen to the Holy Gospel, let us pray to the Lord our God!", and the people sing a **triple** "Lord, have mercy.". The deacon intones, "Wisdom! Let us be attentive! Let us listen to the Holy Gospel!". The celebrant (usually the parish priest) then blesses the people, saying, "Peace be with you all!", and the people sing, "And with your spirit!". The deacon intones, "The Reading is from the Holy Gospel according to Saint John the Theologian!". The people sing, "Glory to You, O Lord, glory to You!". Then, **the deacon** chants the Gospel reading for the washing of the feet, which is John 13:1-11 (ending with the verse, "That was why He said, 'You are not all clean!'". The deacon is standing towards the back of the church, behind the two rows of men seated. The deacon chants this reading **repeatedly** during the washing of the feet, neither going too quickly nor dragging it out too slowly. During this reading, the priest (or, if present, a bishop or Metropolitan) will remove his phelonion, gird a towel onto his priestly belt, and take a pitcher of water and a pan with which to wash the feet of the twelve men. He begins with the row on the right hand side, with the man nearest to the back of the church. After reaching the man in this right hand row on the end (the one nearest the sanctuary), he crosses over to the man in the left hand row on the end (the one nearest the sanctuary) and works his way back to the man in the left hand row nearest to the back of the church. The twelve men, after having sat down, remove their **right** shoe and sock. As the priest comes down the line to each man, this man lifts his right foot slightly, so the priest can pour some water over his right foot, which is at that point over the bowl to catch the falling water. After washing the foot, the celebrant takes the towel, dries the foot of the man, and moves onto the next man.

After he has finished washing the feet of the twelve men, the priest puts his phelonion back on, and goes to the where the deacon has been chanting the Gospel reading. At this point, **the <u>priest</u>** continues with the Gospel reading, starting with John 13:12-17, which begins, "When He had washed their feet, and taken His garments, and resumed His place, He said to them, 'Do you know what I have done to you?'...!". The reading ends with verse 17, which says, "If you know these things, blessed are you if you do them!". **<u>Then</u>**, the people *again* sing, as they do at the end of every Gospel reading, "Glory to You, O Lord, glory to You!".

The deacon intones, "Let us pray to the Lord.". The people sing, "Lord, have mercy.". The celebrant chants the prayer, "O Lord God, because of Your great mercy, You have emptied Yourself and taken on the image of a servant! And, at Your voluntary, saving, and life-creating Passion, condescended to sup with Your Apostles! You have given them an image of wise humility and love towards one another, saying, 'As I have done to you, do likewise to one another!' O holy Master, be now in the midst of Your unworthy servants who have come to imitate Your example and fulfill Your commandments! Wash away all the evil and impurities of our souls! Cleanse us with the towel of love for one another, that we may please You all the days of our lives, and find grace before You! For, You, O Christ our God, do bless and sanctify all things, and to You we ascribe glory, together with Your Father Who is from everlasting, and Your all-Holy, good, and life-creating Spirit, now and ever and unto ages of ages!". The people sing, "Amen.".

The Augmented Litany

Then, the Augmented Litany is celebrated, beginning with the petition, "Have mercy on us, O God, according to Your great goodness,…!", and the people sing, *from the **first** petition*, a **triple** "Lord, have mercy." in a ***non***-Lenten tone.

The Dismissal

The Dismissal is then celebrated. After the Dismissal Prayer ("May our Lord, Who is going to His voluntary Passion on behalf of us men and for our salvation, Christ our true God,....!") and the exclamation ("for He is good and loves mankind!"), the people ***usually*** sing a ***double*** "Amen." ("Amen. Amen.").

[Sermon]

In some parishes, the main celebrant may give a small sermon at this point.

Recessional Hymns

As everyone comes up to venerate the icons and the Holy Cross, this venerating may be done in silence, or some appropriate hymn from the service (such as the Troparion ["When the glorious disciples…!"] or the Exapostilarion ["Your bridal chamber I see adorned, O my Savior,…!"]) may be sung. As always, the local practice should be observed.

● - ● - ●

As previously mentioned, in the **Greek** practice, the Divine Washing of the Feet is *not* celebrated. What *is* celebrated for the end of the service is as follows: 1) Troparion of the Prophecy (tone 3), "You were struck on the face for the sake of mankind, yet were not moved to anger! Deliver our life from corruption, O Lord, and save us!" (sung once, followed by a full "Glory,…now and ever…!", then sung a final time); 2) Prokeimenon (tone 1), "Let the nations know that the Lord is Your Name!" (verse: "O God, Who will be likened to You?");

3) The Prophecy (Jeremiah 11:18-23; 12:1-5, 9-11,24-25); 4) Prokeimenon (tone 6), "In Judah, God is known!"; 5) Augmented Litany; 6) Dismissal and veneration of icons.

D. VESPERAL LITURGY OF HOLY THURSDAY

The Vesperal Liturgy of Holy Thursday, commemorating the Lord's Mystical Supper, is celebrated in the afternoon of Holy Thursday (in the **Byzantine** tradition, this is done in the *morning*). Its order is as follows.[54]

---

[54]*Triodion*, pp. 558-560.

The Doxology, "O Heavenly King!", the Trisagion Prayers, the Lord's Prayer, "Come, Let Us Worship!", and Psalm 103

Since this is a service with Holy Communion, the opening doxology is eucharistic: "Blessed is the Kingdom, of the Father, and of the Son, and of the Holy Spirit, now and ever and unto ages of ages!". A *reader* then chants, "Amen.", "Glory to You, our God, glory to You!", "O Heavenly King!" (in the **Antiochian** tradition, this is all done by the *priest*), the Trisagion Prayers, and the Lord's Prayer. After the exclamation ("For, Yours are the Kingdom, and the power, and the glory,…!"), the reader chants, "Amen." (in the **Greek** practice, "O Heavenly King!", the Trisagion Prayers, and the Lord's Prayer are all ***omitted***), "Come, let us worship…!", and the Vesperal Psalm 103:[55] "Bless the Lord, O my soul! O Lord, my God, You are very great! You are clothed with honor and majesty, Who cover Yourself with light as with a garment,…!". At the conclusion of the Psalm, the reader chants a full "Glory,… now and ever…!", and then, "Alleluia! Alleluia! Alleluia! Glory to You, O God!" ***three*** times.

---

[55] Psalms are numbered according to the Septuagint.

The Great Litany

The Great Litany is then sung, with all of its petitions responded to in a **_non_**-Lenten melody.

"Lord, I Call Upon You!" and Stikhera

Because this is *not* a Vespers on a Saturday evening before a Sunday Liturgy, there is **_no_** singing of Kathisma 1, "Blessed is the Man!". Instead, we **_immediately_** go from the Great Litany to the singing of "Lord, I Call Upon You!", sung here in tone 2. The service books call for 10 stikhera to be sung, 5 different stikhera each sung twice. **However**, in **_most_** parishes (**_especially_** in the **Greek** tradition), this practice is **omitted**, so that there are the 5 stikhera, each **sung once**. They are: "The assembly of the Jews gathers together…!", "The transgressor, Judas, O Lord,…!", "Judas, the treacherous deceiver,…!", "Servant and deceiver, disciple and betrayer, friend and devil,…!", and "The Lamb, Whom Isaiah proclaimed, goes willingly to the slaughter!". A reader then chants a full "Glory,… now and ever…!", and the people then sing the last stikheron, in tone

6, "Truly, Judas is descended from those vipers...!". During the singing of this last stikheron, the clergy and servers exit the sanctuary to the middle of the church for the Vesperal Entrance.

"Gladsome Light!", Prokeimenon 1, and the Reading from Exodus

As the Vesperal Entrance is made, the people sing "Gladsome Light!" (in the **Greek** practice, this hymn, until the last verse ["Therefore, all the world glorifies You!"] is chanted by the **priest**). Then, Prokeimenon 1, in tone 1, is celebrated, "Deliver me, O Lord, from violent men!", with its accompanying verse (**except** in the Greek practice), "Who have schemed unrighteousness in their hearts all the day long!". This is **immediately** followed by the reader chanting the Old Testament reading, Exodus 19:10-19.

Prokeimenon 2, the Reading from Job, and the Reading from Isaiah

Then, usually another reader chants Prokeimenon 2, in tone 7, "Deliver me from my enemies, O God! Save me from those who rise up against me!", with its accompanying verse, "Deliver me from those who work evil!". (In the **Greek** practice, the Prokeimenon **only includes** the first sentence ["Deliver me from my enemies, O God!"], and the accompanying verse is, again, **omitted**.) This is **immediately** followed by the reader chanting the Old Testament reading, Job 38:1-23; 42:1-5.

After this, a reader (usually a third, different reader) **immediately** chants the Old Testament reading, Isaiah 50:4-11.

The Little Litany

After the Prokeimena and Old Testament readings are concluded, a Little Litany is celebrated with a **non**-Lenten melody. (In the **Greek** practice,

only the Doxology of the Little Litany ["For, You are holy, O our God,...!"] is done.)

[The Troparion and the Kontakion]

Even though it is not called for in the service books, at this point, *some* parishes have the people sing the Troparion for the day ("When the glorious disciples...!") in a special tone 8 melody, followed by a full "Glory,... now and ever...!", and then followed by the people singing the Kontakion for the day ("Though I have transgressed more than the harlot, O Good One,...!"). This provides a smooth transition from the Vesperal section of the service to the Liturgy portion. ***Most*** parishes do ***not*** do this, but go ***immediately*** from the Little Litany to the Trisagion. As always, the local liturgical practice should be observed.

The Trisagion, Prokeimenon 3, the Epistle, and the "Alleluia!" Verses

Following either the Little Litany or the Kontakion for the day (depending on the local custom), the Trisagion, "Holy God!" is celebrated. (At this point, in the **Byzantine** practice, the deacon [or, if there is no deacon, the main celebrant] comes out of the sanctuary, stands on the ambo, and intones, "**Dynamis!**" ["**δυναμις**", which means, "With strength!"], before the final singing of "Holy God!".) Then, a reader chants Prokeimenon 3, in tone 7, "The rulers of the people have assembled against the Lord and His Christ!", with the accompanying verse, "Why do the nations conspire, and the peoples plot in vain?"

Then, the reader chants the Epistle reading for the day, 1 Corinthians 11:23-32. After this, the "Alleluia!" verses are celebrated in tone 7. Because there are **three** "Alleluia!" verses instead of the usual **two**, when the celebrant intones, "Peace be with you, Reader!", the reader then chants **all** of the following **at once**: "And with your spirit! Alleluia! Alleluia! Alleluia! Blessed is he who considers the poor and needy! The Lord will deliver him on the day of trouble!". The people then sing a **triple** "Alleluia!". The reader then chants, "My enemies say to me in malice: 'When will he die, and his name perish?'". The people then again sing a **triple** "Alleluia!". The reader then chants, "He who ate my bread has lifted his heel against me!". The people then sing a final **triple** "Alleluia!".

The Gospel

The Gospel is then celebrated, with the usual responses. It is a composite Gospel, chanted as one reading: Matthew 26:1-20; John 13:2-17; Matthew 26:21-39; Luke 22:43-45; and Matthew 26:40-27:2.

[The Sermon]

Even though a sermon is usually done at this point in the Liturgy, in **many** parishes, because of the length of all the Holy Week services, it is omitted from this Vesperal Liturgy (it is **_always omitted_** in the **Greek** practice).

The Augmented Litany, [The Litany of the Catechumens], and the Litanies for the Faithful

At this point, the Augmented Litany is celebrated (***except*** in the Greek practice), with the responses sung, as with *all* litanies from this point onward, in a **non**-Lenten melody. This Litany begins with *two* petitions ("Let us say, with all our soul and with all our mind, let us say:" and "O Lord Almighty, the God of our fathers, we pray You: Hear us and have mercy.") responded to by the singing of a ***single*** "Lord, have mercy." Beginning with the ***third*** petition ("Have mercy on us, O God, according to Your great goodness,…!"), the people respond with a *triple* "Lord, have mercy.".

After the Augmented Litany, some parishes celebrate the Litany of the Catechumens, while other parishes go directly to the Litanies for the Faithful. As always, the local practice should be observed.

Then, ***two*** Litanies for the Faithful are celebrated (the ***Greek*** practice ***omits*** the celebration of the ***first*** one). At the exclamation of the second of these litanies ("that, guarded always by Your might, we may ascribe glory unto You,…!"), ***many*** parishes have the people sing a **double** "Amen." ("Amen. Amen.") to show that this entire liturgical section of litanies has concluded. (In the **Antiochian** tradition, **all** of these litanies are **omitted**.) Again, as always, the local practice should be observed.

"Of Your Mystical Supper"

Then, as the clergy prepare to celebrate the Eucharistic Entrance, the people sing a special Entrance Hymn for the day. Instead of the regular Cherubic Hymn ("Let us, who mystically represent the Cherubim,…!"), the people sing, in tone 6, "Of Your Mystical Supper, O Son of God, accept me today as a communicant! For, I will not speak of Your Mysteries to Your enemies, neither, like Judas, will I give you a kiss! But, like the thief, I will confess You: 'Remember me, O Lord, in Your Kingdom!'". (In the **Antiochian** tradition, the **singing** *stops* at, "But, like the thief, I will confess You:". **After** the Entrance, the **singing continues** with, " 'Remember me, O Lord, in Your Kingdom!'". In the **Greek** practice, the section, "neither, like Judas, will I give you a kiss!", is **omitted**.)

The Entrance is made with the usual commemorations chanted as is the local custom. After the celebrant intones, "You, and all Orthodox Christians,…!", the people sing the *entire* Entrance Hymn ("Of Your Mystical Supper,…!") *again*, followed by, in the same tone 6, a *triple* "Alleluia!".

The Litany of Supplication, "Father, Son, and Holy Spirit!", and the Creed

Following the Entrance, the Litany of Supplication is celebrated. Then, after the celebrant intones, "Let us love one another, that, with one mind and one heart, we may confess:", the people sing, "Father, Son, and Holy Spirit! The Trinity, one in essence, and undivided!". Then, the Creed is sung.

The Anaphora

The Anaphora is then celebrated, with the usual responses. ***Note:*** Even though it does not change or affect what is sung by the singers, this *is* a

Vesperal Liturgy of St Basil the Great. Therefore, the Prayers of the Eucharistic Kanon will be those of that Liturgy, beginning with, "O Existing One, Master, Lord God, Father Almighty and adorable!". Again, **_all_** of the responses are done as with any regular Divine Liturgy.

The Hymn to the Theotokos

Instead of singing "All of Creation!", as would be done at a regular Divine Liturgy of St Basil the Great, the Hymn to the Theotokos at this particular service is Ode 9 of the Matins Kanon celebrated the previous evening, sung in the special tone 6 melody and that begins: "Come, O faithful! Let us enjoy the Master's hospitality,…!". (In the **Byzantine** tradition, the people sing "All of Creation!", as would be done at a regular Divine Liturgy of St Basil the Great.)

"And All Mankind!", the Litany Before the Lord's Prayer, and the Lord's Prayer

The Liturgy then proceeds as usual. When the celebrant intones, "Among the first, remember, O Lord,…!", ending with, "rightly to divide the Word of Your truth!", the people sing, "And all mankind!". Then, the Litany Before the Lord's Prayer is celebrated, followed by the singing of the Lord's Prayer itself.

"One is Holy!" and the Communion Hymn

When the celebrant lifts the Holy Gifts, and intones, "The Holy Things are for the holy!", the people sing, "One is holy! One is the Lord, Jesus Christ, to the glory of God the Father! Amen.", and then, *immediately*, sing the Communion Hymn, which is the same as the Entrance Hymn, sung in tone 6: "Of Your Mystical Supper,…!", ending with a **triple** "Alleluia!" (*except* in the Antiochian tradition). (**Note:** Because this is not a Sunday Divine Liturgy, the usual Communion Hymn, "Praise the Lord from the Heavens!", is **not** sung!)

Communion of the Clergy

During the Communion of the clergy, the people sing the Communion Hymn, "Of Your Mystical Supper,…!", *repeatedly*, with**out** the triple "Alleluia!" at the end.

"Blessed is He!" and the Communion of the Faithful

When the clergy exit the sanctuary and intone, "In the fear of God, and with faith and love, draw near!", the people sing, as usual, "Blessed is He Who comes in the Name of the Lord! God is the Lord and has revealed Himself to us!"

Then, during the Communion of the faithful, the people **again** sing, **repeatedly**, the Communion Hymn, "Of Your Mystical Supper,…!", **again**, with**out** the triple "Alleluia!". After the last of the faithful have received Holy Communion, and (if it is the local custom to do so) the celebrant stands on the ambo and intones, "Lo! This has touched your lips, and shall take away your iniquities, and cleanse your sins!", **then** the people sing the **triple** "Alleluia!" in the same tone 6 as the Communion Hymn (**except** in the Antiochian tradition).

["Having Beheld the Resurrection of Christ"]

At this point, the service books call for the deacon in the sanctuary, during the time that the clergy are getting the Holy Gifts ready to be transferred back to the Table of Oblation, to chant a prayer. This "prayer," however, is actually a **hymn** that is sung as Post-Gospel Stikhera at Resurrectional Matins (this is **never** done in the **Greek** practice). Therefore, in **some** parishes, the practice is for the people to sing these stikhera in the prescribed tone 6. The stikhera are as follows:

> Having beheld the Resurrection of Christ,
> let us worship the holy Lord, Jesus,
> the only sinless One!
> We venerate Your Cross, O Christ,
> and Your holy Resurrection we praise
>   and glorify!
> For, You are our God,
> and we know no other but You.

We call on Your Name.
Come, all you faithful!
Let us venerate Christ's holy Resurrection!
For, behold, through the Cross joy has come
    into all the world!
Let us ever bless the Lord,
praising His Resurrection!
For, by enduring the Cross for us,
He has destroyed death by death!

Shine! Shine, O new Jerusalem!
The glory of the Lord has shone on you!
Exult now and be glad, O Zion!
Be radiant, O pure Theotokos, in the
    Resurrection of your Son!

O Christ, great and most-holy Pascha!
O Wisdom, Word, and Power of God!
Grant that we may more perfectly
    partake of You
in the never-ending Day of Your Kingdom!

Again, in some parishes, it is the practice for the people to sing this hymn. This gives the clergy time to prepare the Holy Gifts to be transferred to the Table of Oblation. As with other liturgical elements, the choir director should check with the bishop, the parish priest, or the main celebrant to follow the local practice in that particular parish.

Liturgy Ending

At this point, the main celebrant comes out onto the ambo, blesses the people, and says, "O God, save Your people and bless Your inheritance!" Then, instead of singing the usual "We have seen the true Light!", the people sing, again in tone 6, "Of Your Mystical Supper,…!", ending with the *triple* "Alleluia!" (*except* in the Antiochian tradition).

The celebrant returns to the sanctuary. When the Holy Gifts are ready to be transferred to the Table of Oblation, the deacon takes the paten over there. The celebrant, holding the chalice, stands in the royal doorway and chants, "Blessed is our God, always now and ever and unto ages of ages!" The people respond with, "Amen." Then, instead of singing the usual "Let our mouths be filled…!", the people sing, again in tone 6, "Of Your Mystical Supper,…!", ending with the *triple* "Alleluia!" (*except* in the Byzantine tradition, where "Let our mouths be filled…!" *is* sung).

The Litany of Thanksgiving, the Prayer Before the Ambo, and "Blessed be the Name of the Lord!"

Then, the Litany of Thanksgiving is celebrated, with the usual responses. As the celebrant exits the sanctuary and intones, "Let us depart in peace!", the people sing, "In the Name of the Lord!". The deacon then intones, "Let us pray to the Lord!", and the people sing, "Lord, have mercy." The celebrant chants a special Prayer Before the Ambo in the middle of the church (*except* in the Byzantine tradition), beginning, "All-good and all-merciful Master, we sing to You, we glorify You, and we thank You, our sinless God!". At the exclamation ("For, Yours are the Kingdom, and the power, and the glory,…!"), the people sing "Amen.", and then, "Blessed be the Name of the Lord, henceforth and forevermore!" *three* times.

The Dismissal

The Dismissal is then celebrated as at all Divine Liturgies. After the exclamation ("for, He is good and loves mankind!"), the people **usually** sing a **double** "Amen." ("Amen. Amen.").

Recessional Hymns

As everyone comes forward to venerate the icons and the Holy Cross, the people **may** sing the Troparion for the day, "When the glorious disciples...!", in tone 8. In **other** parishes, the venerating is done in silence. As always, the local practice should be observed.

E. MATINS OF HOLY FRIDAY

The Matins of Holy Friday is **usually** celebrated in parishes on Thursday evening. This is a **_very long_** service, often referred to as "The 12 Gospels Service," because, during this Matins, the 12 Passion

Gospels are chanted. The order of the service is as follows.[56]

The First Doxology, "O Heavenly King!", the Trisagion Prayers, the Second Doxology

The service begins with the celebrant intoning the first doxology, "Blessed is our God, always now and ever and unto ages of ages!" A reader then chants, "Amen.", "Glory to You, our God, glory to You!", "O Heavenly King!" (in the **Antiochian** tradition, this is all done by the *priest*), the Trisagion Prayers, and the Lord's Prayer. After the exclamation ("For, Yours are the Kingdom, and the power, and the glory…!"), the reader chants, "Amen.". (In the **Antiochian** tradition, this is followed by "Lord, have mercy." **twelve** times, a full "Glory,…now and ever…!", "Come, let us worship…!", Psalms 19 and 20, the Trisagion Prayers again, "O Lord, save Your people!", "Glory…!", "Do You, of Your own good will…!", "Now and ever…!", "O dread champion…!", and petitions with a **triple** "Lord, have mercy.".) Then, in **all** the traditions, the reader chants, "In the Name of the Lord, Father (or, if it be a bishop, "Master"; or, if it be the

---

[56] *Triodion*, pp. 565-600.

Metropolitan, "Most blessed Master"), bless!" The celebrant then intones the second doxology, "Glory to the Holy, consubstantial, life-creating, and undivided Trinity, always now and ever and unto ages of ages!" The reader then chants "Amen.", then "Glory to God in the highest and, on Earth, peace, good will towards men!" **three** times, and "O Lord, open my lips, and my mouth will show forth your praise!" **two** times.

The 6 Psalms

The 6 Psalms of Matins are then chanted: Psalms 3, 37, 62, 87, 102, and 142.[57] It is customary to have two readers chant these Psalms, as follows: the first reader, who has done all the introductory chanting up to now, chants Psalms 3, 37, and 62. He or she then chants a full "Glory,... now and ever...!", "Alleluia! Alleluia! Alleluia! Glory to You, O God!" **three** times, a **triple** "Lord, have mercy.", and, then, the **_first half_** of a "**split** 'Glory!'": "Glory to the Father, and to the Son, and to the Holy Spirit!". The second reader then takes up the chanting at this point with the **_second half_** of the "**split** 'Glory!'": "Now and ever and unto ages of ages! Amen.", and,

---

[57] The Psalms are numbered according to the Septuagint.

then, ***immediately*** chants the remaining three Psalms, Psalms 87, 102, and 142. After the conclusion of the final Psalm, this second reader then chants a full "Glory,… now and ever…!", and "Alleluia! Alleluia! Alleluia! Glory to You, O God!" ***three*** times. (In the ***Antiochian*** tradition, the reader ends with, "O our God and our Hope, glory to You!".)

In ***some*** parishes, because of the length of this service, ***only 3*** of the 6 Psalms are celebrated (either the first three or the last three). If this is the case, then only one reader chants the 3 Psalms, with a full "Glory,… now and ever…!", and "Alleluia! Alleluia! Alleluia! Glory to You, O God!" chanted ***three*** times at the end. Again, the choir director and singers should follow the guidelines of the main celebrant.

The Great Litany

The Great Litany is then celebrated, with ***all*** of its responses sung, as with all other litanies here, in a ***non***-Lenten melody.

"Alleluia!" and Troparion

The deacon then chants a set of Matinal "Alleluia!" petitions, each one followed by the singing by the people of a ***triple*** "Alleluia!", in tone 8. The "Alleluia!" petitions are: "Alleluia! Alleluia! Alleluia! In the night, my soul rises early for You, O God; for, Your commandments are a light on the Earth!", "Learn righteousness, O inhabitants of the Earth!", "Jealousy will grasp an untaught people!", and "Bring more evils on them, O Lord! Bring more evils on those who are glorious on the Earth!".

Following the singing of the last ***triple*** "Alleluia!", the people sing, in tone 8, the Troparion: "When the glorious disciples...!". Then, the people sing, "Glory...Spirit!", then the full Troparion ("When the glorious disciples...!") again, then "Now and ever...Amen.", then the full Troparion "When the glorious disciples...!") one final time. All of this is sung in tone 8. A great censing is done during this singing. In the Greek practice, the rubrics prescribe the Troparion to be sung slowly the first two times and quickly the third and last time.

The Little Litany

A Little Litany is then celebrated, with its usual responses.

The 1st Gospel

The 1st Gospel, John 13:31-18:1, is then chanted. The order for singing for this and the other 11 Gospels in this service is: the deacon intones, "And that we may be accounted worthy to listen to the Holy Gospel, let us pray to the Lord our God!". The people then sing a triple "Lord, have mercy.". The deacon then intones, "Wisdom! Let us be attentive! Let us listen to the Holy Gospel!" The priest (or, bishop) then blesses the people as he chants, "Peace be with you all!" The people sing, "And with your spirit!" The priest then intones, "The Reading is from the Holy Gospel according to Saint [and then, whichever Gospel it is from: Matthew, Mark, Luke, or John the Theologian]!". Then, instead of singing "Glory to You, O Lord, glory to You!", the people sing, **_before_** the chanting of the Gospel, "Glory to Your Passion, O Lord!" (**_except_** in the Greek practice, where "Glory to You, O Lord, glory to You!" *is* sung). The celebrant then chants the Gospel reading. Then, **_after_** the chanting of the Gospel, the people sing, "Glory to Your long-suffering, O Lord!" (in the Antiochian tradition, "Glory to Your Passion, O Lord!" is sung; in the **Greek** practice, "Glory to Your forbearance, O Lord, glory to You!" is sung). Again, this is the pattern celebrated for **_all 12_** Passion Gospels!

Antiphons 1 – 3

Following the 1st Gospel, there are sets of stikhera sung called "antiphons." These are sung in the same stikhera tones that "Lord, I Call Upon You!" and the Apostikha at Vespers are sung in.[58] These antiphons are sung throughout the service in groupings of 3 (Antiphons 1-3, 4-6, 7-9, 10-12, and 13-15). **Therefore**, in **_some_** parishes, only the first antiphon from the first four groupings (Antiphons 1, 4, 7, and 10) are celebrated. In **_most_** parishes, however, **_all_** of the Antiphons are celebrated. Also,

---

[58] Cf., Barrett, David, *Elementary Music Theory for Orthodox Liturgical Singing*, OLP (Orthodox Liturgical Press), January 2014 (hereafter referred to as "*Theory*"), pp. 118-131.

even though the service books call for all the stikhera to be repeated (sung twice), in **_most_** parishes, each stikheron is sung **_only once_**. Because of that, we will treat the explanation of the Antiphons that way (as being sung only once) in our discussion here, knowing that the service books call for them to be sung twice. As always, whatever has been set in place by the main celebrant should be observed.

Antiphon 1, in tone 8, begins, "The rulers of the people have assembled…!" A reader then chants a full "Glory,… now and ever…!", and the people sing, again in tone 8, "As a Virgin, you gave Birth without knowing wedlock,…!". Antiphon 2, in tone 6, starts, "Judas ran to the lawless scribes, and said,…!". A reader then chants a full "Glory,… now and ever…!", and the people sing, again in tone 6, "Do not cease, O Virgin, to pray to Him…!". Antiphon 3 has six stikhera, all in tone 2, beginning, "Because of the raising of Lazarus,…!", "At Your Supper, O Christ our God,…!", "When John asked You, O Lord,…!", "With thirty pieces of silver,…!", "During the washing of the feet,…!", and "You, our God, said to Your disciples,…!". A reader then chants a full "Glory,… now and ever…!", and the people sing, again in tone 2, "Keep your servants safe from danger, O Theotokos!".

[The Little Litany]

Although the service books call for celebrating a Little Litany at this point, because this service is so long, this Little Litany is **omitted** in **many** parishes.

Kathisma Hymn 1

The people then sing Kathisma Hymn 1, in tone 7, beginning, "When You were feeding Your disciples at the Supper,…!".

The 2nd Gospel

The 2nd Gospel reading, John 18:1-28, is then chanted. **Note:** In parishes with many clergy concelebrating (more than one priest, a priest and a deacon, etc.), it is **sometimes** the practice for different members of the clergy to chant the various 12 Passion Gospels. In any case, **_before_** the Gospel is chanted, the people sing, "Glory to Your Passion, O Lord!", and, **_after_** the Gospel is chanted, the people sing, "Glory to Your long-suffering, O Lord!" (in the **Antiochian** tradition, "Glory to Your Passion, O Lord!" is again sung after the Gospel reading).

Antiphons 4 – 6

Antiphon 4, in tone 5, then starts, "Today, Judas forsakes the Master…!", followed by, again in tone 5, "Today, Judas counterfeits piety…!". Then, a stikheron in tone 1 (tone 5 in the **Antiochian** tradition) begins, "As brothers in Christ, let us acquire brotherly love!". A reader then chants a full "Glory,… now and ever…!", and the people sing, again in tone 1 (tone 5 in the **Antiochian** tradition), "Everywhere, glorious things are spoken of you,…!". Antiphon 5, in tone 6, begins, "The disciple agreed upon the price of the Master,…!", followed by, again in tone 6, "Today, the Creator of Heaven and Earth…!". A reader then chants a full "Glory,… now and ever…!", and the people sing, again in tone 6, "O Virgin, who, in the last days,…!". Antiphon 6, in tone

7, starts, "Today, the Jews nailed to the Cross the Lord...!", followed by, again in tone 7, "O Lord, as You came to Your voluntary Passion,...!". ...!". A reader then chants a full "Glory,... now and ever...!", and the people sing, again in tone 7, "Rejoice, Theotokos, who have contained within your womb...!".

[The Little Litany]

Although the service books call for celebrating a Little Litany at this point, because this service is so long, this Little Litany is **omitted** in **<u>many</u>** parishes.

Kathisma Hymn 2

The people then sing Kathisma Hymn 2, in tone 7, beginning, "What caused you to betray the Savior, O Judas?".

The 3rd Gospel

The 3rd Gospel, Matthew 26:57-75, is then chanted. As previously, **_before_** the Gospel is chanted, the people sing, "Glory to Your Passion, O Lord!", and, **_after_** the Gospel is chanted, the people sing, "Glory to Your long-suffering, O Lord!" (in the **Antiochian** tradition, "Glory to Your Passion, O Lord!" is again sung after the Gospel reading).

Antiphons 7 – 9

Antiphon 7, in tone 8, begins, "While permitting transgressors to arrest You,…!", followed by, again in tone 8, "Denying You for the third time,…!". A reader then chants a full "Glory,… now and ever…!", and the people sing, again in tone 8, "Let us praise the holy Virgin,…!". Antiphon 8, in tone 2, starts, "O transgressors,…!", followed by, again in tone 2, "They cried, 'Let Him be Crucified!',…!". A reader then chants a full "Glory,… now and ever…!", and the people then sing, again in tone 2, "As there is no boldness in us…!". Then, Antiphon 9, in tone 3, begins, "They took the thirty pieces of silver,…!", followed by, again in tone 3, "They gave Me gall to eat,…!". A reader then chants a full "Glory,… now and ever…!", and the people sing, again in tone 3, "We Gentiles sing of you, O pure Theotokos…!".

[The Little Litany]

Although the service books call for celebrating a Little Litany at this point, because this service is so long, this Little Litany is **omitted** in **many** parishes.

Kathisma Hymn 3

The people then sing Kathisma Hymn 3, in tone 8, beginning, "How could Judas, who was once Your disciple, plan to betray You?".

The 4ᵗʰ Gospel

The 4ᵗʰ Gospel, John 18:28-19:16, is then chanted. As previously, **_before_** the Gospel is chanted, the people sing, "Glory to Your Passion, O Lord!", and, **_after_** the Gospel is chanted, the people sing, "Glory to Your long-suffering, O Lord!" (in the **Antiochian** tradition, "Glory to Your Passion, O Lord!" is again sung after the Gospel reading).

Antiphons 10 – 12

Antiphon 10, in tone 6, starts, "He Who clothed Himself with light as with a garment…!", followed by, again in tone 6, "The disciple denied Him!". A reader then chants a full "Glory,… now and ever…!", and the people sing, again in tone 6, "O Lord, Who love mankind,…!". Antiphon 11, sung in tone 6, begins, "In return for the blessings You have granted us, O Christ,…!", followed by, sung again in tone 6, "The people of the Hebrews were not satisfied…!", then, again in tone 6, "Neither the quaking of the Earth,…!". A reader then chants a full "Glory,… now and ever…!", and the people sing, again in tone 6, "O Virgin Theotokos, who alone are pure and blessed,…!". Antiphon 12, in tone 8, starts, "Thus says the Lord to the Jews,…!", followed by, again in tone 8, "Today, the curtain of the temple is torn in two,…!", then, again in tone 8, "O lawgivers of Israel,…!". A reader then chants a full "Glory,… now and ever…!", and the people sing, sung again in tone 8, "Rejoice, gate of the King of glory,…!".

[The Little Litany]

Although the service books call for celebrating a Little Litany at this point, because this service is so long, this Little Litany is *omitted* in **_many_** parishes.

Kathisma Hymn 4

The people then sing Kathisma Hymn 4, in tone 8, beginning, "O God, You stood before Caiaphas!".

The 5th Gospel

The 5th Gospel, Matthew 27:3-32, is then chanted. As previously, <u>*before*</u> the Gospel is chanted, the people sing, "Glory to Your Passion, O Lord!", and, <u>*after*</u> the Gospel is chanted, the people sing, "Glory to Your long-suffering, O Lord!" (in the *Antiochian* tradition, "Glory to Your Passion, O Lord!" is again sung after the Gospel reading).

Antiphons 13 – 15

Antiphon 13, in tone 6, begins, "The crowd of the Jews, O Lord,…!", followed by, again in tone 6, "To Christ, the Wisdom and Power of God,…!". !". A reader then chants a full "Glory,… now and ever…!", and the people sing, again in tone 6, "O Theotokos, who, by a Word beyond all words,…!". Antiphon 14, in tone 8, starts, "The thief, whose hands were defiled by blood,…!", followed by, again in tone 8, "The thief on the cross uttered a small cry,…!". !". A reader then chants a full "Glory,… now and ever…!", and the people sing, again in tone 8, "Rejoice! For, through an angel, you received the Joy of the world!".

During the singing of the first stikheron of Antiphon 15, in most churches of the **Byzantine** tradition (as well as **ever-increasing** parishes of the **Slavic** tradition), the cross is brought out in solemn procession from the sanctuary and placed and set up in the middle of the church. The first stikheron of Antiphon 15, in tone 6, in its entirety states, "Today, He Who hung the Earth upon the waters is hung on the Tree! Today, He Who hung the Earth upon the waters is hung on the Tree! Today, He Who hung the Earth upon the waters is hung on the Tree! The King of the angels is decked with a crown of thorns! He Who wraps the Heavens in clouds is wrapped in the purple of mockery! He Who freed Adam in the Jordan is slapped on the face! The Bridegroom of the Church is affixed to the Cross with nails! The Son of the Virgin is pierced by a spear! We worship Your Passion, O Christ! We worship Your Passion, O Christ! We worship Your Passion, O Christ! Show us, also, Your glorious Resurrection!"). This is followed, again in tone 6, with "Let us not keep the feast like the Jews!", and, again in tone 6, "Your Cross, O Lord, is life and resurrection for Your people!". A reader then chants a full "Glory,… now and ever…!", and the people sing, again in tone 6, "When she who Conceived You, O Christ,…!".

[The Little Litany]

Although the service books call for celebrating a Little Litany at this point, because this service is so long, this Little Litany is **_omitted_** in **_many_** parishes.

Kathisma Hymn 5

The people then sing Kathisma Hymn 5, in tone 4, beginning, "By Your precious Blood,…!".

The 6th Gospel

The 6th Gospel, Mark 15:16-32, is then chanted. As previously, **_before_** the Gospel is chanted, the people sing, "Glory to Your Passion, O Lord!", and, **_after_** the Gospel is chanted, the people sing, "Glory to Your long-suffering, O Lord!" (in the

Antiochian tradition, "Glory to Your Passion, O Lord!" is again sung after the Gospel reading).

The Beatitudes

The Beatitudes are then celebrated. The people sing, in tone 4, "In Your Kingdom, remember us, O Lord, when You come in Your Kingdom! Blessed are the poor in spirit; for, theirs is the Kingdom of Heaven! Blessed are those who mourn; for, they shall be comforted! Blessed are the meek; for, they shall inherit the Earth!". Then, the deacon begins chanting a series of verses, in between which the people continue singing the remaining verses of the Beatitudes. So, the deacon begins the verse, "Through a tree, Adam lost his home in Paradise!…". The people then sing, "Blessed are those who hunger and thirst after righteousness; for, they shall be filled!". The deacon then chants, "Lawless men bought the Creator of the Law from a lawless disciple,…!". The people then sing, "Blessed are the merciful; for, they shall obtain mercy!". The deacon then chants, "The swarm of those who would kill God,…!". The people then sing, "Blessed are the pure in heart; for, they shall see God!". The deacon then chants, "From Your life-bearing side, O Christ,…!". The people then sing, "Blessed are the peacemakers; for, they shall be called the sons of God!". The deacon then chants, "You were Crucified for my sake,…!". The people then sing, "Blessed are those who are persecuted for righteousness' sake; for, theirs is the Kingdom of Heaven!". The deacon then chants, "When it beheld You Crucified, O Christ, all creation trembled!". The people then sing, "Blessed are you when men shall revile you and persecute you, and shall say all manner of evil against you falsely, for My sake!". The deacon then chants, "On the Cross, You destroyed the legal bond against us, O Lord!". The people then sing, "Rejoice and be exceeding glad; for, great is your reward in Heaven!". The deacon then chants, "You were lifted up upon the Cross, O Lord!". The people then sing, "Glory to the Father, and to the Son, and to the Holy Spirit!". The deacon then chants, "Let us, the faithful, all pray that,…!". The people then sing, "Now and ever and unto ages of ages! Amen.". The deacon then chants, "We offer to You as an intercessor, O Christ,…!". The Beatitudes are thus concluded.

The Little Litany

A Little Litany is then celebrated, with the responses sung in a **_non_**-Lenten melody.

The Prokeimenon

The Prokeimenon, in tone 4, is then chanted: "They divide My garments among them! And, for My raiment, they cast lots!", with the accompanying verse, "My God, My God, look upon Me! Why have You forsaken Me?".

The 7th Gospel

The 7th Gospel, Matthew 27:33-54, is then chanted. As previously, **_before_** the Gospel is chanted, the people sing, "Glory to Your Passion, O Lord!", and, **_after_** the Gospel is chanted, the people sing, "Glory to Your long-suffering, O Lord!" (in the **_Antiochian_** tradition, "Glory to Your Passion, O Lord!" is again sung after the Gospel reading).

Psalm 50

A reader then chants Psalm 50: "Have mercy on me, O God, according to Your steadfast love. According to Your abundant mercy, blot out my transgressions!...!".

The 8th Gospel

The 8th Gospel, Luke 23:32-49, is then chanted. As previously, **_before_** the Gospel is chanted, the people sing, "Glory to Your Passion, O Lord!", and, **_after_** the Gospel is chanted, the people sing, "Glory to Your long-suffering, O Lord!" (in the **Antiochian** tradition, "Glory to Your Passion, O Lord!" is again sung after the Gospel reading).

The Kanon, [The Little Litany], the Kontakion, and the Oikos

The Kanon is then celebrated, in a special melody in tone 6. Even though the service books call for each ode to be sung twice and the troparia to be repeated three or six times, in **most** parishes, this is **not** done. Instead, each ode is **sung once**, and each troparion is **chanted once** by a reader, with another reader chanting the refrain, "Glory to You, our God, glory to You!" until the final troparion is chanted, and then the final refrain is a full "Glory,... now and ever...!".

    Ode 5 begins, "Early will I seek You, O Word of God,...!". After this, the service books call for a Little Litany to be celebrated, but **most** parishes **omit** this. Then, the Kontakion, in tone 8, is sung, "Come, let us sing the praises of Him Who was crucified for us!...!". Then, a reader chants the Oikos, beginning, "Behold her own Lamb led to the slaughter, Mary followed with the other women,...!". After the reader chants the phrase, "Do not pass me by in silence, O You Who kept me pure!", the people sing the cadence phrase, in the same tone 8 of the Kontakion, "For, You are my Son and my God!". This is followed by Ode 8, beginning, "The godly youths exposed a monument of godless wickedness!". After the second troparion, instead of chanting "Glory...Spirit!", the reader chanting the refrains intones, "Let us bless the Father, and the Son, and the Holy Spirit, the Lord!". The other reader then chants a troparion. The first reader then chants "Now and ever…Amen.", and the other reader chants a final troparion. Then, the people sing, in the same special tone 6 melody of the Kanon, "We praise, bless, and worship the Lord, singing and exalting Him throughout all ages!". Then, Ode 9 begins, "More honorable than the Cherubim,…!". After the final troparion is chanted, Ode 9, "More honorable than the Cherubim,…!" is sung one more time as the katavasia.

In the **Greek** practice, after the Kontakion and Oikos, the Synaxaria for the Day from the Menaion and the Triodion are chanted, followed by the Stikhera for the Crucifixion and the Wise Thief.

The Exapostilarion

Following the Kanon, the Exapostilarion is celebrated, in a special melody in tone 8 or tone 3. In **many** parishes, this is sung by a single chanter, or, more commonly, by a trio. The full Exapostilarion is, "The wise thief, You made worthy of Paradise in a single moment (or, in the Greek practice, "on this very day"), O Lord! By the Wood of Your Cross, also (in the **Greek** practice, adding, at this point, "on this very day") illumine me and save me!" This is sung once, then a reader chants, "Glory...Spirit!". The full Exapostilarion is sung again, and then the reader chants, "Now and ever...Amen.". The full Exapostilarion is then sung a third and final time.

The 9th Gospel

The 9th Gospel, John 19:25-37, is then chanted. As previously, ***before*** the Gospel is chanted, the people sing, "Glory to Your Passion, O Lord!", and, ***after*** the Gospel is chanted, the people sing, "Glory to Your long-suffering, O Lord!" (in the **Antiochian** tradition, "Glory to Your Passion, O Lord!" is again sung after the Gospel reading).

The Praises

The Praises (Psalms 148, 149, and 150) are then chanted by a reader. After the phrase, "Praise Him with lute and harp!", the people sing, in tone 3, "Israel, My first-born son,...!". The service books call for this stikheron to be sung twice, but, in **most** parishes, it is sung **only once** (**except** in the **Greek** practice, where it *is* sung twice). The next stikheron, also in tone 3, begins, "Every member of Your holy flesh endured dishonor for us,…!". The third stikheron, again in tone 3, says, "Behold You Crucified, O Christ,…!". The reader then chants, "Glory…Spirit!", and the people sing, in tone 6, "They have stripped Me of My garments and clothed Me in a purple robe!". The reader then chants, "Now and ever…Amen.", and the people sing, still in tone 6, "I gave My back to scourging!".

The 10th Gospel

The 10th Gospel, Mark 15:43-47, is then chanted. As previously, **_before_** the Gospel is chanted, the people sing, "Glory to Your Passion, O Lord!", and, **_after_** the Gospel is chanted, the people sing, "Glory to Your long-suffering, O Lord!" (in the **Antiochian** tradition, "Glory to Your Passion, O Lord!" is again sung after the Gospel reading).

The Lesser Doxology

After the 10th Gospel, the reader who had chanted the verses for the Praises intones, "To You, O Lord our God, belongs glory, and to You we send up glory: to the Father, and to the Son, and to the Holy Spirit, now and ever and unto ages of ages! Amen.".

The celebrant then intones, "Glory to You, Who have shown us the Light!" (**except** in the Antiochian tradition). A **different** reader then chants the Lesser Doxology, "Glory to God in the highest and, on Earth, peace, good will towards men! We praise You! We bless You! We worship You! We glorify You! We give thanks to You for Your great glory!…!".

The Litany of Matins

The Litany of Matins is then celebrated, responded to in a **_non_**-Lenten melody.

The 11th Gospel

The 11th Gospel, John 19:38-42, is then chanted. As previously, **_before_** the Gospel is chanted, the people sing, "Glory to Your Passion, O Lord!", and, **_after_** the Gospel is chanted, the people sing, "Glory to Your long-suffering, O Lord!" (in the **Antiochian** tradition, "Glory to Your Passion, O Lord!" is again sung after the Gospel reading).

The Apostikha

The Apostikha follows the 11th Gospel. Starting in tone 1, the first stikheron begins, "All creation was changed by fear when it saw You hanging upon the Cross, O Christ!". A reader then chants the verse, "They divided My garments among them! And, for My raiment, they cast lots!". The next stikheron, in tone 2, starts, "An impious and transgressing people,…!". The reader then chants the verse, "They gave Me gall for food! And, for My thirst, they gave Me vinegar to drink!". The third stikheron, also in tone 2, begins, "Today, the blameless Virgin saw You suspended upon the Cross,

O Lord!". The reader then chants the verse, "God is our King before the ages! He has worked salvation in the midst of the Earth!". The next stikheron, staying in tone 2, starts, "When she who Bore You without seed saw You suspended upon the Tree,…!". The reader then chants, "Glory…Spirit!". The people then sing, in tone 8, "When You ascended the Cross, O Lord, fear and trembling fell upon creation!". The reader then chants, "Now and ever…Amen.", and the people sing, still in tone 8, "Now, the unjust judges dip the pen of judgment!". (In *some Slavic* service books, this *last* stikheron is called to be sung in tone 6.)

The 12th Gospel

The 12th Gospel, Matthew 27:62-66, is then chanted. As previously, ***before*** the Gospel is chanted, the people sing, "Glory to Your Passion, O Lord!", and, ***after*** the Gospel is chanted, the people sing, "Glory to Your long-suffering, O Lord!" (in the ***Antiochian*** tradition, "Glory to Your Passion, O Lord!" is again sung after the Gospel reading).

Prayer, the Trisagion Prayers, and the Lord's Prayer

Following the Apostikha, a reader chants the prayer, "It is good to give thanks to the Lord, to sing praises to Your Name, O Most High, to declare Your steadfast love in the morning, and Your truth by night!". The reader then chants the Trisagion Prayers and the Lord's Prayer. After the exclamation ("For, Yours are the Kingdom, and the power, and the glory,…!"), the reader chants an "Amen.".

The Troparion

The people then sing the Troparion, in tone 4: "By Your precious Blood, You have redeemed us from the curse of the Law! By being nailed to the Cross and pierced by a spear, You have poured forth immortality for man! O our Savior, glory to You!". This is usually sung in a special melody for tone 4. In the **Greek** practice, it is usually sung **three** times.

The Augmented Litany

Then, the Augmented Litany is celebrated, beginning with the petition, "Have mercy on us, O God, according to Your great goodness,...!", and the people sing, *from the <u>first</u> petition*, a **triple** "Lord, have mercy." in a **<u>non</u>**-Lenten tone.

The Dismissal

The Dismissal is then celebrated. After the Dismissal Prayer ("May He Who endured spitting and scourging, the Cross and death, for the salvation of the world, Christ our true God,...!") and the exclamation ("for He is good and loves mankind!"), the people **usually** sing a **double** "Amen." ("Amen. Amen.").

Recessional Hymns

As everyone comes up to venerate the icons and the Holy Cross, this venerating may be done in silence, or some appropriate hymn from the service (such as the Troparion ["When the glorious disciples...!"] or the Exapostilarion ["The wise thief, You made worthy of Paradise in a single moment, O Lord,...!"]) may be sung. As always, the local practice should be observed.

F. ROYAL HOURS OF HOLY FRIDAY

The Royal Hours of Holy Friday, when celebrated in a parish, are usually done early on Holy Friday morning (the **Greek** practice allows any time of day prior to the Vespers of Holy Friday). Also, although the rubrics in the **Greek** practice call for the entire service (with the exception of the stikhera, **none** of which are **repeated**) to be chanted rather than sung, it is customary, in parish practice, to celebrate the service as described here. The order for them is as follows.[59]

---

[59] *Triodion*, pp. 600-611.

The 1ˢᵗ Hour

The service begins with the celebrant intoning the first doxology, "Blessed is our God, always now and ever and unto ages of ages!" A reader then chants, "Amen.", "Glory to You, our God, glory to You!", "O Heavenly King!" (done by the priest), the Trisagion Prayers, and the Lord's Prayer. After the exclamation ("For, Yours are the Kingdom, and the power, and the glory…!"), the reader then chants, "Amen.", "Lord, have mercy." *twelve* times, a full "Glory,… now and ever…!", and "Come, let us worship God, our King…!".

The reader then chants three Psalms for the 1ˢᵗ Hour: Psalm 5 ("Give ear to my words, O Lord!"), Psalm 2 ("Why do the nations conspire, and the peoples plot in vain?"), and Psalm 21 ("My God, my God, why have You forsaken me?").[60] Then, the reader chants a full "Glory,… now and ever…!", "Alleluia! Alleluia! Alleluia! Glory to You, O God!" **three** times, a **triple** "Lord, have mercy.", and "Glory…Spirit!".

---

[60] The Psalms are numbered according to the Septuagint.

The people then sing, in tone 1, the Troparion, "When You were Crucified, O Christ,...!". The same reader then chants, "Now and ever...Amen.", and the people sing, still in tone 1, the theotokion, "What should we call you, O full of grace?".

The people then sing a set of stikhera, the first one, in tone 8, beginning, "The curtain of the temple was torn in two,...!". A reader then chants, "Why do the nations conspire, and the peoples plot in vain?". The people then sing, again in tone 8, "You were led as a Sheep to the slaughter, O Christ our King,...!". The reader then chants, "The rulers of the people have assembled against the Lord and His Christ!". The people then **_repeat the singing_** of "You were led as a Sheep to the slaughter, O Christ our King,...!", in tone 8. (**_Note:_** In some parishes, which do **not** repeat the singing of **any** stikhera, when the reader chants, "Why do the nations conspire,...?", he or she then **_immediately_** chants, "The rulers of the people have assembled...!", and the people sing "You were led as a Sheep to the slaughter,...!" **_only once!_**) The reader chants a full "Glory,... now and ever...!", and the people sing, still in tone 8, "While permitting transgressors to arrest You, You cried out to them, O Lord,...!". **_Note:_** The service books call for the reader to chant, "Glory...Spirit!", then the singing of

"While permitting transgressors...!", then the reader chanting, "Now and ever...Amen.", then the **_singing again_** of "While permitting transgressors...!". Although this is what is called for in the service books, *most* parishes have the reader chant a **_full_** "Glory,... now and ever...!", and the singing of "While permitting transgressors...!" **_only once!_** Again, in the **Greek** practice, **none** of the stikhera is repeated.

The Prokeimenon of the Prophecy, in the 4th tone, is then celebrated: "His heart gathers mischief! When he goes out, he tells it abroad!", with its accompanying verse, "Blessed is he who considers the poor and needy!". Then, the same reader who chants this Prokeimenon of the Prophecy chants the Old Testament reading, Zechariah 11:10-13. The chanting of the Epistle reading, Galatians 6:14-18, is usually done by a **_different_** reader. Following the Epistle, the Gospel reading, Matthew 27:1-56, is chanted.

Then, a reader chants a prayer that states, "Order my steps, and let no iniquity have dominion over me! Deliver me from the false accusation of men, so I will keep Your commandments! Make Your Face to shine upon Your servant, and teach me Your statutes! Let my mouth be filled with Your praise, O Lord, that I may sing of Your glory and majesty all the day long!". Then, this same reader chants the Trisagion Prayers and the Lord's Prayer. After the exclamation ("For, Yours are the Kingdom, and the power, and the glory,...!"), this **same** reader chants "Amen.".

The people then sing, in tone 8, the Kontakion, "Come, let us sing the praises of Him Who was Crucified for us!". A reader then chants "Lord, have mercy." **forty** times, followed by the prayer that begins, "You, Who at every season and every hour,...!", followed by a **triple** "Lord, have mercy.", a full "Glory,... now and ever...!", "More honorable than the Cherubim,...!", and, "In the Name of the Lord, Father (or, if it be a bishop, "Master"; or, if it be the Metropolitan, "Most blessed Master"), bless!". The celebrant then intones, "God be bountiful to us, and bless us and show the light of His countenance on us, and be merciful unto us!". The reader then chants "Amen.", followed by, "O Christ, the true Light, Who enlighten and sanctify everyone who comes into the world: Let the light of Your countenance shine upon us; that, in it, we may behold the unapproachable Light, and guide our footsteps aright to the keeping of Your commandments, through the prayers of Your most-pure Mother, and of all Your saints! Amen." (in the

Byzantine tradition, the priest chants "O Christ, the true Light,...).

The 3rd Hour

The rest of the Hours, the 3rd, the 6th, and the 9th, all begin with a reader chanting "Come, let us worship God, our King!". Then, in the 3rd Hour, the reader continues with the chanting of Psalm 34 ("Contend, O Lord, with those who contend with me! Fight against those who fight against me!"), Psalm 108 ("Be not silent, O God of my praise!"), and Psalm 50 ("Have mercy on me, O God, according to Your steadfast love! According to Your abundant mercy, blot out my transgressions!"). Then, the reader chants a full "Glory,... now and ever...!", "Alleluia! Alleluia! Alleluia! Glory to You, O God!" **three** times, a **triple** "Lord, have mercy.", and "Glory...Spirit!".

The people then sing, in tone 6, the Troparion, "O Lord, the Jews condemned You to death,...!". The reader then chants, "Now and ever...Amen.", and the people sing the theotokion, also in tone 6, "O Theotokos, you are the true vine who have put forth the Fruit of Life!". This is followed by the singing of some stikhera. First, in tone 8, we sing, "Through the fear of the Jews, Your friend and companion, Peter, denied You, O Lord,…!". The service books call for this to be sung twice, but, in **most** parishes, it is sung **only once**. A reader then chants, "Give ear to my words, O Lord! Attend to my cry!". The people then sing, still in tone 8, "When the soldiers mocked You, O Lord,…!". The reader then chants, "Hearken to the voice of my prayer, my King and my God!". The people then **repeat the singing** of "When the soldiers mocked You, O Lord,…!". (**Note:** In **some** parishes, which do *not* repeat the singing of *any* stikhera, when the reader chants, "Give ear to my words, O Lord!", he or she then **immediately** chants, "Hearken to the voice of my prayer,…!", and the people sing "When the soldiers mocked You, O Lord,…!" **only once!**) The reader chants a full "Glory,… now and ever…!", and the people sing, in tone 5, "When You were led to Crucifixion,…!". **Note:** The service books call for the reader to chant, "Glory…Spirit!", then the singing of "When You were led to Crucifixion…!", then the reader chanting, "Now and ever…Amen.", then the **singing again** of "When You were led to Crucifixion,…!". Although this is what is called for in the service books, **most** parishes have the reader chant a full "Glory,... now and ever...!", and the singing of "When You were led to Crucifixion ...!" **_only once!_** Again, in the **Greek** practice, **none** of the stikhera is repeated.

The Prokeimenon of the Prophecy, in the 4th tone, is then celebrated: "I am ready for scourging, and my pain is ever with me!", with its accompanying verse, "O Lord, rebuke me not in Your anger, nor chasten me in Your wrath!". Then, the same reader who chants this Prokeimenon of the Prophecy chants the Old Testament reading, Isaiah 50:4-11. The chanting of the Epistle reading, Romans 5:6-10, is usually done by a *different* reader. Following the Epistle, the Gospel reading, Mark 15:16-41, is chanted.

Then, a reader chants a prayer that states, "Blessed be the Lord God! Blessed be the Lord from day to day, and may the God of our salvation prosper us! For, He is our God, the God of salvation!". Then, this same reader chants the Trisagion Prayers and the Lord's Prayer. After the exclamation ("For, Yours are the Kingdom, and the power, and the glory,...!"), this *same* reader chants "Amen.".

The people then sing, in tone 8, the Kontakion, "Come, let us sing the praises of Him Who was Crucified for us!". A reader then chants "Lord, have mercy." **forty** times, followed by the prayer that begins, "You, Who at every season and every hour,…!", followed by a **triple** "Lord, have mercy.", a full "Glory,… now and ever…!", "More honorable than the Cherubim,…!", and, "In the Name of the Lord, Father (or, if it be a bishop, "Master"; or, if it be the Metropolitan, "Most blessed Master"), bless!". The celebrant then intones, "God be bountiful to us, and bless us and show the light of His countenance on us, and be merciful unto us!". The reader then chants "Amen.", followed by, "O God the Master, Father Almighty! O Lord, Jesus Christ, the only-begotten Son, and You, O Holy Spirit, one Godhead, one Power: Have mercy upon me, a sinner, and, according to Your divine judgment, save me, Your unworthy servant! For, You are blessed unto ages of ages! Amen." (in the **Byzantine** tradition, the priest chants this prayer that begins, "O God the Master, Father Almighty!").

The 6ᵗʰ Hour

The 6ᵗʰ Hour begins with a reader chanting "Come, let us worship God, our King!". Then, the reader continues with the chanting of Psalm 53 ("Save me, O God, by Your Name, and vindicate me by Your might!"), Psalm 139 ("Deliver me, O Lord, from evil men!"), and Psalm 90 ("He who dwells in the shelter of the Most High, who abides in the shadow of the Almighty, will say to the Lord,...!"). Then, the reader chants a full "Glory,... now and ever...!", "Alleluia! Alleluia! Alleluia! Glory to You, O God!" **three** times, a **triple** "Lord, have mercy.", and "Glory...Spirit!".

The people then sing, in tone 2, the Troparion, "O Christ our God, You have worked salvation in the midst of the Earth!". The reader then chants, "Now and ever...Amen.", and the people sing the theotokion, also in tone 2, "As there is no boldness in us because of the multitude of our sins,...!". This is followed by the singing of some stikhera. First, in tone 8, we sing, "Thus says the Lord to the Jews,...!". The service books call for this to be sung twice, but, in *most* parishes, it is sung **only once**. A reader then chants, "They gave Me gall to eat! And, for My thirst, they gave Me vinegar to drink!". The people then sing, still in tone 8, "O lawgivers of Israel,...!". The reader then chants, "Save me, O God! For, the water have come up to my neck!". The people then **repeat the singing** of "Thus says the Lord to the Jews,...!". (**Note:** In **some** parishes, which do **not** repeat the singing of **any** stikhera, when the reader chants, "They gave Me gall to eat!", he or she then **immediately** chants, "Save me, O God!", and the people sing "Thus says the Lord to the Jews,...!" **only once!**) The reader chants a full "Glory,... now and ever...!", and the people sing, in tone 5, "Come, O Christ-bearing people,...!". **Note:** The service books call for the reader to chant, "Glory...Spirit!", then the singing of "Come, O Christ-bearing people ...!", then the reader chanting, "Now and ever...Amen.", then the **singing again** of "Come, O Christ-bearing people,...!". Although this is what is called for in the service books, *most* parishes have the reader chant a full "Glory,... now and ever...!", and the singing of "Come, O Christ-bearing people ...!" **only once!** Again, in the **Greek** practice, **none** of the stikhera is repeated.

The Prokeimenon of the Prophecy, in the 4th tone, is then celebrated: "O Lord, our Lord, how majestic is Your Name in all the Earth!", with its accompanying verse, "For, Your majesty is lifted high above the Heavens!". Then, the same reader who chants this Prokeimenon of the Prophecy chants the Old Testament reading, Isaiah 52:13-54:1. The chanting of the Epistle reading, Hebrews 2:11-18, is usually done by a ***different*** reader. Following the Epistle, the Gospel reading, Luke 23:32-49, is chanted.

Then, a reader chants a prayer that states, "Let Your tender mercies, O Lord, go speedily before us! For, we have become exceedingly poor! Help us, the God of our salvation, for the glory of Your Holy Name! O Lord, deliver us and purge away our sins, for Your Name's sake!". Then, this same reader chants the Trisagion Prayers and the Lord's Prayer. After the exclamation ("For, Yours are the Kingdom, and the power, and the glory,…!"), this ***same*** reader chants "Amen.".

The people then sing, in tone 8, the Kontakion, "Come, let us sing the praises of Him Who was Crucified for us!". A reader then chants "Lord, have mercy." ***forty*** times, followed by the prayer that begins, "You, Who at every season and every hour,…!", followed by a ***triple*** "Lord, have mercy.", a full "Glory,… now and ever…!", "More honorable than the Cherubim,…!", and, "In the Name of the

Lord, Father (or, if it be a bishop, "Master"; or, if it be the Metropolitan, "Most blessed Master"), bless!". The celebrant then intones, "God be bountiful to us, and bless us and show the light of His countenance on us, and be merciful unto us!". The reader then chants "Amen.", followed by, "O God, the Lord of hosts and Author of all creation; Who, in Your ineffable and tender mercy, have sent down Your only-begotten Son, our Lord, Jesus Christ, for the salvation of our kind; and, through His precious Cross, have torn up the handwriting of our sins and, thereby, triumphed over the princes and dominions of darkness: Do You, O Master Who love mankind, accept these prayers of thanksgiving and supplication even from us sinners, and deliver us from every dark and deadly transgression and from all the visible and invisible enemies who seek to do us harm! Nail our flesh with the fear of You, and let not our hearts incline to evil words or thoughts! But, wound our souls with Your love, that, ever gazing upon You, guided by Your light and beholding You, the eternal Light Whom no man can approach, we may offer up unceasing praises and thanksgiving to You: the Father without beginning, together with Your only-begotten Son, and Your most-Holy, good, and life-creating Spirit, now and ever and unto ages of ages! Amen" (in the **Byzantine** tradition, this prayer is chanted by the **priest**).

The 9th Hour

The 9th Hour begins with a reader chanting "Come, let us worship God, our King!". Then, the reader continues with the chanting of Psalm 68 ("Save me, O God! For, the waters have come up to my neck!"), Psalm 69 ("Be pleased, O God, to deliver me! O Lord, make haste to help me!"), and Psalm 85 ("Incline Your ear, O Lord, to answer me, for I am poor and needy!"). Then, the reader chants a full "Glory,... now and ever...!", "Alleluia! Alleluia! Alleluia! Glory to You, O God!" **three** times, a **triple** "Lord, have mercy.", and "Glory...Spirit!".

The people then sing, in tone 8, the Troparion, "When the thief beheld the Author of life hanging upon the Cross,...!". The reader then chants, "Now and ever...Amen.", and the people sing the theotokion, also in tone 8, "O loving Lord, for our sake, You were Born of a Virgin,...!". This is followed by the singing of some stikhera. First, in tone 7, we sing, "A strange wonder it was to behold the

Creator...!". The service books call for this to be sung twice, but, in **most** parishes, it is sung **only once**. A reader then chants, "They parted My garments among them, and, for My raiment, they cast lots!". The people then sing, in tone 2, "When the transgressors nailed You, O Lord of glory, to the Cross,...!". The reader then chants, "They gave Me gall to eat! And, for My thirst, they gave Me vinegar to drink!". The people then **repeat the singing** of "When the transgressors...!". (*Note:* In some parishes, which do **not** repeat the singing of *any* stikhera, when the reader chants, "They parted My garments...!", he or she then **immediately** chants, "They gave Me gall to eat!", and the people sing "When the transgressors...!" **only once!**) The reader chants a full "Glory,... now and ever...!", and the people (in the Greek practice, a lone canonarch) sing, in tone 6, "Today, He Who hung the Earth upon the waters!". Again, in the **Greek** practice, **none** of the stikhera is repeated.

The Prokeimenon of the Prophecy, in the 6th tone, is then celebrated: "The fool says in his heart, 'There is no God!'", with its accompanying verse, "There is no one who does good, no, not one!". Then, the same reader who chants this Prokeimenon of the Prophecy chants the Old Testament reading,

Jeremiah 11:18-23; 12:1-15 (in the **Greek** practice, it is Jeremiah 12:5-8, 12-13). The chanting of the Epistle reading, Hebrews 10:19-31, is usually done by a ***different*** reader. Following the Epistle, the Gospel reading, John 18:28-19:37 (in the **Greek** practice, it is John 19:23-37), is chanted.

Then, a reader chants a prayer that states, "Do not deliver us up to the end, for Your Holy Name's sake, neither annul Your covenant, and do not cause Your steadfast love to depart from us, for the sake of Abraham, Your beloved, and Isaac, Your servant, and Israel, Your holy one!". Then, this same reader chants the Trisagion Prayers and the Lord's Prayer. After the exclamation ("For, Yours are the Kingdom, and the power, and the glory,…!"), this ***same*** reader chants "Amen.".

The people then sing, in tone 8, the Kontakion, "Come, let us sing the praises of Him Who was Crucified for us!". A reader then chants "Lord, have mercy." ***forty*** times, followed by the prayer that begins, "You, Who at every season and every hour,…!", followed by a ***triple*** "Lord, have mercy.", a full "Glory,… now and ever…!", "More honorable than the Cherubim,…!", and, "In the Name of the Lord, Father (or, if it be a bishop, "Master"; or, if it be the Metropolitan, "Most blessed Master"), bless!". The celebrant then intones, "God be bountiful to us, and bless us and show the light of His countenance on us, and be merciful unto us!". The reader then chants "Amen.", followed by, "O Master and Lord, Jesus Christ our God, Who are long-suffering towards our faults and have brought us even to this present hour, in which, hanging upon the life-giving Cross, You have opened to the wise thief the way into Paradise, and destroyed death by death: Be merciful to us, Your sinful and unworthy servants! For, we have sinned and transgressed, and we are not worthy to lift up our eyes and look at the height of Heaven, since we have forsaken the path of Your righteousness and have walked according to the desires of our own hearts! But, we pray to You out of Your boundless goodness: Spare us, O Lord, according to the abundance of Your steadfast love, and save us for Your Holy Name's sake, for our days have been consumed in vanity! Deliver us from the hand of the adversary! Forgive us our sins, and kill our fleshly and carnal desires, that, putting off the old man, we may put on the New Man, and may live for You, our Master and Benefactor; that, following Your ordinances, we may attain to eternal rest, in the place where all the righteous dwell! For, You, O Christ our God, are, indeed, the true Joy and

Gladness of those who love You, and to You we ascribe glory, together with Your Father, Who is from ever-lasting, and Your all-Holy, good, and life-creating Spirit, now and ever and unto ages of ages! Amen." (in the **Byzantine** tradition, this prayer is chanted by the **_priest_**).

The Typika

After the 9th Hour, the Typika are celebrated (*except* in the Greek practice). First, a reader chants the full Beatitudes, beginning with, "In Your Kingdom, remember us, O Lord, when You come in Your Kingdom!". Then, **another** reader chants the series of verses, as follows: "The heavenly choir sings Your praises, saying, 'Holy! Holy! Holy! Lord of Sabaoth! Heaven and Earth are full of Your glory!'". **Another** reader (**or**, perhaps, the **_first reader_**) then chants the verse, "Draw near to Him, and be enlightened, and, so, your faces will never be ashamed!". The previous reader then again chants, "The heavenly choir sings Your praises, saying, 'Holy! Holy! Holy! Lord of Sabaoth! Heaven and Earth are full of Your glory!'". The other reader then chants, "Glory...Spirit!". The previous reader then chants,

Holy Week and Pascha

"The choir of the holy angels and archangels, with all the powers of Heaven, sings Your praises, saying, 'Holy! Holy! Holy! Lord of Sabaoth! Heaven and Earth are full of Your glory!'". The other reader then chants, "Now and ever…Amen."

A third reader then chants the Nicene Creed ("I believe in one God, the Father Almighty, Maker of Heaven and Earth, and of all things, visible and invisible!…!"). A fourth reader then chants, "Forgive, remit, and pardon, God, our sins, both voluntary and involuntary, in word, deed, or thought, committed in knowledge or in ignorance, by night or by day! Forgive us all of them! For, You are good and love mankind!". The first reader then chants the Lord's Prayer. After the exclamation ("For, Yours are the Kingdom, and the power, and the glory,…!"), this same first reader then chants, "Amen.".

The people then sing, in tone 8, the Kontakion of the day, "Come, let us sing the praises of Him Who was Crucified for us!". A reader then chants "Lord, have mercy." **forty** times, followed by the prayer, "Most Holy Trinity, consubstantial Power, undivided Kingship, the Cause of all good: Be gracious to us sinners! Confirm and instruct our hearts, and take away from us every defilement! Enlighten our minds, that we may ever glorify, praise, and worship You, saying: 'One is Holy! One is Lord, Jesus Christ, to the glory of God the Father! Amen!'". The people then sing, "Blessed be the Name of the Lord, henceforth and forevermore!", *three* times.

A reader then chants a full "Glory,... now and ever...!", and then Psalm 33 ("I will bless the Lord at all times! His praise will continually be in my mouth!"). The people then sing the Hymn to the Theotokos, "It is truly meet...!" (in the **Antiochian** tradition, the priest chants, "Wisdom!" and a **reader** chants, "It is truly meet...!". The priest then chants, "Most holy Theotokos, save us!", and the reader chants, "More honorable than the Cherubim...!"). The Dismissal is then celebrated. After the Dismissal Prayer ("May He Who endured spitting and scourging, the Cross and death, for the salvation of the world, Christ our true God,...!") and the exclamation ("for He is good and loves mankind!"), the people **usually** sing a **double** "Amen." ("Amen. Amen."). As everyone comes up to venerate the icons and the Holy Cross, this venerating may be done in silence, or some appropriate hymn from the service (such as the Troparion ["When the glorious disciples...!"] or the Exapostilarion ["The wise thief, You made worthy of Paradise in a single moment, O

Lord,…!"]) may be sung. As always, the local practice should be observed.

G. VESPERS OF HOLY FRIDAY

The Vespers of Holy Friday is celebrated in the late afternoon. The order of the service is as follows.[61]

The Doxology, "O Heavenly King!", the Trisagion Prayers, the Lord's Prayer, "Come, Let Us Worship!", and Psalm 103

The opening doxology is, "Blessed is our God, always now and ever and unto ages of ages!". A **reader** then chants, "Amen.", "Glory to You, our God, glory to You!", "O Heavenly King!" (in the **Antiochian** tradition, all of this is done by the **priest**),

---

[61]*Triodion*, pp. 611-616.

the Trisagion Prayers, and the Lord's Prayer in the **Greek** practice, "O Heavenly King!", the Trisagion Prayers, and the Lord's Prayer are ***all omitted***). After the exclamation ("For, Yours are the Kingdom, and the power, and the glory,…!"), the reader chants, "Amen.", "Come, let us worship…!", and the Vesperal Psalm 103:[62] "Bless the Lord, O my soul! O Lord, my God, You are very great! You are clothed with honor and majesty, Who cover Yourself with light as with a garment,…!". At the conclusion of the Psalm, the reader chants a full "Glory,… now and ever…!", and then, "Alleluia! Alleluia! Alleluia! Glory to You, O God!" *three* times (in the *Antiochian* tradition, this is concluded with, "O our God and our Hope, glory to You!").

The Great Litany

The Great Litany is then sung, with all of its petitions responded to in a ***non***-Lenten melody.

---

[62] Psalms are numbered according to the Septuagint.

"Lord, I Call Upon You!" and Stikhera

Because this is **not** a Vespers on a Saturday evening before a Sunday Liturgy, there is **no** singing of Kathisma 1, "Blessed is the Man!". Instead, we **immediately** go from the Great Litany to the singing of "Lord, I Call Upon You!", sung here in tone 1. After that, a reader chants the full, longer prayer before the verses, beginning with, "Set a guard over my mouth, O Lord! Keep watch over the door of my lips! Incline not my heart to any evil, to busy myself with wicked deeds, in company with men who work iniquity, and let me not join their chosen ones….!"

Though the service books call for 6 stikhera to be sung, the first one, in tone 1, "All creation was changed by fear…!", is called for to be sung twice. In **many** parishes, however, it is **usually** sung **only once**. Therefore, there end up being 5 stikhera. Again, the first one, in tone 1, is, "All creation was changed by fear…!". The next three stikhera are all in tone 2: "An impious and transgressing people!", "Today, the blameless Virgin saw You suspended on the Cross, O Word!", and "When she who Born You without seed saw You suspended upon the Tree,…!". Then, there is a stikheron in tone 6, "Today, the

Master of creation stands before Pilate!". The reader chants, "Glory...Spirit!", and the people sing, still in tone 6, "See how the lawless assembly condemns the King of Creation to death!". The reader chants, "Now and ever...Amen.", and the people sing, again in tone 6, "We see a strange and fearful mystery accomplished today!". As the people sing this final stikheron, the clergy and servers exit the sanctuary for the Vesperal Entrance.

"Gladsome Light"

Once the prayer for the Entrance has been chanted and "Wisdom! Let us be attentive!" has been intoned, the people sing, "Gladsome Light!" as the clergy and servers enter the sanctuary.

1st Prokeimenon and the Reading from Exodus

Following "Gladsome Light", the 1st Prokeimenon, in tone 4, is celebrated: "They divided My garments among them, and, for My raiment, they cast lots!", along with its accompanying verse,

"My God, my God, look upon Me! Why have You forsaken Me?". The same reader who has chanted this Prokeimenon then chants the first Old Testament reading, Exodus 33:11-23.

2nd *Prokeimenon and the Readings from Job and Isaiah*

Following the reading from Exodus, a different reader chants the 2nd Prokeimenon, in tone 4: "Judge, O Lord, those who wrong Me! Fight against those who fight against Me!", along with its accompanying verse, "They rewarded Me evil for good! My soul is forlorn!" (in the **Greek** practice, the accompanying verse is abbreviated to be **only**, "They rewarded me evil for good!"). The same reader who has chanted this Prokeimenon then chants the second Old Testament reading, Job 42:12-17 (in the **Greek** practice, this reading from Job is chanted in tone 4).

Then, a third reader chants the third Old Testament reading, Isaiah 52:13-54:1 (in the **Greek** practice, this reading from Isaiah is chanted in tone 4).

3rd Prokeimenon, the Epistle, and the "Alleluia!" Verses

Then, a different reader chants the 3rd Prokeimenon, in tone 6: "They have laid Me in the depths of the pit, in the regions dark and deep!", with its accompanying verse, "O Lord, God of My salvation, I call for help by day! I cry out in the night before You!". The same reader who has chanted this Prokeimenon then chants the Epistle Reading, which is 1 Corinthians 1:18-2:2. After the Epistle is concluded, the "Alleluia!" verses are in tone 1. Since there are **three** "Alleluia!" verses instead of the customary **two**, the chanting of them is as follows: "And with your spirit! Alleluia! Alleluia! Alleluia! Save me, O God! For, the waters have come up to My neck!". The people then sing a *triple* "Alleluia!". The reader then chants, "They gave Me gall for food! And, for My thirst, they gave Me vinegar to drink!". The people again sing a *triple* "Alleluia!". The reader then chants, "Let their eyes be darkened, so that they cannot see!". The people then sing a *triple* "Alleluia!" for the third and final time. In the **Greek** practice, these "Alleluia!"'s and verses are done slowly and with great solemnity, as was done earlier in the week with the Bridegroom Matins.

The Gospel

The Gospel for the Vespers of Holy Friday is then celebrated. This is a long composite Gospel reading, consisting of the following: Matthew 27:1-38; Luke 23:39-43; Matthew 27:39-54; John 19:31-37; and Matthew 27:55-61. Since the beginning section of the composite Gospel reading is from Matthew, the announcement is, "The Reading is from the Holy Gospel according to Saint Matthew!". Again, just as at the Matins of Holy Friday service the evening before (Thursday evening), at the **_beginning_** of the Gospel reading, the people sing, "Glory to Your Passion, O Lord!", and, at the **_end_** of the Gospel reading, the people sing, "Glory to Your long-suffering, O Lord!" (in the **Antiochian** tradition, "Glory to Your Passion, O Lord!" is again sung after the Gospel reading; in the **Greek** practice, before and after the Gospel reading, the people sing the standard, "Glory to You, O Lord! Glory to You!").

In the **Byzantine** tradition, if there is more than one priest serving at this Vespers, when the final verses of the composite Gospel reading are chanted (Matthew 27:55-61), one of the priests exits the sanctuary and, taking down the figure of Christ from the crucifix in the center of the church, wraps it in a white cloth, carries it into the sanctuary, and places it on the Altar.

The Augmented Litany, "Vouchsafe, O Lord!", and the Litany of Supplication

At this point, the Augmented Litany is celebrated, with the responses sung, as with **all** litanies from this point onward, in a **_non_**-Lenten melody. This Litany begins with **two** petitions ("Let us say, with all our soul and with all our mind, let us say:" and "O Lord Almighty, the God of our fathers, we pray You: Hear us and have mercy.") responded to by the singing of a **single** "Lord, have mercy." Beginning with the **third** petition ("Have mercy on us, O God, according to Your great goodness,....!"), the people respond with a **triple** "Lord, have mercy.".

A reader then chants, "Vouchsafe, O Lord!". After this, the Litany of Supplication is celebrated, again in a **_non_**-Lenten melody.

The Apostikha

The Apostikha is then celebrated. In the **Antiochian** tradition, the Shroud (Epitaphion, Platchenitsa) is processed to the middle of the church and placed on the Tomb during the singing of the tone 5 stikheron after the "Glory,…now and ever…!". In the **Greek** practice, this begins at the start of the Apostikha. In the *Slavic* tradition, this takes place towards the end of the service, with the singing of the Troparion, "The Noble Joseph!".

There are 4 stikhera of the Apostikha that are sung to a special melody in tone 2: The first stikheron begins, "Joseph of Arimathea took You down from the Tree,…!". A reader then chants the verse, "The Lord is King! He is robed in majesty!". The people then sing, "When You, the Redeemer of all, were placed in a tomb,…!". The reader then chants, "For, He has established the world, so that it will never be moved!". The people then sing, "In the flesh, You were willingly enclosed in the tomb,…!". The reader then chants, "Holiness befits Your house, O Lord, forevermore!". The people then sing, "The Powers of Heaven shook with fear,…!". **Note:** The verses chanted here by the reader ("The Lord is

King!", "For, He has established...!", "Holiness befits Your house,....!") are the same verses as chanted for the Apostikha every Saturday evening of the year at **<u>Resurrectional</u>** *Vespers*, manifesting here, liturgically, that, even on Holy Friday, the Cross is **<u>never</u>** contemplated in the Church apart from the Resurrection!

The reader then chants a full "Glory,... now and ever...!", and the people sing, to a special melody in tone 5, "Joseph, together with Nicodemus, took You down from the Tree,...!".

St Symeon's Prayer, the Trisagion Prayers, and the Lord's Prayer

A reader then chants St Symeon's Prayer ("Lord, now let Your servant depart in peace,...!"), the Trisagion Prayers, and the Lord's Prayer. After the exclamation ("For, Yours are the Kingdom, and the power, and the glory,...!"), the reader chants, "Amen.".

"The Noble Joseph!"

The people then sing, to a special melody in tone 2, the Troparion, "The Noble Joseph!". As the people begin to sing the Troparion, the priest takes the Gospel Book, while other members of the clergy or the laity take the Shroud, which they hold above the priest's head. They go around the right and behind the altar and out of the sanctuary via the north deacon's door. The Shroud is preceded with processional candles and incense. The procession goes to the center of the church, where there stands a Tomb decorated with flowers. The Shroud is placed here, and, on top of it, the Gospel Book. The priest censes around it three times.

The text of the longer singing of this Troparion is as follows: "The noble Joseph, when he had taken down Your most pure Body from the Tree, wrapped it in fine linen and anointed it with spices and placed it in a new tomb! Glory to the Father, and to the Son, and to the Holy Spirit! When You descended to death, O Life Immortal, You slew hell with the splendor of Your Godhead! And when, from the depths, You raised the dead, all the powers of Heaven cried out: 'O Giver of Life, Christ our God, glory to You!' Now and ever and unto ages of ages! Amen. The angel came to the myrrh-bearing women at the tomb, and said: 'Myrrh is fitting for the dead! But, Christ has shown Himself a Stranger to corruption!'". This longer version is **not** done in the **Byzantine** tradition.

The Dismissal

The Dismissal is then celebrated. After the Dismissal Prayer ("May He Who endured fearful suffering, the life-creating Cross, and voluntary burial in the flesh for us men and our salvation, Christ our true God,….!" [in the **Greek** practice, this Dismissal Prayer begins, "May He Who endured spittings, scourging, buffetings, the Cross, and death for the salvation of the world, Christ our true God,….!") and the exclamation ("Have mercy on us and save us, for He is good and loves mankind!"), the people **usually** sing a **double** "Amen." ("Amen. Amen.").

Recessional Hymn

In **many** parishes, as everyone comes forward to venerate the icons, the Shroud, the Gospel Book, and the Holy Cross, the people sing a hymn to a special melody in tone 5: "Come, let us bless Joseph of eternal memory, who came by night to Pilate and begged for the Life of all: 'Give me this Stranger, Who has no place to lay His head! Give me this Stranger, Whom an evil disciple betrayed to death! Give me this Stranger, Whom His Mother saw hanging upon the Cross, and with a Mother's sorrow cried, weeping: "Woe to me, O my Child, Light of my eyes and beloved of my bosom! For, what Symeon foretold in the temple now has come to pass: A sword has pierced my heart! But, change my grief to gladness By Your Resurrection!"' We worship Your Passion, O Christ! We worship Your Passion, O Christ! We worship Your Passion, O Christ, and Your Holy Resurrection!". In the **Antiochian** tradition, this hymn is sung after the procession with the shroud at the end of Matins of Holy Saturday. In the Greek practice, instead of singing, "Come, let us bless Joseph of eternal memory,…!", a chanter sings the entire first part of the Apostikha, there is a hymn addressed directly to the Savior as a lengthy lamentation, singing to Him the sorrows of Joseph and Nicodemus.

Since the Little Compline of Holy Friday is **almost _never_** celebrated in parishes, it will **_not_** be covered here.

H. MATINS OF HOLY SATURDAY

Even though the service books call for this service to be celebrated at about 1 o'clock in the morning on Holy Saturday, in **most** parishes, the Matins of Holy Saturday is celebrated Friday evening. The order of the service is as follows.[63]

The First Doxology, "O Heavenly King!", the Trisagion Prayers, the Second Doxology

The service begins with the celebrant intoning the first doxology, "Blessed is our God, always now and ever and unto ages of ages!" A reader then

---

[63] *Triodion*, pp. 622-655.

chants, "Amen.", "Glory to You, our God, glory to You!", "O Heavenly King!" (in the Antiochian tradition, all of this is done by the priest), the Trisagion Prayers, and the Lord's Prayer. After the exclamation ("For, Yours are the Kingdom, and the power, and the glory...!"), the reader chants, "Amen." (In the **Antiochian** tradition, this is followed by "O Lord, save Your people!", "Glory...!", "Do You, of Your own good will...!", "Now and ever...!", "O dread champion...!", and petitions with a **triple** "Lord, have mercy.".) Then, in **all** the traditions, the reader chants, "In the Name of the Lord, Father (or, if it be a bishop, "Master"; or, if it be the Metropolitan, "Most blessed Master"), bless!" The celebrant then intones the second doxology, "Glory to the Holy, consubstantial, life-creating, and undivided Trinity, always now and ever and unto ages of ages!" The reader then chants "Amen.", then "Glory to God in the highest and, on Earth, peace, good will towards men!" **three** times, and "O Lord, open my lips, and my mouth will show forth your praise!" **two** times.

The 6 Psalms

The 6 Psalms of Matins are then chanted: Psalms 3, 37, 62, 87, 102, and 142.[64] It is customary to have two readers chant these Psalms, as follows: the first reader, who has done all the introductory chanting up to now, chants Psalms 3, 37, and 62. He or she then chants a full "Glory,... now and ever...!", "Alleluia! Alleluia! Alleluia! Glory to You, O God!" **three** times, a **triple** "Lord, have mercy.", and, then, the **_first half_** of a "**split** 'Glory!'": "Glory to the Father, and to the Son, and to the Holy Spirit!". The second reader then takes up the chanting at this point with the **_second half_** of the "**split** 'Glory!'": "Now and ever and unto ages of ages! Amen.", and, then, **_immediately_** chants the remaining three Psalms, Psalms 87, 102, and 142. After the conclusion of the final Psalm, this second reader then chants a full "Glory,... now and ever...!", and "Alleluia! Alleluia! Alleluia! Glory to You, O God!" **three** times. (In the **Antiochian** tradition, this section concludes with, "O our God and our Hope, glory to You!".)

In **some** parishes, because of the length of this service, **_only 3_** of the 6 Psalms are celebrated (either the first three or the last three). If this is the case,

---

[64] The Psalms are numbered according to the Septuagint.

then only one reader chants the 3 Psalms, with a full "Glory,… now and ever…!", and "Alleluia! Alleluia! Alleluia! Glory to You, O God!" chanted **three** times at the end. Again, the choir director and singers should follow the guidelines of the main celebrant.

The Great Litany

The Great Litany is then celebrated, with **all** of its responses sung, as with all other litanies here, in a **non**-Lenten melody.

"God is the Lord!" and "The Noble Joseph!"

Following the Great Litany, "God is the Lord!" is intoned to the same special melody in tone 2 as "The Noble Joseph!" is sung to (**except** in the Greek tradition, where, in contrast to the more solemn tone 2 setting sung at the Vespers service earlier, a more joyful setting is used here). After the various verses are chanted by the deacon and "God is the Lord!" has been sung for the final time, the longer version of the Troparion, "The Noble Joseph!", is sung, as follows: "The noble Joseph, when he had taken down Your most pure Body from the Tree, wrapped it in fine linen and anointed it with spices and placed it in a new tomb! Glory to the Father, and to the Son, and to the Holy Spirit! When You descended to death, O Life Immortal, You slew hell with the splendor of Your Godhead! And when, from the depths, You raised the dead, all the powers of Heaven cried out: 'O Giver of Life, Christ our God, glory to You!' Now and ever and unto ages of ages! Amen. The angel came to the myrrh-bearing women at the tomb, and said: 'Myrrh is fitting for the dead! But, Christ has shown Himself a Stranger to corruption!'". During this long singing, a great censing of the entire church is done, concluding in front of the Tomb in the middle of the church.

In the **Byzantine** tradition, before the following section of the Praises, the Kathisma Hymns, Psalm 50, and the Kanon (which **follow** the Praises in the other traditions and are presented as such here) are done at this point, **before** the Praises.

The Praises: The 1ˢᵗ Stasis and the Little Litany

The following troparia, known as "The Praises", are then chanted between the verses of Psalm 118, in three sections, or stases. This is one of the main liturgical elements of this service, which is often referred to as "the Lamentations", named after these states. (In the **Greek** practice, **only** about a third of the actual composed hymns are sung, and none of the Psalm verses are taken.) These are celebrated as follows:

    The main celebrant (priest or bishop) chants a series of troparia (as is done with the Kanon at Matins), and then the verses of Psalm 118 are interspersed with these troparia. The manner of celebrating the Psalm verses varies from parish to parish. In some communities, a reader (or, with the three stases, a set of readers) will chant the Psalm verses. In other parishes, the people sing the Psalm verses, in tone 5. As always, the local custom of the community should be observed. During the celebration of this stasis, a great censing of the entire church is done, beginning with the censing of the Tomb and the Shroud.

    The 1st Stasis intersperses the troparia with verses from Psalm 118 that begin with verse 1 through verse 72. Then, the reader chants or the people sing, "Glory…Spirit!", the celebrant chants a troparion, the reader chants or the people sing, "Now and ever…Amen.", and the celebrant chants a theotokion. In the service books, it is called for the celebrant to chant the first troparion of the 1st Stasis ("In a Tomb, they laid You, O Christ the Life!") immediately after the theotokion. However, in **some** parishes, this repeated chanting of the first troparion is **omitted**.

This is followed by a Little Litany is celebrated, with the responses sung in a **_non_**-Lenten melody.

The Praises: The 2nd Stasis and the Little Litany

At the beginning of the 2nd Stasis, a lesser censing is done: the Tomb and the Shroud, the iconostasis, and the people. If there is more than one clergyman celebrating the service (a priest and a deacon, or two or more priests), it is customary in **many** of these parishes to have the deacon or a second priest chant the troparia of the 2nd stasis. The verses of Psalm 118 are again either chanted by a reader or sung by the people in tone 5. Again, the local parish custom should prevail.

The 2nd stasis intersperses the troparia with verses from Psalm 118 that begin with verse 73 through verse 131. Then, the reader chants or the people sing, "Glory…Spirit!", the celebrant chants a troparion, the reader chants or the people sing, "Now and ever…Amen.", and the celebrant chants a theotokion. In the service books, it is called for the celebrant to chant the first troparion of the 2nd Stasis ("It is right to magnify You, O Life-giving Lord!")

immediately after the theotokion. However, in **some** parishes, this repeated chanting of the first troparion is **omitted**.

This is followed by a Little Litany is celebrated, with the responses sung in a **_non_**-Lenten melody.

The Praises: The 3ʳᵈ Stasis

At the beginning of the 3ʳᵈ Stasis, a lesser censing is done: the Tomb and the Shroud, the iconostasis, and the people. If there is more than one clergyman celebrating the service (a priest and a deacon, or two or more priests), it is customary in **many** of these parishes to have either the first priest or a third priest chant the troparia of the 3ʳᵈ stasis. The verses of Psalm 118 are again either chanted by a reader or sung by the people, but, instead of being sung in tone 5 (as with the celebration of the 1ˢᵗ and 2ⁿᵈ Stases), the singing of the Psalm verses for the 3ʳᵈ Stasis is done in **_tone 3_**. Again, the local parish custom should prevail.

The 3ʳᵈ stasis intersperses the troparia with verses from Psalm 118 that begin with verse 132 through the end of the Psalm, verse 176. Then, the reader chants or the people sing, "Glory...Spirit!", the celebrant chants a troparion, the reader chants or the people sing, "Now and ever...Amen.", and the celebrant chants a theotokion. In the **Greek** practice, after the singing of the stanza, "O Maker of Creation, minds must tremble seeing Your strange and dreadful Burial...!", the singing stops and the priest sprinkles the Epitaphion and the people with rose water. In the service books, unlike the celebration of the 1st and 2nd Stases, it is **_not_** called for the celebrant to chant the first troparion of the 3rd Stasis (**_except_** in the Byzantine tradition), nor is the celebration of a Little Litany called for. Instead, the Troparia of the Resurrection **_immediately_** follows the theotokion.

Troparia of the Resurrection

The Troparia of the Resurrection, sung in tone 5, are now celebrated: "Blessed are You, O Lord! Teach me Your statutes! The assembly of angels was amazed beholding You among the dead! By destroying the power of death, O Savior, You raised Adam with Yourself and freed all men from hell! Blessed are You, O Lord! Teach me Your statutes! In the tomb, the radiant angel cried to the Myrrhbearers: 'Why do you women mingle myrrh with your tears? Look at the tomb and understand! The Savior has risen from the tomb!' Blessed are

You, O Lord! Teach me Your statutes! Very early in the morning, the Myrrhbearers ran with sorrow to Your tomb! But, an angel came and said to them: 'The time for sorrow has come to an end! Do not weep, but announce the Resurrection to the Apostles!' Blessed are You, O Lord! Teach me Your statutes! The Myrrhbearers were sorrowful as they neared Your tomb! But, the angel said to them: 'Why do you number the Living among the dead? As God, He has risen from the tomb!' Glory to the Father, and to the Son, and to the Holy Spirit! We worship the Father, and His Son, and the Holy Spirit! The Holy Trinity, one in essence! We cry with the Seraphim: 'Holy! Holy! Holy! are You, O Lord!' Now and ever and unto ages of ages. Amen! Since you gave birth to the Giver of Life, O Virgin, you delivered Adam from his sin! You gave joy to Eve, instead of sadness! The God–Man Who was born of you has restored to life those who had fallen from it! Alleluia! Alleluia! Alleluia! Glory to You, O God! Alleluia! Alleluia! Alleluia! Glory to You, O God! Alleluia! Alleluia! Alleluia! Glory to You, O God!

(Again, in the ***Antiochian*** tradition, this is concluded with, "O our God and our Hope, glory to You!".)

[The Little Litany]

Although the service books call for a Little Litany to be celebrated at this point, **many** parishes **omit** this. If it **is** to be celebrated, though, the responses are sung in a **_non_**-Lenten melody.

Kathisma Hymns

Then, Kathisma Hymns are sung, in tone 1 (**except** in the Antiochian tradition, where this is done **before** the Praises). The first hymn begins, "Joseph begged Your holy body from Pilate!". The service books then call for a reader to chant "Glory…Spirit!", the people to sing, again in tone 1, the cadence phrase of this first hymn ("As You have foretold us, O Christ, show us the Resurrection!"), then the reader to chant "Now and ever…Amen.", and then the people to sing, still in tone 1, the hymn that begins "The choirs of angels were filled with awe,…!". **However**, in **many** parishes, the people sing the first hymn ("Joseph begged Your holy body from Pilate!"), the reader chants a **_full_** "Glory,… now and ever…!", and the people **then** sing "The choirs of angels were filled with awe,…!". As always, the local practice should be observed. In the **Greek** practice, there are **two** Kathisma Hymns chanted in a special variant of tone 1, with a full "Glory,…now and ever…!" in between them.

Psalm 50

On this day, we do **_not_** sing the Post-Gospel Stikhera ("Having Beheld the Resurrection of Christ!"). Instead, a reader chants Psalm 50: "Have mercy on me, O God, according to Your steadfast love. According to Your abundant mercy, blot out my transgressions!…!" (**except** in the Antiochian tradition, where this is done **before** the Praises).

Also, the prayer of intercession, "O Lord, save Your people", is **_not_** said on this day. **Instead**, the Kanon begins **immediately**!

The Kanon

The Kanon is sung to a special melody sung in tone 6 (**except** in the Antiochian tradition, where this is done **before** the Praises). Even though the service books call for each ode to be sung twice and the troparia to be repeated four times, with the ode repeated at the end as the katavasia, in **_most_** parishes this is **_not_** done (**_except_** in the Greek practice). Instead, each ode (and its accompanying troparia) is sung **_only once_**, and the **_only_** katavasia sung is at the end of Ode 9.

Ode 1 starts, "Of old, You buried the pursuing tyrant beneath the waves of the sea!". Two readers usually share the chanting of the troparia and the refrain ("Glory to You, our God, glory to You!" until the full "Glory,… now and ever…!"). Ode 3 begins, "You suspended the Earth immovably upon the waters!". A Little Litany is called for at this point in the service books, but, again, this is **_omitted_** in **_many_** parishes. A Kathisma Hymn, in tone 1, is then sung: "The soldiers guarding Your tomb, O Savior,…!". The service books then call for a reader to chant a full "Glory,… now and ever…!", followed by the repeat singing of "The soldiers guarding Your tomb, O Savior,…!". In **_most_** parishes, however, this is **_not_** done, and the Kathisma Hymn is sung **_only once_**, with**out** any intervening "Glory,… now and ever…!".

Ode 4 starts, "Foreseeing Your divine humiliation on the Cross, Habak'kuk cried out, trembling,…!". Ode 5 begins, "Isaiah saw the never-setting Light of Your compassionate manifestation to us as God, O Christ!". Ode 6 starts, "Jonah was caught, but not held fast, in the belly of the whale!".

After this ode is concluded, a Little Litany is called for in the service books, but, again, this is **omitted** in **many** parishes. The Kontakion, sung to a special melody in tone 6, is then sung: "He Who shut in the depths is beheld dead, wrapped in fine linen and spices!". A reader then chants the Oikos, which begins, "He Who holds all things together has been lifted up on the Cross,...!". After the reader chants the verse, "but the women cried out,", the people sing, again to the same special melody in tone 6 of the Kontakion, the cadence phrase of the Kontakion: "This is the blessed Sabbath, on which Christ has fallen asleep to arise on the third day!".

Ode 7 begins, "O inexpressible wonder! In the furnace, You saved the holy youths from the flame!". Ode 8 starts, "Be amazed, O Heavens! Be shaken, O foundations of the Earth!". After the final troparion, instead of chanting a full "Glory,... now and ever...!", the reader chanting the refrains chants, "Let us bless the Father, and the Son, and the Holy Spirit, the Lord, now and ever and unto ages of ages. Amen.". The people then sing, in the same special tone 6 melody of the Kanon, "We praise, bless, and worship the Lord, singing and exalting Him throughout all ages!". Ode 9 is then sung: "Do not lament Me, O Mother, seeing Me in the tomb, the Son, Conceived in the womb without seed! For, I will arise and be glorified with eternal glory as God! I will exalt all who magnify you in faith and in love!". After the final troparion and the chanting of a full "Glory,… now and ever…!", the people then *again* sing, "Do not lament Me, O Mother,…!" as the katavasia.

The Little Litany and "Holy is the Lord, our God!"

Following the Kanon, a Little Litany is celebrated in a **non**-Lenten melody. Then, the deacon chants, "Holy is the Lord, our God!". The people then sing, "Holy is the Lord, our God!". The deacon chants, "For, holy is the Lord, our God!". The people then *again* sing, "Holy is the Lord, our God!". The deacon chants, "Over all people is our God!". The people then *again* sing, "Holy is the Lord, our God!" one final time. In the **Byzantine** tradition, the people simply sing this **three** times, with **no** chanting done by a deacon.

The Praises

Even though the celebration of the 3 stases of Psalm 118 from earlier in the service, often called "the Lamentations", is also referred to as "the Praises", what is *usually* called "the Praises" at this point of Matins is celebrated here, as well. The people sing, in tone 2, the beginning of the Praises ("Let every breath praise the Lord!...", and "Praise Him, all you angels of His!..."), and then a reader chants verses from Psalms 148, 149, and 150 in between the stikhera on the Praises. The first stikheron, in tone 2, begins, "Today, a tomb holds Him Who holds creation in the hollow of His hand!". The next stikheron, also in tone 2, starts, "What is this sight we behold? What is this present rest?". The third stikheron, still in tone 2, begins, "Come, let us see our Life lying in the tomb,...!". The next stikheron, in tone 6 (tone 2 in the **Antiochian** tradition), starts, "Joseph asked for the body of Jesus and placed it in his own new tomb!". The reader then chants "Glory...Spirit!", and the people sing, in tone 6, "The great Moses mystically foreshadowed this day, when he said,...!". The reader then chants "Now and ever...Amen.", and the people sing, in tone 2 (tone 6 in the **Antiochian** tradition), "You are most blessed, O Virgin Theotokos!".

The Great Doxology

During the singing of the Great Doxology, the priest and deacon go around the Shroud three times, censing it from the four sides! The priest chants, "Glory to You, Who have shone us the Light!", and the people sing the Great Doxology, beginning, "Glory to God in the highest, and on Earth peace, good will towards men! We praise You! We bless You! We worship You! We glorify You! We give thanks to You for Your great glory!" After singing, "Continue Your steadfast love to those who know You!", the people sing "Holy God! Holy Mighty! Holy Immortal! Have mercy on us!" *three* times, followed by a *full* "Glory,... now and ever...!", and, then, "Holy Immortal! Have mercy on us!".

Then, the people begin singing the Processional Trisagion, which is "Holy God! Holy Mighty! Holy Immortal! Have mercy on us!" in a slowly-sung manner. As the Processional Trisagion is sung, the priest takes the Book of the Gospels, and four laymen take the Shroud and hold it above his head. They go in procession once around the outside of the church, while the people continue to sing the Processional Trisagion. The Cross, with the processional candles, leads the procession, followed by the choir, the deacon with the censer, the servers, then the Shroud, and then all the members of the congregation, holding lighted candles. In the **Antiochian** tradition, when the procession reaches the front doors of the church, the shroud is held very high as the people process under it to go back into the church, and, at this point, sing (in tone 5), "Give me this Stranger...!". When the procession returns to the interior of the church, the Shroud is carried to the Royal Doors, and the priest exclaims, "Wisdom! Let us be attentive!" **Note:** In the **Byzantine** tradition, at the end of the procession, the Shroud is **not** placed again in the center of the church, **but** carried into the **sanctuary**: the clergy proceed once around the Altar with the Shroud, and then place it on the Altar itself. Here it will remain until the eve of the Ascension, when the Leavetaking of Pascha occurs. In the **Slavic** tradition, the Shroud is left in the **center** of the church until the evening of Holy Saturday: it is taken into the sanctuary and placed on the Altar at the end of Nocturns, immediately preceding Paschal Matins, where it will remain until the eve of the Ascension, when the Leavetaking of Pascha occurs.

The Troparion

As the people sing the troparion, the Shroud is returned to its place in the center of the church, the Book of the Gospels is placed on it, and the priest and deacon cense around it once. The people then sing the ***shorter*** version of the Troparion for Holy Saturday, to the special melody in tone 2: "The noble Joseph, when he had taken down Your most-pure Body from the Tree, wrapped it in fine linen, and anointed it with spices, and placed it in a new tomb!"

The Troparion of the Prophecy

After the Troparion, the priest intones, "Wisdom!", and then a reader chants, "The Troparion of the Prophecy is in the 2nd tone!". The people then sing the Troparion of the Prophecy, in tone 2: "O Christ, Who hold fast the ends of the Earth, You have consented to be held fast in the tomb, to deliver man from his fall into hell, and, as Immortal God, You have given us life and immortality!". The service books then call for a reader to chant a full "Glory,… now and ever…!", and then the people to repeat the singing of "O Christ, Who hold fast the ends of the Earth,…!". **However**, in **most** parishes, this Troparion of the Prophecy is sung **only once**, with**out** the intervening chanting of the "Glory,… now and ever…!". In the **Antiochian** tradition, the Troparion of the Prophecy is **omitted entirely**.

Prokeimenon 1 and the Reading from Ezekiel

Then, Prokeimenon 1 is celebrated, in tone 4: "Arise, O Lord, and help us! Deliver us for Your Name's sake!", with its accompanying verse, "We have heard with our ears, O God! Our fathers have told us what deeds You performed in their days, in the days of old!"

Then, this same reader chants the Old Testament reading, Ezekiel 37:1-14. Some parishes chose a reader who is proficient in his or her voice to chant this reading melodically, using a higher range of notes or tones for when God is speaking in the reading as to when Ezekiel is speaking. In any case, the reading, though done melodically, should be done in a way that those listening to the reading are not distracted from the content of the reading itself because of the flamboyant manner in which the reading is being celebrated. As always, a somber respective for the Scriptures should always be shown.

Prokeimenon 2 the Epistle Reading, and the "Alleluia!" Verses

After this, another reader chants, along with the singing of the people, Prokeimenon 2, in tone 7: "Arise, O Lord my God! Lift up Your hand! Forget not Your poor forever!", with its accompanying verse, "I will praise You, O Lord my God, with my whole heart! I will make all Your wonders known!"

Then, this same reader chants a composite Epistle reading, 1 Corinthians 5:6-8 and Galatians 3:13-14. ***Note:*** Being a composite reading, which is read as though it were one continuous text, the reader does **not** make a separate announcement of the reading at the point that the portion from Galatians begins. Rather, he or she **only** announces, at the beginning of the entire composite reading, "The Reading is from the First Epistle of the holy Apostle Paul to the Corinthians!". After the celebrant intones, "Let us be attentive!", the reader then intones, "Brethren!" and chants the entire composite reading.

      The "Alleluia!" verses, in tone 5, are then celebrated. Since there are **three** "Alleluia!" verses instead of the customary **two**, the celebration of these verses is as follows: The celebrant intones, "Peace be with you, Reader!", and then the reader chants, **all together**, "And with your spirit! Alleluia! Alleluia! Alleluia! Let God arise! Let His enemies be scattered! Let those who hate Him flee from before His Face!" The people then sing a *triple* "Alleluia!". The reader then chants, "As smoke vanishes, so let them vanish, as wax melts before the fire!". The people then again sing a *triple* "Alleluia!". The reader then chants, "So, the sinners will perish before the Face of God! But, let the righteous be glad!". The people then again sing a *triple* "Alleluia!" one final time.

The Matins Gospel

The Matins Gospel for Holy Saturday is then celebrated, Matthew 27:62-66, with the usual responses.

The Augmented Litany and the Litany of Supplication

While remaining in their place before the Shroud and the Tomb, the priest and the deacon, along with the people, celebrate the Augmented Litany and the Litany of Supplication, **both** celebrated in a **_non_**-Lenten melody. The Augmented Litany begins with the petition, "Have mercy on us, O God, according to Your great goodness, we pray You: Hear us and have mercy." The people then respond, **_from the first petition_**, with a **triple** "Lord, have mercy.". After the Augmented Litany, the Litany of Supplication is celebrated.

The Dismissal

Following the two litanies, the Dismissal is celebrated. The deacon intones, "Wisdom!" The people sing, "Father (or, if it be a bishop, "Master"; or, if it be the Metropolitan, "Most blessed Master"), bless!". The celebrant intones, "Christ, the One Who Is, is blessed always, now and ever and unto ages of ages!". The people sing, "Amen. Preserve, O God, the holy Orthodox Faith and Orthodox Christians, unto ages of ages!". The celebrant intones, "Most holy Theotokos, save us!". The people sing, "More honorable than the Cherubim,...!". The celebrant intones, "Glory to You, O Christ, our God and our Hope, glory to You!". The people sing a full "Glory,... now and ever...!", a *triple* "Lord, have mercy.", and, then, "Father (or, if it be a bishop, "Master"; or, if it be the Metropolitan, "Most blessed Master"), bless!". The celebrant then chants the Dismissal Prayer, beginning, "May He Who endured fearful suffering, the life-creating Cross, and voluntary burial in the flesh on behalf of us men and for our salvation, Christ our true God,...!". The people then *usually* sing a *double* "Amen." ("Amen. Amen.").

Recessional Hymn

Everyone then comes forward to prostrate before and venerate the Tomb, the Shroud, and the Gospel Book, and then venerate the icons. With everyone prostrating, this usually takes a while. During this time, the people sing a hymn to a special melody in tone 5: "Come, let us bless Joseph of eternal memory, who came by night to Pilate and begged for the Life of all: 'Give me this Stranger, Who has no place to lay His head! Give me this Stranger, Whom an evil disciple betrayed to death! Give me this Stranger, Whom His Mother saw hanging upon the Cross, and with a Mother's sorrow cried, weeping: "Woe to me, O my Child, Light of my eyes and beloved of my bosom! For, what Symeon foretold in the temple now has come to pass: A sword has pierced my heart! But, change my grief to gladness By Your Resurrection!" ' We worship Your Passion, O Christ! We worship Your Passion, O Christ! We worship Your Passion, O Christ, and Your Holy Resurrection!". In the **Antiochian** tradition, a vigil is held in the church throughout the night into the next morning.

I. VESPERAL LITURGY OF HOLY SATURDAY

Although the service books call for the Vesperal Liturgy of Holy Saturday to be celebrated that day at about 4 o'clock in the afternoon, depending on the parish and the availability of parishioners to celebrate the service, it ***may*** begin as early as 10 o'clock in the morning. ***Note:*** Since the canons of the Church forbid the celebration of the Eucharist on Holy Saturday, the feast of Pascha itself, the Feast of feasts, is so full that it functions as ***two days***: Pascha itself, ***and*** Bright Sunday. Therefore, Pascha has ***two Liturgies celebrated*** on it: the Vesperal Liturgy of Holy Saturday (and, Vespers is ***always*** considered the liturgical beginning of the *next* day!) ***and*** the Divine Liturgy that follows Paschal Matins. Therefore, the Vesperal Liturgy of Holy Saturday is really ***the first Paschal service!***   In many parishes, the Liturgy is celebrated in the center of the church, on the Tomb of Christ. The order for the service is as follows.[65]

The Doxology, "O Heavenly King!", the Trisagion Prayers, the Lord's Prayer, "Come, Let Us Worship!", and Psalm 103

The opening doxology is, "Blessed is the Kingdom of the Father, and of the Son, and of the Holy Spirit, always now and ever and unto ages of ages!". A **reader** then chants, "Amen.", "Glory to You, our God, glory to You!", "O Heavenly King!" (in the **Antiochian** tradition, all of this is done by the **priest**; in the **Greek** practice, "O Heavenly King!", the Trisagion Prayers, and the Lord's Prayer are *all omitted*), the Trisagion Prayers, and the Lord's Prayer. After the exclamation ("For, Yours are the Kingdom, and the power, and the glory,…!"), the reader chants, "Amen.", "Come, let us worship…!", and the Vesperal Psalm 103:[66] "Bless the Lord, O my soul! O Lord, my God, You are very great! You are clothed with honor and majesty, Who cover Yourself

---

[65] *Triodion*, pp. 665-670.
[66] Psalms are numbered according to the Septuagint.

with light as with a garment,...!". At the conclusion of the Psalm, the reader chants a full "Glory,... now and ever...!", and then, "Alleluia! Alleluia! Alleluia! Glory to You, O God!" *three* times. (In the **Antiochian** tradition, this is concluded with, "O our God and our Hope, glory to You!".)

The Great Litany

The Great Litany is then sung, with all of its petitions responded to in a **_non_**-Lenten melody.

"Lord, I Call Upon You!" and Stikhera

"Lord, I Call Upon You!" is then sung by the people, in tone 1. There then follow 8 stikhera, the first 4 being the same as those sung for the weeks of tone 1 throughout the year at Resurrectional Vespers: "Accept our evening prayers, O holy Lord!", "Encircle Zion and surround her, O people!", "Come, O people!", and "We have been freed from suffering by Your sufferings, O Christ!". Then, a stikheron in tone 8 is sung **_twice_**: "Today, hell cries out, groaning: 'I should not have accepted the Man Born of Mary!'". After the second singing of this stikheron, two stikhera, also in tone 8, are sung: "Today, hell cries out, groaning: 'My dominion has been shattered!'" "Today, hell cries out, groaning: 'My power has been trampled upon!'". Then, the reader chants "Glory…Spirit!", and the people sing, in tone 6, "The great Moses mystically foreshadowed this day when he said,…!". The reader then chants "Now and ever…Amen.", and the people sing the Dogmatikon in tone 1: "Let us praise the Virgin Mary, the gate of Heaven, the glory of the world,…!".

"Gladsome Light"

During the singing of the Dogmatikon, the clergy and servers exit the sanctuary for the Vesperal Entrance. After the deacon intones, "Wisdom! Let us be attentive!", the people sing the Vesperal Entrance Hymn, "Gladsome Light".

The 15 Old Testament Readings

At this point, unique to this service, there is **_no_** Prokeimenon celebrated. Instead, the 15 Old Testament Readings for this Vesperal Liturgy are chanted. Ideally, whenever possible, it is good to have 15 different readers chanting, one for each reading. The 15 Old Testament Readings are as follows:

1. Genesis 1:1-13 (the first three days of creation).
2. Isaiah 60:1-16 (the glory of God upon His people).
3. Exodus 12:1-11 (the institution of Passover).
4. Jonah 1:1-4:11 (Jonah in the whale and Tarshish).
5. Joshua 5:10-15 (the Passover at Gilgal and God's army).
6. Exodus 13:20-15:19 (crossing the Red Sea).
7. Zephaniah 3:8-15 (the Day of the Lord).

8. 1 Kings 17:8-24 (Elijah and the widow at Zar'ephath).

9. Isaiah 61:10-62:5 (God as the Bridegroom).

10. Genesis 22:1-18 (the sacrificing of Isaac).

11. Isaiah 61:1-9 (the Spirit of God upon the people).

12. 2 Kings 4:8-37 (Elisha and the Shu'nammite woman).

13. Isaiah 63:11-64:5 (the Suffering Servant of the Lord).

14. Jeremiah 31:31-34 (God's Law on the peoples' hearts).

15. Daniel 3:1-91 [or, Daniel 3:1-23 and The Song of the Three Youths 1:1-68] (the three youths in the fiery furnace in Babylon).

In the **Byzantine** tradition, **only** readings 1, 4, and 15 are celebrated.

During the 6th Reading (Exodus 13:20-15:19), when the reader chants, "Then Moses and the people of Israel sang this song to the Lord, saying, 'Let us sing to the Lord!'", the people then sing the refrain, "For, gloriously has He been glorified!". Then, the reader chants the Song of Moses (Exodus 13:2-18), as the people **_repeatedly_** sing this same refrain, "For, gloriously has He been glorified!". This can be done one of two ways: Either the chanter can chant one or two verses of the song, the people then singing the refrain, and then the chanter continuing (whereby the verses of the Song of Moses is **_not_** covered over by the singing of the refrain), or the people can sing the refrain, quietly and continuously, while the reader chants the verses of the Song of Moses. In any case, the local custom should be observed. Following the conclusion of the Song of Moses and the singing of the refrain, the reader chants the closing verse of this reading (Exodus 15:19).

During the 15th Reading (Daniel 3:1-91 [or, Daniel 3:1-23 and The Song of the Three Youths 1:1-68]), when the reader chants, "Blessed are You in the firmament of Heaven, and to be praised and glorified forever!", the people then sing the refrain, "Praise the Lord! Sing and exalt Him throughout all the ages!". Then, the reader chants the Song of the Three Youths (The Song of the Three Youths 1:1-68), as the people **_repeatedly sing_** this same refrain, "Praise the Lord! Sing and exalt Him throughout all the ages!". This can be done one of two ways: Either the chanter can chant one or two verses of the song, the people then singing the refrain, and then the chanter continuing (whereby the verses of the Song of the Three Youths is **_not_** covered over by the singing of the refrain), or the people can sing the refrain, quietly and continuously, while the reader chants the verses of the Song of the Three Youths. In any case, the local custom should be observed.

The Little Litany and "As Many As Have Been Baptized"

Following the last of the 15 Old Testament Readings, a Little Litany is celebrated. Then, instead of the usual Trisagion ("Holy God!"), the people sing, "As Many As Have Been Baptized", as follows: "As many as have been Baptized into Christ have put on Christ! Alleluia!" is sung by the people *three* times. Then, the people sing a full "Glory,… now and ever…!", followed by "Have put on Christ! Alleluia!", and then, the full "As Many As Have Been Baptized", as follows: "As many as have been Baptized into Christ have put on Christ! Alleluia!" is sung by the people one final time (in the **Greek** practice, before the final singing of "As Many As Have Been Baptized", the deacon (or, if there is no deacon, the main celebrant) comes out of the sanctuary, stands on the ambo, and intones, "*Dynamis*!" ("*δυναμις*", which means, "With strength!"). During the singing of the full "Glory,… now and ever…!", the reader goes to the celebrant for a blessing to read the Epistle.

The Prokeimenon, the Epistle, and "Arise, O God!" and Verses

The Prokeimenon is then celebrated in tone 5: "Let all the Earth worship You and praise You! Let it praise Your Name, O Most High!", with its accompanying verse, "Sing praises to the Lord, all the Earth! Sing praises to His Holy Name!".

The reader then chants the Epistle reading, Romans 6:3-11.

_No_ "Alleluia!" is sung here at this service. **_Instead_**, what is sung is "Arise, O God!". At the conclusion of the Epistle reading, the celebrant intones, "Peace be with you, Reader!". The reader (in the **Greek** practice, the **priest**) then chants, "And with your spirit! Arise, O God! Judge the Earth! For, You, belong all the nations!". The people then sing, to a special melody in tone 7, "Arise, O God! Judge the Earth! For, to You, belong all the nations!" Then, a set of verses is chanted by the reader, while the people **_repeatedly_** sing, "Arise, O God! Judge the Earth! For, to You, belong all the nations!" This can be done one of two ways: Either the chanter can chant one or two verses of the song, the people then singing the "Arise, O God!", and then the chanter continuing (whereby the verses of "Arise, O God!" chanted by the reader are **_not_** covered over by the singing by the people), or the people can sing "Arise, O God!", quietly and continuously, while the reader chants the verses of "Arise O God!". The verses for "Arise, O God!" that the reader chants are as follows:

- God has taken His place in the divine counsel! In the midst of the gods, He holds judgment!

- How long will You judge unjustly and accept the faces of sinners?

- Give justice to the weak and the fatherless! Maintain the right of the afflicted and the destitute!

- Rescue the weak and the needy! Deliver them from the hand of the sinner!

- They have neither knowledge nor understanding! They walk about in darkness!

- Let all the foundations of the Earth be shaken! I say: "You are gods, sons of the Most High, all of you! Nevertheless, you will die like men, and fall like any prince!"

- Arise, O God! Judge the Earth!

Note: It is at **_this_** time, during the singing of "Arise, O God!" and the chanting of its verses, that the clergy and servers switch from their dark vestments to the white vestments for Pascha. In any case, the local custom should be observed. **_Also_**, during this time, lay people go around the church, changing the coverings on the icon stands from dark to white, and changing the votive glass candles before the icons from dark to white. **_Therefore_**, the choir director and singers **_must_** take this into account, and give plenty of time for **_all_** of these changes to take place! This **_may_** involve having the reader **_repeat_** the verses to "Arise, O God!" until everything is completed.

The Gospel

The Gospel Reading for the Vesperal Liturgy of Holy Saturday is then celebrated, Matthew 28:1-20, with the usual responses.

[The Sermon]

Usually, in **_most_** parishes, there is **_no_** sermon at this point in the service.

The Augmented Litany and the Litanies for the Faithful

At this point, the Augmented Litany is celebrated. This Litany begins with *two* petitions ("Let us say, with all our soul and with all our mind, let us say:" and "O Lord Almighty, the God of our fathers, we pray You: Hear us and have mercy.") responded to by the singing of a *single* "Lord, have mercy." Beginning with the *third* petition ("Have mercy on us, O God, according to Your great goodness,…!"), the people respond with a *triple* "Lord, have mercy.".

Then, *two* Litanies for the Faithful are celebrated. At the exclamation of the second of these litanies ("that, guarded always by Your might, we may ascribe glory unto You,…!"), *many* parishes have the people sing a *double* "Amen." ("Amen. Amen.") to show that this entire liturgical section of litanies has concluded. Again, as always, the local practice should be observed.

In the *Byzantine* tradition, these litanies are *not* celebrated in this manner. Rather, the petition beginning, "Help us! Save us!" is chanted, followed by the exclamation, "that, guarded always by Your might, we may ascribe glory unto You,...!", followed by "Let All Mortal Flesh Keep Silent!" is sung.

"Let All Mortal Flesh Keep Silent!"

After the two Litanies for the Faithful, the people sing the Entrance Hymn, "Let All Mortal Flesh Keep Silent!". This is usually sung in a special melody. This Entrance Hymn is in two sections: **Before** the actual Entrance itself, the people sing, "Let all mortal flesh keep silent, and, in fear and trembling, stand, pondering nothing earthly minded! For, the King of kings, and Lord of lords, comes to be slain, to give Himself as Food to the faithful!". **After** the Entrance, the people sing, "Before Him go the ranks of angels: all the Principalities and Powers; the many-eyed Cherubim and the six-winged Seraphim, covering their faces, singing their hymn: 'Alleluia! Alleluia! Alleluia!'". (In the **Greek** practice, the phrase, "Before Him go the ranks of angels" is done in the first half [**before** the Entrance], and the section sung **after** the Entrance begins with, "All the Principalities and Powers...!".) As with the Entrance at the Liturgy of the Presanctified Gifts during Great Lent, **this** Entrance, on Holy Saturday, is done **in** ___complete___ silence, with **_no_** commemorations made! **_Therefore_**, as the title of the Entrance Hymn suggests, "Let All Mortal Flesh Keep **_Silent!_**"), the first portion of the Hymn (**_before_** the Entrance) should be sung through **_only once_**, and then **_the singing stops!_** The second portion of the Hymn (**_after_** the Entrance) does **_not_** begin with an "Amen.", since **_no_** commemorations have been made! **_Instead_**, the people **_immediately_** take up the singing with, "Before Him go the ranks of angels,...!".

The Litany of Supplication, "Father, Son, and Holy Spirit!", and the Creed

Following the Entrance, the Litany of Supplication is celebrated. Then, after the celebrant intones, "Let us love one another, that, with one mind and one heart, we may confess:", the people sing, "Father, Son, and Holy Spirit! The Trinity, one in essence, and undivided!". Then, the Creed is sung.

The Anaphora

The Anaphora is then celebrated, with the usual responses. **<u>Note:</u>** Even though it does not change or affect what is sung by the singers, this *<u>is</u>* a Vesperal Liturgy of St Basil the Great. Therefore, the Prayers of the Eucharistic Kanon will be those of that Liturgy, beginning with, "O Existing One, Master, Lord God, Father Almighty and adorable!". Again, *<u>all</u>* of the responses are done as with any regular Divine Liturgy.

The Hymn to the Theotokos

Instead of singing "All of Creation!", as would be done at a regular Divine Liturgy of St Basil the Great (and which the **Byzantine** tradition *still* follows at this point), the Hymn to the Theotokos at this particular service is Ode 9 of the Matins Kanon celebrated the previous evening, sung in the special tone 6 melody and that begins: "Do not lament Me, O Mother, seeing Me in the tomb, the Son, Conceived in the womb without seed! For, I will arise and be glorified with eternal glory as God! I will exalt all who magnify you in faith and in love!".

"And All Mankind!", the Litany Before the Lord's Prayer, and the Lord's Prayer

The Liturgy then proceeds as usual. When the celebrant intones, "Among the first, remember, O Lord,…!", ending with, "rightly to divide the Word of Your truth!", the people sing, "And all mankind!". Then, the Litany Before the Lord's Prayer is celebrated, followed by the singing of the Lord's Prayer itself.

"One is Holy!" and the Communion Hymn

When the celebrant lifts the Holy Gifts, and intones, "The Holy Things are for the holy!", the people sing, "One is holy! One is the Lord, Jesus Christ, to the glory of God the Father! Amen.", and then, ***immediately***, sing the Communion Hymn, "The Lord awoke as One asleep, and arose from the dead, saving me ("us" in the **Greek** practice)! Alleluia! Alleluia! Alleluia!".

The Communion of the Clergy

As the clergy receive Holy Communion, the people sing hymns appropriate for the day. **Many** parishes, at this point, for instance, sing the odes from the Matins Kanon of the previous evening.

"Blessed is He!" and the Communion of the Faithful

When the clergy exit the sanctuary and intone, "In the fear of God, and with faith and love, draw near!", the people sing, as usual, "Blessed is He Who comes in the Name of the Lord! God is the Lord and has revealed Himself to us!" (*except* in the Greek practice).

As the faithful come up to receive Holy Communion, the people sing, as usual, "Receive the Body of Christ! Taste the Fountain of Immortality!" After the last of the faithful have received the

Eucharist and the celebrant chants the prayer, "Lo! This has touched your lips,…!" (if that is the local parish practice), the people then sing a **triple** "Alleluia!".

["Having Beheld the Resurrection of Christ"]

At this point, the service books call for the deacon in the sanctuary, during the time that the clergy are getting the Holy Gifts ready to be transferred back to the Table of Oblation, to chant a prayer. This "prayer," however, is actually a **hymn** that is sung as the Post-Gospel Stikhera at Resurrectional Matins. Therefore, in **some** parishes, the practice is for the people to sing these stikhera in the prescribed tone 6. The stikhera are as follows:

> Having beheld the Resurrection of Christ,
> let us worship the holy Lord, Jesus,
> the only sinless One!
> We venerate Your Cross, O Christ,
> and Your holy Resurrection we praise
> > and glorify!
> For, You are our God,
> and we know no other but You.

We call on Your Name.
Come, all you faithful!
Let us venerate Christ's holy Resurrection!
For, behold, through the Cross joy has come
    into all the world!
Let us ever bless the Lord,
praising His Resurrection!
For, by enduring the Cross for us,
He has destroyed death by death!

Shine! Shine, O new Jerusalem!
The glory of the Lord has shone on you!
Exult now and be glad, O Zion!
Be radiant, O pure Theotokos, in the
    Resurrection of your Son!

O Christ, great and most-holy Pascha!
O Wisdom, Word, and Power of God!
Grant that we may more perfectly
    partake of You
in the never-ending Day of Your Kingdom!

    Again, in some parishes, it is the practice for the people to sing this hymn. This gives the clergy time to prepare the Holy Gifts to be transferred to the Table of Oblation. As with other liturgical elements, the choir director should check with the bishop, the parish priest, or the main celebrant to follow the local practice in that particular parish.

Liturgy Ending

At this point, the main celebrant comes out onto the ambo, blesses the people, and says, "O God, save Your people and bless Your inheritance!" The people then sing, "We have seen the true Light!" (**except** in the **Byzantine** tradition, where the people sing, "Remember us, merciful One, as You remembered the thief in the Kingdom of Heaven!").

The celebrant returns to the sanctuary. When the Holy Gifts are ready to be transferred to the Table of Oblation, the deacon takes the paten over there. The celebrant, holding the chalice, stands in the royal doorway and chants, "Blessed is our God, always now and ever and unto ages of ages!" The people respond with, "Amen." and "Let our mouths be filled…!". The celebrant (or, some junior priest) comes out into the middle of the church, and, on his way out there, intones, "Let us depart in peace!" The people respond, "In the Name of the Lord!" The deacon, still on the solea, intones, "Let us pray to the Lord." The people sing, "Lord, have mercy." The celebrant in the center of the church then chants the Prayer Before the Ambo When he chants the exclamation, the people respond with, "Amen."

The Blessing of Loaves and Wine

After this, the celebrant blesses loaves of bread and wine for the people to partake of after the Liturgy, with the usual responses ("Lord, have mercy." and "Amen.") sung at their proper places. This practice is *not* done in the **Byzantine** tradition.

"Blessed Be the Name of the Lord"

The people then sing, "Blessed be the Name of the Lord, henceforth and forevermore!" *three* times.

The Dismissal

The Dismissal is celebrated as usual, with the Dismissal Prayer beginning as it does on Pascha and every Sunday Divine Liturgy, "May He Who arose from the dead, Christ our true God,...!". The people then *usually* sing a *double* "Amen." ("Amen. Amen.").

Recessional Hymns

Everyone then comes forward to prostrate before and venerate the Tomb, the Shroud, and the Gospel Book, and then venerate the icons. With everyone prostrating, this usually takes a while. During this time, the people *may* sing the odes from the Matins Kanon of the previous evening.

[Vigil Reading from the Acts of the Apostles]

In many parishes, between the conclusion of the Vesperal Liturgy and the celebration of Nocturns that night, some people of the parish remain in the church, keeping a kind of "vigil" before the Tomb of Christ, and quietly chanting from the Acts of the Apostles in the New Testament. (This is *not* done in the *Greek* practice.)

J. NOCTURNS OF HOLY SATURDAY

The Nocturns of Holy Saturday are celebrated late at night, usually beginning at 11:30 pm. The order of the service is as follows.[67]

Doxology, "O Heavenly King!", the Trisagion Prayers, the Lord's Prayer, "Come, Let Us Worship!", and Psalm 50

The service begins with the doxology, "Blessed is our God, always now and ever and unto ages of ages!". A reader chants, "Amen.", then, "Glory to

---

[67] *Triodion*, pp. 660-661.

You, our God, glory to You!", then "O Heavenly King!" (in the *Antiochian* tradition, all of this is done by the **priest**), the Trisagion Prayers, and the Lord's Prayer. After the exclamation ("For, Yours are the Kingdom, and the power, and the glory,…!"), the reader chants, "Amen.", then "Lord, have mercy." *twelve* times, a full "Glory,… now and ever,…!", and then, "Come, let us worship God, our King!". The reader then chants Psalm 50: "Have mercy on me, O God, according to Your steadfast love. According to Your abundant mercy, blot out my transgressions!…!".[68]

In **some** parishes, this section ("O Heavenly King!", the Trisagion Prayers, the Lord's Prayer, "Come, Let Us Worship!", and Psalm 50) is **omitted**. Again, the local parish custom should be observed.

["The Noble Joseph"]

In those parishes that **may** omit the previous section, after the celebrant intones, "Blessed is our God,…!", the people sing "Amen." and then the

---

[68] The Psalm numbering is according to the Septuagint.

Troparion for Holy Saturday, "The Noble Joseph", to the special melody in tone 2. Again, this is *not* called for in the service books. As always, the local parish practice should be observed.

The Kanon

Ode 1 starts, "Of old, You buried the pursuing tyrant beneath the waves of the sea!". Two readers usually share the chanting of the troparia and the refrain ("Glory to You, our God, glory to You!" until the full "Glory,... now and ever...!"). Ode 3 begins, "You suspended the Earth immovably upon the waters!". A Little Litany is called for at this point in the service books, but, again, this is *omitted* in *many* parishes (the *Greek* practice includes the Little Litany *only* after the 3rd and 6th odes of the Kanon). A Kathisma Hymn, in tone 1, is then sung: "The soldiers guarding Your tomb, O Savior,...!". The service books then call for a reader to chant a full "Glory,... now and ever...!", followed by the repeat singing of "The soldiers guarding Your tomb, O Savior,...!". In *most* parishes, however, this is *not* done (*except* in the Greek practice), and the Kathisma Hymn is sung *only once*, with*out* any intervening "Glory,... now and ever...!" (in the

Antiochian tradition, the Kathisma Hymn is also **omitted**).

Ode 4 starts, "Foreseeing Your divine humiliation on the Cross, Habak'kuk cried out, trembling,…!". Ode 5 begins, "Isaiah saw the never-setting Light of Your compassionate manifestation to us as God, O Christ!". Ode 6 starts, "Jonah was caught, but not held fast, in the belly of the whale!". After this ode is concluded, a Little Litany is called for in the service books, but, again, this is **omitted** in **many** parishes. The Kontakion, sung to a special melody in tone 6, is then sung: "He Who shut in the depths is beheld dead, wrapped in fine linen and spices!". A reader then chants the Oikos, which begins, "He Who holds all things together has been lifted up on the Cross,…!" (in the *Antiochian* tradition, the Kontakion and Oikos are **omitted**). After the reader chants the verse, "but the women cried out,", the people sing, again to the same special melody in tone 6 of the Kontakion, the cadence phrase of the Kontakion: "This is the blessed Sabbath, on which Christ has fallen asleep to arise on the third day!".

Ode 7 begins, "O inexpressible wonder! In the furnace, You saved the holy youths from the flame!". Ode 8 starts, "Be amazed, O Heavens! Be shaken, O foundations of the Earth!". After the final troparion, instead of chanting a full "Glory,... now and ever...!", the reader chanting the refrains chants, "Let us bless the Father, and the Son, and the Holy Spirit, the Lord, now and ever and unto ages of ages. Amen.". The people then sing, in the same special tone 6 melody of the Kanon, "We praise, bless, and worship the Lord, singing and exalting Him throughout all ages!". Ode 9 is then sung: "Do not lament Me, O Mother, seeing Me in the tomb, the Son, Conceived in the womb without seed! For, I will arise and be glorified with eternal glory as God! I will exalt all who magnify you in faith and in love!". After the final troparion and the chanting of a full "Glory,... now and ever...!", the people then *again* sing, "Do not lament Me, O Mother,...!" as the katavasia.

In the *Slavic* tradition, during the singing of Ode 9 of the Kanon, the priest and deacon exit the sanctuary and come to the Shroud on the Tomb in the center of the church. The priest censes around all four sides of the Shroud three times and, with either other priests or deacons (if they are available) or servers holding the Shroud by its four corners over the head of the main celebrate, proceed into the sanctuary, where the Shroud is laid upon the Altar. Again, the priest censes around all four sides of the Shroud three times.

The Trisagion Prayers and the Lord's Prayer

A reader (the ***priest*** in the ***Greek*** practice) then chants the Trisagion Prayers and the Lord's Prayer. After the exclamation ("For, Yours are the Kingdom, and the power, and the glory,…!"), the reader chants, "Amen.".

The Troparion

Then, the people (the ***priest*** in the ***Greek*** practice) sing the Troparion to the special melody in tone 2 that was used at Matins of Holy Saturday for singing "The Noble Joseph": "When You descended to death, O Life Immortal, You slew hell with the splendor of Your Godhead! And when, from the depths, You raised the dead, all the powers of Heaven cried out: 'O Giver of Life, Christ our God, glory to You!'".

[The Augmented Litany]

The Augmented Litany is then celebrated. It begins with the petition, "Have mercy on us, O God, according to Your great goodness, we pray You: Hear us and have mercy." The people then respond, *from the first petition*, with a **triple** "Lord, have mercy." Even though the service books call for this Augmented Litany to be celebrated, in *some* parishes, it is *omitted* altogether. Again, the local parish practice should be observed.

The Dismissal

The Dismissal is celebrated as usual, with the Dismissal Prayer beginning as it does on Pascha and every Sunday Divine Liturgy, "May He Who arose from the dead, Christ our true God,...!". The people then **usually** sing a **double** "Amen." ("Amen. Amen."). In the **Greek** practice, this is followed by the priest chanting, "Behold! The darkness and the morning! Why are you at the tomb, O Mary, with great darkness filling your mind?...!".

Then, **_all_** lights and candles are extinguished in the church before the celebration of Paschal Matins.

K. PASCHAL MATINS

The order for Paschal Matins is as follows.[69]

"Come, and Receive the Light!"

Following the Dismissal of Nocturns and the extinguishing of the lights and candles, there are a few moments of silence. Then, the main celebrant lights one candle and, coming out of the sanctuary and standing on the ambo of the solea, he chants, sometimes in a special melody, "Come, and receive the Light that is never overtaken by the night! Come, and glorify the Christ, Who is Arisen from the dead!" (in the **Greek** practice, this is sung in tone 5).

---

[69] Nassar, pp. 920-930.

A person from the parish comes forward with a candle and lights his or her candle from the priest's candle, then lights another person's candle, and so forth and so on throughout the parish.

"Your Resurrection!"

Then, the singing of "Your Resurrection!" commences, in tone 6. This is done in different ways in various parishes. It *may* start out as a quartet of men in the sanctuary, singing it *three* times (softly, medium volume, and then, the third time, loudly), before the rest of the congregation sings it. It *may* start out with just a choir singing it, and then the rest of the people in the parish joining in. As always, the local liturgical practice should be observed.

The people then gather at the back of the church for the *triple* procession around the outside of the church, going out the front doors and then **_counter-clockwise_** around the church (around the south side of the church, to the back of the church on the east side, around the north side of the church, and to the front of the church on the west side). The order for the procession is: a man carrying the Holy Cross, men carrying the banners, people carrying the holy icons, the Gospel Book (usually carried by a deacon, a priest, or altar servers), the choir director and the choir, and then all of the people of the congregation, carrying candles. This same Resurrectional Stikheron, in tone 6, is sung repeatedly throughout the **triple** procession around the church: "Your Resurrection, O Christ our Savior, the angels in Heaven sing! Enable us on Earth to glorify You in purity of heart!".

The Doxology and "Christ is Risen!" with the Paschal Verses

After the third time around the church, everyone gathers at the front doors of the church. The priest censes the Gospel Book, the icons and banners, the choir, and all the people. Then, standing before and facing the doors of the church, he lifts the censer in front of the doors and makes the sign of the cross with it, three times. He holds the precious Cross and the three-branched candlestick in his left hand. The altar servers stand on both sides. The priest then intones, in a loud voice, "Glory to the Holy, consubstantial, life-creating and undivided Trinity, always now and ever and unto ages of ages!". The people sing, "Amen."

The priest then chants the Troparion of Pascha: "Christ is Risen from the dead, trampling down death by death, and, upon those in the tombs, bestowing life!" ***three*** times. The people then sing this same Troparion, "Christ is Risen!", ***three*** times. The priest then chants the verses from Psalm 67:1-3 and Psalm 117:24 as he censes the Holy Table and the sanctuary in the usual manner.[70] The people then respond each time by singing, "Christ is Risen" *once*. The Paschal Verses are: "Let God Arise! Let His enemies be scattered! Let those who hate Him flee from before His Face!", "As smoke vanishes, so, let them vanish, as wax melts before the fire!", "So, the sinners will perish before the Face of God! But, let the righteous be glad!", "This is the Day that the Lord has made! Let us rejoice and be glad in it!", "Glory to the Father, and to the Son, and to the Holy Spirit!", and, finally, "Now and ever and unto ages of ages! Amen.". Then, the priest chants the ***<u>first half</u>*** of the Troparion, "Christ is Risen from the dead, trampling down death by death!". The people then sing the ***<u>second half</u>*** of the Troparion, "And, upon those in the tombs, bestowing life!".

---

[70] The Psalms are numbered according to the Septuagint.

Holy Week and Pascha

The Matins Gospel

Even though the service books call for it to be celebrated **before** the Doxology, the Paschal Troparion, and the Paschal Verses, **many** parishes will celebrated the chanting of the Matins Gospel at this point, *after* those initial liturgical elements (which, actually, makes more sense liturgically). Furthermore, the chanting of this Matins Gospel is part of the **Byzantine** tradition and **not** often a part of the **Slavic** tradition. **However**, more and more parishes of the **Slavic** tradition are embracing the chanting of this Gospel, which is a good thing, since, by omitting it, it seems to be the **only** Matins service *of the entire liturgical year* that is celebrated with**out** a Matins Gospel!

The Matins Gospel called for here is the 2nd of the 11 Resurrectional Matins Gospels, Mark 16:1-8 (in the Greek practice, the Gospel reading is Matthew 28:1-20). It is celebrated in the usual manner: The deacon intones, "And, that we may be accounted worthy of listening to the Holy Gospel, let us pray to the Lord our God!". The people then sing a **triple** "Lord, have mercy.". The deacon then chants, "Wisdom! Let us be attentive! Let us listen to the Holy Gospel!". The priest then blesses the people, and intones, "Peace be with you all!". The people sing, "And with your spirit!". The priest then chants, "The Reading is from the Holy Gospel according to Saint Mark!". The people sing, "Glory to You, O Lord, glory to You!". The deacon intones, "Let us be attentive!". The priest chants the Gospel reading. After he finishes, the people again sing, "Glory to You, O Lord, glory to You!". **Note:** In the **Byzantine** tradition, this Gospel reading is done **before** the "Christ is Risen!" with the accompanying verses.

The Entrance into the Church

The priest turns and knocks on the front doors of the church three times, each time intoning, "Christ is Risen!", and the people responding each time, "Truly, He is Risen!". The doors of the church are opened. The priest enters with the precious Cross, with two servers, holding lit candles, preceding him. Then, those carrying the Holy Cross, the banners, and the icons, enter the church, followed by the choir director, the choir, and the rest of the faithful. As then enter the church, all the people repeatedly sing the Troparion, "Christ is Risen...!". Then, all the bells are rung. The priest and the concelebrants enter the sanctuary. The choir and the people take their places within the church. In the **Antiochian** tradition, the priest does not knock on the door, but exchanges verses from Psalm 24 with someone inside the church ("Lift up your gates, princes, and be lifted up, everlasting doors,...!", etc.). In the **Greek** practice, the entrance into the church occurs only with the beginning of the singing of the Paschal Kanon.

The Great Litany

The Great Litany is then celebrated, with the usual responses.

The Kanon: Odes 1 and 3

During the celebration of the Kanon, the priest censes the church many times, preceded by the deacon carrying a lit candle. As he does the censing, the priest greets the people many times with, "Christ is Risen!", and the people respond with, "Truly, He is Risen!".

Being Pascha, the Feast of feasts, **_every_** part of the Kanon is sung! Therefore, there is **_no_** chanting of troparia by a reader. Rather, the troparia are sung in the same melody as the odes of the Kanon. The Kanon is sung in tone 1. In the **Greek** practice, **only** the odes (heirmoi) of the Kanon are sung, **not** the troparia.

Ode 1 chants, "This is the Day of Resurrection! Let us be illumined, O people! Pascha, the Pascha of the Lord! For, from death to life, and from Earth to Heaven, has Christ our God led us, as we sing the song of victory!". The refrain, sung throughout the **_entire_** Kanon, is then sung, "Christ is Risen from the dead!". Then, the troparia are sung: "Let us purify our senses,…!", "Let the Heavens be glad,…!". After the first troparion, the refrain is sung **once**, and, after the final troparion ("Let us purify our senses,…!"), "Christ is Risen!" is sung **three** times. In the **Antiochian** tradition, after the triple "Christ is Risen!" at the end of **each** ode, the people sing, "Truly, Jesus is Risen from the tomb, as He foretold, granting us eternal life and great mercy!".

Ode 3 chants, "Come, let us drink, not miraculous water drawn forth from a barren stone, but a new vintage from the fount of incorruption, springing from the tomb of Christ! In Him, we are established!". Then, the refrain, "Christ is Risen from the dead!". The troparia for this ode are: "Now, all is filled with light,…!", and "Yesterday, I was buried with You, O Christ!…!". After this last troparion, "Christ is Risen…!" is sung **three** times.

The Hypakoe

The Hypakoe, in tone 8, is then sung: "Before the dawn, Mary and the women came and found the stone rolled away from the tomb! They heard the angelic voice: 'Why do you seek among the dead, as a man, the One Who is ever-lasting Light? Behold! The clothes in the grave! Go! And proclaim to the world: "The Lord is Risen! He has slain death, as He is the Son of God, saving the race of man!"'". Even though the service books call for the Hypakoe to be sung in tone 4, it is **almost always** sung in tone 8 (**except** in the **Antiochian** tradition, where it is sung in tone 4). In the **Greek** practice, the Hypakoe is sung **after** ode 6.

The Kanon: Odes 4, 5, and 6

Ode 4 chants, "The inspired prophet, Habbak'kuk, now stands with us in holy vigil! He is like a shining angel, who cries with a piercing voice: 'Today, salvation has come to the world! For, Christ Risen as all-powerful!'". The refrain is then sung. The troparia for this ode are: "Christ, our Pascha, has appeared as a male Child,…!", "Christ, the Crown with Whom we are blest,…!", and "David, the ancestor of God,…!". After this last troparion, "Christ is Risen…!" is sung **three** times.

Ode 5 chants, "Let us arise at the arising of the sun, and bring to the Master a hymn, instead of myrrh! And, we will see Christ, the Sun of righteousness, Who causes life to dawn for all!". The refrain is then sung. The troparia for this ode are: "We celebrate the death of death…!", and, "This is the bright and saving night,…!". After this last troparion, "Christ is Risen…!" is sung **three** times.

Ode 6 chants, "You descended, O Christ, into the depths of the Earth! You broke the everlasting bars, which held death's captives! And, like Jonah, from the whale on the third day, You arose from the grave!". The refrain is then sung. The troparia for this ode are: "You arose, O Christ, and, yet, the tomb remained sealed,…!", and, "O my Savior! As God, You brought Yourself freely to the Father,…!". After this last troparion, "Christ is Risen…!" is sung **three** times.

The Kontakion and the Oikos

The Kontakion is then sung, in tone 8: "You descended into the tomb, O Immortal! You destroyed the power of death! In victory, You arose, O Christ God, proclaiming, 'Rejoice!' to the myrrh-bearing women, granting peace to Your Apostles, and bestowing resurrection on the fallen!". (Again, in the **Greek** practice, the Hypakoe is sung between ode 6 and the Kontakion.)

The Oikos is then sung, in tone 8: "Before the dawn, the myrrh-bearing women sought, as those who seek the day, their Sun, Who was before the sun, yet had descended to the grave! And they cried to each other, 'O friends, come, let us anoint with spices His life-bearing yet buried Body, the flesh that raised the fallen Adam and now lies in the tomb! Let us assemble and, like the Magi, let us hasten and let us worship! Let us bring myrrh as a gift to Him Who is wrapped now, not in swaddling clothes, but in a winding sheet! Let us lament and cry: "Arise, O Master, and bestow resurrection on the fallen!" ' "

[The Synaxarion]

The service books call for the Synaxarion of Pascha to then be chanted, beginning, "On the Holy and Great Sunday of Pascha, we celebrate the life-giving Resurrection of our Lord and God and Savior, Jesus Christ!". **However**, in **many** parishes, this is **omitted** (**except** in the *Greek* practice).

Post – Gospel Stikhera

Following either the Oikos or the Synaxarion, the people sing the Post-Gospel Stikhera, in tone 6: "Having beheld the Resurrection of Christ, let us worship the holy Lord, Jesus, the only sinless One! We venerate Your Cross, O Christ, and Your holy Resurrection we praise and glorify! For, You are our God, and we know no other but You! We call on

Your Name! Come, all you faithful! Let us venerate Christ's holy Resurrection! For, behold! Through the Cross, joy has come into all the world! Let us ever bless the Lord, praising His Resurrection! For, by enduring the Cross for us, He has destroyed death by death! Jesus has Risen from the tomb, as He foretold, granting us eternal life, and great mercy!"

The Kanon: Odes 7, 8, and 9

Ode 7 chants, "He Who saved the three young men in the furnace became incarnate and suffered as a mortal Man! Through His sufferings, He clothed what is mortal in the robe of immortality! He, alone, is blessed and most glorious, the God of our fathers!" The refrain is then sung. The troparia for this ode are: "The godly women had hastened to Your with myrrh, O Christ!", "We celebrate the death of death and the overthrow of hell,...!", and "This is the bright and saving night, sacred and supremely festal!". After this last troparion, "Christ is Risen...!" is sung *three* times.

Ode 8 chants, "This is the chosen and holy Day, first of Sabbaths, king and lord of days, the

Feast of feast, Holy Day of holy days! On this Day, we bless Christ forevermore!". The refrain is then sung. The troparia for this ode are: "Come, on this chosen Day of the Resurrection!", and, "Lift up your, O Zion, round about and see,…!". The people then sing, "O Most-Holy Trinity, our God, glory to You!". Then, the final troparion begins, "Father Almighty, Word, and Spirit!". After this last troparion, "Christ is Risen…!" is sung **three** times. In the service books, before Ode 9, the deacon stands before the icon of the Theotokos on the iconostasis, and intones, "The Theotokos, and the Mother of the Light, let us honor and magnify in song!". In **many** parishes, however, this is **omitted** (**except** in the **Antiochian** tradition), and the people go **immediately** from singing "Christ is Risen…!" **three** times to the singing of Ode 9.

Ode 9 is usually sung in a special melody all its own. The service books call for to be sung as follows: Heirmos 1: "Shine! Shine! Shine, O new Jerusalem! The glory of the Lord has shone on you! Exult, now, exult, and be glad, O Zion! Be radiant, O pure Theotokos, in the Resurrection of your Son!"; Troparion 1: "How divine! How beloved! How sweet is Your voice, O Christ! For, You have promised faithfully to be with us to the end of the world! Having You as our Anchor of hope, we, the faithful, rejoice!"; Troparion 2: "O Christ, great and most holy Pascha! The Wisdom, Word, and Power of God, grant that we more perfectly may partake of You in the never-ending Day of Your Kingdom!"; Refrain 1: "My soul magnifies Him Who voluntarily endured death, was buried, and rose from the dead on the third day!"; Refrain 2: "My soul magnifies Him Who rose from the dead on the third day: Christ, the Giver of life!"; Refrain 3: "Christ, the New Pascha! The Living Sacrifice! The Lamb of God, Who takes away the sins of the world!"; Refrain 4: "Today, all creation rejoices and is glad! For, Christ is Risen, and He has despoiled hell!"; "Glory...Spirit!"; Refrain 5: "My soul magnifies the might of the indivisible and Tri-Personal Godhead!"; "Now and ever...Amen."; Refrain 6: "Rejoice, O Virgin, rejoice! Rejoice, O blessed one! Rejoice, O glorified one! For, Your Son is Risen from His three days in the tomb!"; and, Refrain 7: "The angel cried to the Lady full of grace: 'Rejoice! Rejoice, O pure Virgin! Again, I say, "Rejoice!" Your Son is Risen from His three days in the tomb! With Himself, He has raised all the dead! Rejoice! Rejoice, O you people!'".

In the **Byzantine** tradition, the people first sing, "Magnify, O my soul, Him Who died of His own free will, was buried, and Arose from the dead on the third day!", then, "Shine! Shine!". After the first two refrains, the people sing, "Shine! Shine!". After the second two refrains, the people sing Troparion 1. After *both* the "Glory,...!" and 5th refrain *and* the "Now and ever...!" and 6th refrain, the people sing Troparion 2. Then, the people sing, "The angel cried...!" and "Shine! Shine!".

However, **many** parish communities *only* sing the following **shortened** version of this Ode 9: "The angel cried to the Lady full of grace: 'Rejoice! Rejoice, O pure Virgin! Again, I say, "Rejoice!" Your Son is Risen from His three days in the tomb! With Himself, He has raised all the dead! Rejoice! Rejoice, O you people!' Shine! Shine! Shine, O new Jerusalem! The glory of the Lord has shone on you! Exult, now, exult, and be glad, O Zion! Be radiant, O pure Theotokos, in the Resurrection of your Son!".

[The Little Litany]

In the **Greek** practice, the Kanon is followed by the Little Litany.

The Exapostilarion

Even though the service books call for this in tone 2 (which the **Byzantine** tradition follows), the Exapostilarion of Pascha is *usually* sung in tone 3: "In the flesh, You fell asleep as a mortal Man, O King and Lord! You arose on the third day, raising Adam from corruption, and destroying death! O Pascha of incorruption, the salvation of the world!". This is called for to be sung *three* times.

The Praises and "Let God Arise!"

Following the Exapostilarion, the Praises are sung in tone 1: "Let every breath praise the Lord! Praise the Lord in Heaven! Praise Him in the highest! To You, O God, is due a song!", and, "Praise Him, all you angels of His! Praise Him, all His hosts! To You, O God, is due a song!". In the **Antiochian** tradition, this is followed by the first four Resurrectional stikhera of the Praises from tone 1.

Then, "Let God Arise!" is sung in tone 5: "Let God Arise! Let His enemies be scattered! Today, a sacred Pascha is revealed to us! A new and holy Pascha! A mystical Pascha! A Pascha worthy of veneration! A Pascha Who is Christ, the Redeemer! A blameless Pascha! A great Pascha! A Pascha of the faithful! A Pascha Who has opened for us the gates of Paradise! A Pascha Who sanctifies all the faithful! As smoke vanishes, so, let them vanish! Come from that scene, O women bearers of glad tidings, and say to Zion: 'Receive from us the glad tidings of joy of Christ's Resurrection: "Exult and be glad, and rejoice, O Jerusalem, seeing Christ, the King, Who comes forth from the tomb, like a Bridegroom in procession!"' So, the sinners will perish before the Face of God! But, let the righteous be glad! The myrrh-bearing women, at the break of dawn, drew near to the tomb of the Life-Giver! There, they found an angel sitting upon the stone! He greeted them with these words: 'Why do you seek the Living among the dead? Why do you mourn the Incorrupt amid corruption? Go! Proclaim the glad tidings to His disciples!' This is the Day that the Lord has made! Let us rejoice and be glad in it! Pascha of beauty! The Pascha of the Lord! A Pascha worthy of all honor has dawned for us! Pascha! Let us embrace each other joyously! Pascha, ransom from affliction! For, today, as from a bridal chamber, Christ has shone forth from the tomb, and filled the women with joy, saying: 'Proclaim the glad tidings to the Apostles!' Glory to the Father, and to the Son, and to the Holy Spirit, now and ever and unto ages of ages! Amen. This is the Day of Resurrection! Let us be illumined by the Feast! Let us embrace each other! Let us call 'brothers' even those who hate us, and forgive all by the Resurrection, and, so, let us cry: 'Christ is Risen from the dead, trampling down death by death, and, upon those in the tombs, bestowing life! Christ is Risen from the dead, trampling down death by death, and, upon those in the tombs, bestowing life! Christ is Risen from the dead, trampling down death by death, and, upon those in the tombs, bestowing life!'". In the *Greek* practice, at the conclusion of this hymnology, the priest stands on the solea with the Gospel Book while all the people come forward to venerate it at this point.

The Paschal Sermon of St John Chrysostom

The Paschal Sermon of St John Chrysostom is then chanted by the priest. No one sits during the sermon, but all stand and listen. Though this is not called for in the service books, it is **almost <u>always</u>** done in most parishes.

The Troparion of St John Chrysostom

The Troparion of St John Chrysostom is then sung, in tone 8, beginning, "Grace shining forth from your lips like a beacon has enlightened the universe!". Though this is not called for in the service books, it is *almost <u>always</u>* done in most parishes.

This concludes Paschal Matins. The Paschal Divine Liturgy then begins ***immediately*** following.

L.   PASCHAL DIVINE LITURGY

The order for the Paschal Divine Liturgy is as follows.[71]

---

[71] Nassar, pp. 930-935.

The Doxology and "Christ is Risen!"

The eucharistic doxology, "Blessed is the Kingdom of the Father, and of the Son, and of the Holy Spirit, now and ever and unto ages of ages!" is chanted by the celebrant. The people sing, "Amen."

The celebrant then chants, *three* times, the Paschal Troparion: "Christ is Risen from the dead, trampling down death by death, and, upon those in the tombs, bestowing life!". Then, the people sing, *three* times, this *same* Paschal Troparion: "Christ is Risen from the dead, trampling down death by death, and, upon those in the tombs, bestowing life!". In the **Antiochian** tradition, the priest then chants the Resurrectional stikhera ("Let God Arise!", etc.), followed by the people singing "Christ is Risen!" once, and quickly.

[The Great Litany]

The service books call for the Great Litany to then be celebrated (as the **Antiochians** do), with its usual responses. However, **many** parishes, having sung the Great Litany at Paschal Matins, **omit and eliminate** it here at the beginning of the Paschal Divine Liturgy.

The 1ˢᵗ Antiphon and the Little Litany

The 1ˢᵗ Antiphon of Pascha is then celebrated. After each verse, the refrain is sung, "Through the prayers of the Theotokos, O Savior, save us!". The verses are: "Make a joyful noise to God, all the Earth! Sing of His Name! Give glory to His praise!"; "Say to God: 'How awesome are Your deeds! So great is Your power that Your enemies cringe before You!"; "Let all the Earth worship You and praise You! Let it praise Your Name, O Most High!"; and, "Glory to the Father, and to the Son, and to the Holy Spirit, now and ever and unto ages of ages! Amen."

After this, a Little Litany is celebrated, with the usual responses.

The 2nd Antiphon, "Only – Begotten Son!", and the Little Litany

Then, the 2nd Antiphon of Pascha is celebrated. After each verse, the refrain is sung, "O Son of God, Who Arose from the dead: Save us who sing to You: 'Alleluia!'". The verses are: "God be bountiful to us and bless us! Show the light of Your countenance upon us and have mercy on us!" (these two sentences are **split** in the **Greek** practice, with the refrain sung in between); "That we may know Your way upon the Earth, and Your salvation among all nations!"; and, "Let the people give thanks to You, O God! Let all the people give thanks to You!".

Then, a full "Glory,... now and ever...!" is sung, followed *immediately* by the singing of "Only-Begotten Son!". After this, a Little Litany is celebrated, with the usual responses.

The 3rd Antiphon

Following this is the celebration of the 3rd Antiphon. A reader chants the verses, and, after each of them, the people sing the Troparion of Pascha: "Christ is Risen from the dead, trampling down death by death, and, upon those in the tombs, bestowing life!". In most parishes, a different setting or arrangement from various tone traditions is used to sing this Troparion. The verses the reader chants are: "Let God Arise! Let His enemies be scattered! Let those who hate Him flee from before His Face!"; "As smoke vanishes, so, let them vanish, as wax melts before the fire!"; and, "So, the sinners will perish before the Face of God! But, let the righteous be glad!". During the last verse and singing of the Troparion, the clergy and servers exit the sanctuary for the Gospel Entrance.

When the clergy and servers reach the middle of the church, the deacon raises up the Gospel Book, and intones the Little Introit: "Wisdom! Let us be attentive! Bless God in the churches, the Lord, O you who are of Israel's fountain!" (in the **Antiochian** tradition, this is followed by, "O Son of God, Who Arose from the dead, save us who sing to You: 'Alleluia!'"). The people then sing the Troparion of Pascha one final time.

The Hypakoe and the Kontakion

The people then sing the Hypakoe, in tone 8 (in the **Greek** practice, "Christ is Risen!" is sung here one more time): "Before the dawn, Mary and the women came and found the stone rolled away from the tomb! They heard the angelic voice: 'Why do you seek among the dead, as a man, the One Who is ever-lasting Light? Behold! The clothes in the grave! Go! And proclaim to the world: "The Lord is Risen! He has slain death, as He is the Son of God, saving the race of man!"'". Even though the service books call for the Hypakoe to be sung in tone 4 (which the **Byzantines** follow), it is *almost **always*** sung in tone 8.

The people then sing a full "Glory,... now and ever...!", followed by the Kontakion, in tone 8: "You descended into the tomb, O Immortal! You destroyed the power of death! In victory, You arose, O Christ God, proclaiming, 'Rejoice!' to the myrrh-bearing women, granting peace to Your Apostles, and bestowing resurrection on the fallen!".

"As Many As Have Been Baptized!"

Instead of singing the regular Trisagion ("Holy God!"), at this point, the people sing, "As Many As Have Been Baptized!", as follows: "As many as have been Baptized into Christ have put on Christ! Alleluia!" is sung by the people **three** times. Then, the people sing a full "Glory,… now and ever…!", followed by "Have put on Christ! Alleluia!", and then, the full "As Many As Have Been Baptized", as follows: "As many as have been Baptized into Christ have put on Christ! Alleluia!" is sung by the people one final time. During the singing of the full "Glory,… now and ever…!", the reader goes to the celebrant for a blessing to read the Epistle.

The Prokeimenon, the Epistle, and the "Alleluia!" Verses

The Prokeimenon is then chanted, in tone 8: "This is the Day that the Lord has made! Let us rejoice and be glad in it!", with its accompanying verse, "O give thanks to the Lord, for He is good! For, His steadfast love endures forever!".

Then, the reader chants the Epistle reading, Acts 1:1-8. He or she introduces this reading as follows: "The Reading is from the Acts of the holy Apostles!". When the deacon intones, "Let us be attentive!", the reader does **_not_** say, "Brethren!", as is usually the case, but begins the reading by chanting, "In those days!" (for this first reading, at the beginning of Acts, the reader just starts with verse 1, "In the first Book, O Theophilus,…!).

Following the Epistle are the "Alleluia!" verses, in tone 4: "You Arose and had mercy on Zion!", and, "The Lord looked down from Heaven and saw all the sons of men!".

The Gospel

The Gospel is then celebrated, John 1:1-18. First, it is celebrated in its usual way, with either the priest, or, if there be one present, a deacon chanting the reading. At the conclusion of the reading, the people sing, as usual, "Glory to You, O Lord, glory to You!".

Then, as is the case in **many** if not **most** parishes nowadays, parishioners (baptized Orthodox

Christians who are active and regular communicants of the Eucharist in the parish) who have prepared themselves come forward and chant the Gospel in various languages. The specifics of this varies from parish to parish. In some communities, each person reads the entire Gospel reading, John 1:1-18. In other parishes, only a few verses are chanted by each reader (such as, say, only John 1:1-5). Whatever the local practice is should be observed. Once the last person chants the Gospel reading in their particular language, the people ***again, one final time***, sing, "Glory to You, O Lord, glory to You!". In the **Byzantine** tradition, this reading in various languages is done at the Gospel for Paschal Vespers.

There is ***no sermon*** called for at this time, nor is there usually one given at this Paschal Divine Liturgy.

The Augmented Litany and the Litanies for the Faithful

The Augmented Litany is then celebrated, beginning with two petitions ("Let us say, with all our soul and with all our mind, let us say!", and, "O

Lord Almighty, the God of our fathers, we pray You: Hear us and have mercy!") that are responded to by the singing of a *single* "Lord, have mercy.". Starting with the third petition ("Have mercy on us, O God, according to Your steadfast love, we pray You: Hear us and have mercy!"), the people sing a *triple* "Lord, have mercy." for this and the subsequent petitions.

There is no Litany of the Catechumens celebrated at this service. Instead, the two Litanies for the Faithful are celebrated. After the exclamation for the second of these litanies ("that, guarded always by Your might, we may ascribe glory to You,….!"), the people usually sing a *double* "Amen." ("Amen. Amen.").

The Cherubic Hymn and the Litany of Supplication

Then, for the Eucharistic Entrance, the people sing the Cherubic Hymn, the *__first__ half* ("Let us who mystically represent the Cherubim…!") sung *before* the Entrance, and the *__second__ half* ("That we may receive the King of all…!") sung *after* the Entrance. In the *Greek* practice, "That we may receive the King of all" is included in the ***first*** half (***before*** the Entrance), and the ***second*** half (***after*** the Entrance) begins with, "Who comes invisibly upborne...!".

Following the Cherubic Hymn, the Litany of Supplication is celebrated, with its usual responses.

"Father, Son, and Holy Spirit!" and the Creed

After this, the people sing, "Father, Son, and Holy Spirit...!", followed by the singing of the Creed ("I believe in one God, the Father Almighty,...!").

The Anaphora

The Anaphora is then celebrated. Even though it does not affect anything that the people sing, from this point on until the eve of Christmas, ***every*** Divine Liturgy will be that of St John Chrysostom and, therefore, his Anaphora and Eucharistic Kanon.

The Hymn to the Theotokos

Instead of singing the regular Hymn to the Theotokos ("It is truly meet…!"), the people sing, from Pascha through its Leavetaking, as the Hymn to the Theotokos, the **shortened** version of Ode 9 sung in many parishes at Paschal Matins: "The angel cried to the Lady full of grace: 'Rejoice! Rejoice, O pure Virgin! Again, I say, "Rejoice!" Your Son is Risen from His three days in the tomb! With Himself, He has raised all the dead! Rejoice! Rejoice, O you people!' Shine! Shine! Shine, O new Jerusalem! The glory of the Lord has shone on you! Exult, now, exult, and be glad, O Zion! Be radiant, O pure Theotokos, in the Resurrection of your Son!".

"And All Mankind!", the Litany Before the Lord's Prayer and the Lord's Prayer

Then, the people sing, "And all mankind!", followed by the Litany Before the Lord's Prayer, and then the Lord's Prayer itself.

"One is Holy!" and the Communion Hymn

The people then sing, "One is holy!", followed *immediately* by the Communion Hymn. Here, for Pascha, the situation with the Communion Hymn is unique. For many feasts of the year that fall on a Sunday, the people first sing, "Praise the Lord from the Heavens! Praise Him in the highest!", and then sing the special Communion Hymn for the feast. For Pascha, however, the situation is reversed: The people *first* sing, "Receive the Body of Christ! Taste the Fountain of immortality!", *then*, they sing (*except* in the *Byzantine* tradition), "Praise the Lord from the Heavens! Praise Him in the highest!", and, *then*, sing a *triple* "Alleluia!". This will be the pattern for singing the Communion Hymn every Sunday through the Leavetaking of Pascha.

The Communion of the Clergy

During the communion of the clergy, the people sing hymns appropriate for the feast. In *many* parishes, the people will the sing the Heirmi for the odes of the Paschal Kanon. In the **Greek** practice, **only** "Receive the Body of Christ!" is sung.

"Blessed is He!" and "Receive the Body of Christ!"

When the clergy emerge from the sanctuary for the communion of the faithful, the people sing, "Blessed is He Who comes in the Name of the Lord! God is the Lord and has revealed Himself to us!".

While everyone receives Holy Communion, the people **repeatedly** sing, "Receive the Body of Christ! Taste the Fountain of immortality!" After the last of the faithful receives the Eucharist, and the celebrant intones the prayer, "Lo! This has touched your lips...!" (if this is done in that particular parish), then, the people sing a **triple** "Alleluia!".

["Having Beheld the Resurrection of Christ"]

At this point, the service books call for the deacon in the sanctuary, during the time that the clergy are getting the Holy Gifts ready to be transferred back to the Table of Oblation, to chant a prayer. This "prayer," however, is actually a **hymn** that is sung as Post-Gospel Stikhera at Resurrectional Matins. Therefore, in **some** parishes, the practice is for the people to sing these stikhera in the prescribed tone 6. The stikhera are as follows:

> Having beheld the Resurrection of Christ,
> let us worship the holy Lord, Jesus,
> the only sinless One!
> We venerate Your Cross, O Christ,
> and Your holy Resurrection we praise
> > and glorify!
> For, You are our God,
> and we know no other but You.
> We call on Your Name.
> Come, all you faithful!
> Let us venerate Christ's holy Resurrection!
> For, behold, through the Cross joy has come
> > into all the world!
> Let us ever bless the Lord,
> praising His Resurrection!
> For, by enduring the Cross for us,
> He has destroyed death by death!
>
> Shine! Shine, O new Jerusalem!
> The glory of the Lord has shone on you!
> Exult now and be glad, O Zion!

Be radiant, O pure Theotokos, in the
	Resurrection of your Son!

O Christ, great and most-holy Pascha!
O Wisdom, Word, and Power of God!
Grant that we may more perfectly
	partake of You
in the never-ending Day of Your Kingdom!

Again, in some parishes, it is the practice for the people to sing this hymn. This gives the clergy time to prepare the Holy Gifts to be transferred to the Table of Oblation. As with other liturgical elements, the choir director should check with the bishop, the parish priest, or the main celebrant to follow the local practice in that particular parish.

The Liturgy Ending and the Ending Litany

For the Liturgy Ending, when the celebrant intones, "O God, save Your people and bless Your inheritance!", the people do **_not_** sing, "We have seen the true Light!", but, **_instead_**, sing the full Troparion of Pascha, ***once***: "Christ is Risen from the dead, trampling down death by death, and, upon those in the tombs, bestowing life!".

Then, when the celebrant intones, "Blessed is our God, always now and ever and unto ages of ages!", the people do <u>***not***</u> sing, "Let our mouths be filled...!" (***except*** in the ***Byzantine*** tradition), but, <u>***instead***</u>, ***again*** sing the full Troparion of Pascha, ***once***: "Christ is Risen from the dead, trampling down death by death, and, upon those in the tombs, bestowing life!".

After this, the Ending Litany is celebrated, with its appropriate responses.

"Blessed Be the Name of the Lord!"

Following the prayer of the ambo and its exclamation, the people sing, "Amen.", and then, "Blessed be the Name of the Lord, henceforth and forevermore!" ***three*** times. In the ***Byzantine*** tradition, this is replaced by the ***triple*** singing of "Christ is Risen!" on Pascha, during Bright Week, and on the Leavetaking of Pascha.

The Dismissal

For the Dismissal, instead of intoning, "Glory to You, O Christ, our God and our Hope, glory to You!", the celebrant intones the **full** Troparion of Pascha ("Christ is Risen…!") *three* times. Then, the people sing this **same full** Troparion of Pascha ("Christ is Risen…!") *three* times. After the Dismissal Prayer ("May He Who Arose from the dead,…!"), the people **usually** sing a **double** "Amen." ("Amen. Amen."), followed **immediately** by, in tone 8: "And, unto us, He has given eternal life! Let us worship His Resurrection on the third day!".

The service books then call for the chanting of the Paschal Sermon of St John Chrysostom. **However**, in **almost all** parishes, the chanting of the Pascal Sermon is transferred to and has already been celebrated in Paschal Matins, immediately following the singing of "Let God Arise!".

Recessional Hymns

As everyone comes forward to venerate the holy icons, the people sing any variety of hymns appropriate for the day. This could include the Troparion, the Kontakion, the Hypakoe, and/or the odes of the Paschal Kanon.

M. PASCHAL VESPERS

The time for the celebration for Paschal Vespers varies widely from parish to parish and between the Byzantine and Slavic practices, anywhere from 11 o'clock in the morning to around 5 o'clock in the evening. The order for the service is as follows:[72]

---

[72] Ibid, pp. 936-937.

The Doxology, "Christ is Risen!", The Paschal Verses and Troparion

The celebrant intones the **_Matinal_** doxology, "Glory to the Holy, consubstantial, life-creating and undivided Trinity, always now and ever and unto ages of ages!". The people respond by singing, "Amen.".

The celebrant then chants, *three* times, the Paschal Troparion (**except** in the **Antiochian** tradition): "Christ is Risen from the dead, trampling down death by death, and, upon those in the tombs, bestowing life!". Then, the people sing, **three** times, this **same** Paschal Troparion: "Christ is Risen from the dead, trampling down death by death, and, upon those in the tombs, bestowing life!".

Then, the celebrant chants the verses from Psalm 67:1-3 and Psalm 117:24 as he censes the Holy Table and the sanctuary in the usual manner.[73] The people then respond each time by singing, "Christ is Risen" once. The Paschal Verses are: "Let God Arise! Let His enemies be scattered! Let those who hate Him flee from before His Face!", "As

---

[73] The Psalms are numbered according to the Septuagint.

smoke vanishes, so, let them vanish, as wax melts before the fire!", "So, the sinners will perish before the Face of God! But, let the righteous be glad!", "This is the Day that the Lord has made! Let us rejoice and be glad in it!", "Glory to the Father, and to the Son, and to the Holy Spirit!", and, finally, "Now and ever and unto ages of ages! Amen.". Then, the priest chants the ***first half*** of the Troparion, "Christ is Risen from the dead, trampling down death by death!". The people then sing the ***second half*** of the Troparion, "And, upon those in the tombs, bestowing life!".

The Great Litany

The Great Litany is then celebrated, with the usual responses.

"Lord, I Call Upon You!" and Stikhera

Unlike Resurrectional Vespers celebrated on Saturday evenings throughout the year, there is no Kathisma 1 ("Blessed is the man…!") or any other

Kathisma celebrated at Paschal Vespers. Instead, the people go from the conclusion of the Great Litany into immediately singing, "Lord, I Call Upon You!", in tone 2. There are then 6 stikhera sung. Again, since this is Paschal Vespers, **everything** is sung! In other words, there is **no** chanting of the interspersed verses by a reader. Therefore, after singing, "Let my prayer arise…!", the people sing, "If You, O Lord, should mark iniquities,…!", and then the stikheron in tone 2 that begins, "Come, let us worship the Word of God, begotten of the Father before all ages…!". Then, the people sing the verse, "For Your Name's sake, I wait for You, O Lord!" Then, the next stikheron in tone 2 begins, "Christ our Savior nailed to the Cross the bond against us!". The people then sing the verse, "From the morning watch until night,…!", followed by, in tone 2, "With the archangels, let us praise the Resurrection of Christ!". The people then sing the verse, "For, with the Lord, there is mercy,…!", followed by, still sung in tone 2, "The angel proclaimed You, the Crucified and buried Master!". The people then sing the verse, "Praise the Lord, all nations! Praise Him, all peoples!", and, in tone 2, "By Your Cross, You destroyed the curse of the tree!". The people then sing the verse, "For, His mercy is confirmed on us,...!", and, in tone 2, "The gates of death opened to You from fear, O Lord!".

Then, the people sing, "Glory to the Father, and to the Son, and to the Holy Spirit!", followed by, still in tone 2, "Let us come and worship in the house of the Lord,...!". The people then sing, "Now and ever and unto ages of ages! Amen.", and then, in tone 2, the Dogmatikon, "The shadow of the Law passed when grace came!". During the singing of the Dogmatikon, the clergy and servers exit the sanctuary for the Vesperal Entrance.

"Gladsome Light"

At the Vesperal Entrance, when the deacon raises up the Gospel Book and intones, "Wisdom! Let us be attentive!", the people sing the Vesperal Entrance Hymn, "Gladsome Light!". The clergy and servers then enter the sanctuary (**except** in the **Antiochian** tradition, where they **remain** on the solea until after the Great Prokeimenon has been chanted).

The Great Prokeimenon

After the Vesperal Entrance, the Great Prokeimenon is celebrated in tone 7. The deacon intones this Great Prokeimenon, "Who is so great a God as our God? You are the God Who do wonders!". The people then sing this full Prokeimenon, "Who is so great a God as our God? You are the God Who do wonders!" to a special melody in tone 7. They sing this full Great Prokeimenon after the subsequent verses chanted by the deacon, which are as follows: "You have made known Your power among the peoples!"; "And I said, 'Now, I have begun! This is the change of the right hand of the Most High!'"; and, "I remembered the works of the Lord! For, from the beginning, I will remember all Your wonders!" (in the *Greek* practice, *only* the first sentence of this last verse ["I remembered the works of the Lord!"] is chanted). Then, the deacon intones the ***first* half** of the Great Prokeimenon, "Who is so great a God as our God?", followed by the people singing the ***second* half** of this ***same*** Great Prokeimenon, "You are the God Who do wonders!".

The Gospel

The Gospel reading for the Paschal Vespers, John 20:19-25, is then celebrated, with the usual responses (in the **Greek** practice, this Gospel reading is done in **three** sections, as follows: John 20:19-20; John 20:21-23; and John 20:24-25). In the **Byzantine** tradition, <u>**this**</u> is the Gospel Reading that is then said at this point in **various languages**.

The Augmented Litany, "Vouchsafe, O Lord!", and the Litany of Supplication

Then, the Augmented Litany is celebrated, beginning with the petition, "Have mercy on us, O God, according to Your great goodness,…!", and the people sing, **from the <u>first</u> petition**, a **triple** "Lord, have mercy.". In the **Antiochian** tradition, this Litany begins with the **two single** "Lord, have mercy." petitions ("Let us say, with all our heart…!" and "O Lord Almighty, the God of our fathers,…!").

The people then sing, "Vouchsafe, O Lord!", in the usual melodic setting.

After "Vouchsafe, O Lord!", the Litany of Supplication is celebrated, with the usual responses sung.

The Apostikha and the Paschal Stikhera

Following the "Amen." at the conclusion of the Litany of Supplication, the people sing the first stikheron of the Apostikha from the tone 2 Resurrectional Vespers: "Your Resurrection, O Christ our Savior, has enlightened the whole universe, recalling Your creation! Glory to You, O Almighty Lord!". In the **Byzantine** tradition, there is a **procession** around the church, with each parishioner holding a lighted candle.

Then, the people ***immediately*** sing the Paschal Stikhera that begin, "Let God Arise! Let His enemies be scattered! Let those who hate Him flee from before His Face!". These stikhera are concluded in the usual manner, with the **triple** singing of the joyous, majestic, and victorious Troparion of Pascha, "Christ is Risen from the dead, trampling down death by death, and, upon those in the tombs, bestowing life!".

The Dismissal

Following the Paschal Stikhera, the Dismissal is celebrated. The deacon intones, "Wisdom!", and the people sing, "Father (or, if it be a bishop, "Master"; or, if it be the Metropolitan, "Most blessed Master"), bless!" The celebrant then chants, "Christ, the One Who is, is blest always, now and ever and unto ages of ages!". The people sing, "Amen. Preserve, O God, the holy Orthodox Faith and Orthodox Christians, unto ages of ages!". The celebrant then intones, "Most holy Theotokos, save us!" The people sing, "More honorable...!" (in the *Greek* practice, "Shine! Shine! O New Jerusalem!"). The celebrant then chants, **three** times, the **full** Paschal Troparion, "Christ is Risen from the dead, trampling down death by death, and, upon those in the tombs, bestowing life!". The people then sing, **three** times, this **same full** Paschal Troparion, "Christ is Risen from the dead, trampling down death by death, and, upon those in the tombs, bestowing life!". The celebrant then chants the Dismissal Prayer that begins, "May He Who is Risen from the dead, trampling down death by death and, upon those in the tombs, bestowing life, Christ our true God,...!". At the conclusion of the prayer, the people

usually sing a ***double*** "Amen." ("Amen. Amen."), followed by, in tone 8: "And, unto us, He has given eternal life! Let us worship His Resurrection on the third day!".

In the ***Antiochian*** tradition, the Dismissal begins with the priest chanting, "Glory to You, O Christ, our God and our Hope, glory to You!", with the people responding with a full "Glory,...now and ever...!", a triple "Lord, have mercy.", and "Father, bless!".

Recessional Hymns

As everyone comes forward to venerate the holy icons, the people repeatedly sing different settings of the Paschal Troparion, "Christ is Risen...!".

N.   PASCHAL HOURS

Although this service is referred to in the service books as Paschal Compline, in **almost all** parishes, it is considered to be the Paschal Hours, celebrated immediately before the Divine Liturgy on the days of Bright Week (in most parishes of the **Greek** practice, **Paschal Matins** is celebrated **instead**). The order for the service is as follows.[74]

The Doxology, "Christ is Risen!", and the Resurrectional Post – Gospel Stikhera

The celebrant chants the doxology, "Blessed is our God, always now and ever and unto ages of ages!". The people sing, "Amen.". The celebrant then chants, **three** times, the **full** Paschal Troparion, "Christ is Risen from the dead, trampling down death by death, and, upon those in the tombs, bestowing life!". The people then sing, **three** times, this **same full** Paschal Troparion, "Christ is Risen

---

[74] Nassar, pp. 935-936.

from the dead, trampling down death by death, and, upon those in the tombs, bestowing life!".

The people then ***immediately*** sing, in tone 6, the Post-Gospel Stikhera from Resurrectional Matins: "Having beheld the Resurrection of Christ, let us worship the holy Lord, Jesus, the only sinless One! We venerate Your Cross, O Christ, and Your holy Resurrection we praise and glorify! For, You are our God, and we know no other but You. We call on Your Name. Come, all you faithful! Let us venerate Christ's holy Resurrection! For, behold, through the Cross joy has come into all the world! Let us ever bless the Lord, praising His Resurrection! For, by enduring the Cross for us, He has destroyed death by death!" (this is sung **three times** in the **Greek** practice).

The Hypakoe and the Kontakion

The people then ***immediately*** sing the Hypakoe, in tone 8: "Before the dawn, Mary and the women came and found the stone rolled away from the tomb! They heard the angelic voice: 'Why do you seek among the dead, as a man, the One Who is ever-lasting Light? Behold! The clothes in the grave! Go! And proclaim to the world: "The Lord is Risen!

He has slain death, as He is the Son of God, saving the race of man!"""". Even though the service books call for the Hypakoe to be sung in tone 4, it is **almost always** sung in tone 8 (in the **Greek** practice, the Hypakoe, the Kontakion, and the Concluding Troparia are all chanted by a **reader** instead).

The people then ***immediately*** sing the Kontakion, in tone 8: "You descended into the tomb, O Immortal! You destroyed the power of death! In victory, You arose, O Christ God, proclaiming, 'Rejoice!' to the myrrh-bearing women, granting peace to Your Apostles, and bestowing resurrection on the fallen!".

Concluding Troparia

The people then ***immediately*** sing, in tone 8, the Concluding Troparia of the Paschal Hours: "In the tomb with the body and in hell with the soul, in Paradise with the thief and on the throne with the Father and the Spirit, were You, O boundless Christ, filling all things! Glory to the Father, and to the Son, and to the Holy Spirit! Bearing life and more fruitful than Paradise, brighter than any royal chamber: Your tomb, O Christ, is the fountain of our resurrection! Now and ever and unto ages of ages!

Amen. Rejoice, O holy and divine abode of the Most High! For, through you, O Theotokos, joy is given to those who cry: 'Blessed are you among women, O all-undefiled Lady!'".

The Dismissal

Then, the people sing "Lord, have mercy." *forty* times, followed by a full "Glory,…now and ever…!", "More honorable…!", and, "In the Name of the Lord, Father (or, if it be a bishop, "Master"; or, if it be the Metropolitan, "Most blessed Master"), bless!". The celebrant intones, "Through the prayers of our holy fathers,…!". The people then sing, "Amen.", followed by a *triple* "Lord, have mercy.", and then, again, "Father (or, if it be a bishop, "Master"; or, if it be the Metropolitan, "Most blessed Master"), bless!". The celebrant again intones, "Through the prayers of our holy fathers,…!". The people then *usually* sing a *double* "Amen." ("Amen. Amen."). Then, the celebration of the Divine Liturgy begins.

O. BRIGHT WEEK

The services of Bright Week (also called, "New Week") continue through the week following Pascha, culminating in the Divine Liturgy celebrated on Bright Saturday morning. They basically follow the services for Pascha itself. In *most* parishes, these *may* consist of celebrating Paschal Vespers in the evening, and then Paschal Hours and the Paschal Divine Liturgy each morning of Bright Week. The specifics of the differing elements of these services for Bright Week are as follows.[75]

Paschal Vespers

Paschal Vespers for Bright Week are celebrated the same every day, with the ***following two*** differences: First of all, each day of Bright Week celebrates the "Lord, I Call!" and Apostikha stikhera from each successive tone of Resurrectional Vespers celebrated throughout the liturgical year. Therefore, Paschal Vespers for Bright Monday (celebrated on

---

[75] Ibid, pp. 937-939.

Sunday, as indicated above), these stikhera are in tone 2; for Bright Tuesday (celebrated on Monday evening), these stikhera are in tone 3; for Bright Wednesday (celebrated on Tuesday evening), these stikhera are in tone 4; for Bright Thursday (celebrated on Wednesday evening), these stikhera are in tone 5; for Bright Friday (celebrated on Thursday evening), these stikhera are in tone 6; and, for Bright Saturday (celebrated on Friday evening), these stikhera are in tone 7.

Second of all, the Great Prokeimenon celebrated at Pascha Vespers throughout Bright Week differs from day to day. For the Paschal Vespers for Bright Monday (celebrated on Sunday), the Great Prokeimenon, sung in tone 7, is "Who is so great a God as our God? You are the God Who do wonders!", with its accompanying verses, as indicated above.

For the Paschal Vespers for Bright Tuesday (celebrated on Monday evening), the Great Prokeimenon, sung in tone 7, is "Our God is in Heaven and on Earth! He does whatever He pleases!", with its accompanying verses, "When Israel went forth from Egypt, the house of Jacob from a strange people, Judah became His sanctuary!"; "The sea looked and fled! Jordan turned back!"; and, "What ails you, O sea, that you flee? O Jordan, that you turn back?".

For the Paschal Vespers for Bright Wednesday (celebrated on Tuesday evening), the Great Prokeimenon, sung in tone 8, is "I cried aloud with my voice to the Lord, with my voice to God, and He heard me!", with its accompanying verses, "I sought God in the day of my affliction, with my hands lifted up in the night before Him, and was not deceived!"; "When my soul refused to be comforted, I remembered God, and was made glad!"; and, "Your way, O God, is in the sanctuary!".

For the Paschal Vespers for Bright Thursday (celebrated on Wednesday evening), the Great Prokeimenon, sung in tone 7, is "Hearken to my prayer, O God, and hide not Yourself from my supplications!", with its accompanying verses, "Attend to me and answer me!"; "For, they bring iniquity upon me!"; and, "I cried unto God, and the Lord heard me, in the evening and in the morning and at noontime!".

For the Paschal Vespers for Bright Friday (celebrated on Thursday evening), the Great Prokeimenon, sung in tone 7, is "I will love You, O Lord, my Strength and my Confirmation!", with its accompanying verses, "My God, my Helper, in

Whom I trust!"; "With praise, I will call upon the Lord and will be saved from my enemies!"; and, "From His holy temple, He has heard my voice!".

    For the Paschal Vespers for Bright Saturday (celebrated on Friday evening), the Great Prokeimenon, sung in tone 8, is "You have given an inheritance, O Lord, to those who fear Your Name!", with its accompanying verses, "From the ends of the Earth, I have called to You!"; "I will be safe under the shelter of Your wings!"; and, "So, I will sing praises to Your Name forever!".

    The only other difference of Paschal Vespers during Bright Week is that, unlike Pascha, there is **_no_** Gospel reading on the other days. Therefore, at the Vesperal Entrance on these other days, the censer is carried, rather than the Gospel Book. **_All other_** liturgical elements of Paschal Vespers remain **_exactly the same!_**

Paschal Hours

    For the remaining days of Bright Week (Bright Tuesday through Bright Saturday), the Paschal Hours are celebrated **_exactly the same_** as for Bright

Monday, as indicated above, with **_no_** liturgical differences **_whatsoever!_**

Paschal Divine Liturgy

The **_only_** basic differences in the Paschal Divine Liturgy on the days of Bright Week are the Prokeimenon, the Epistle reading, the "Alleluia!" verses, and the Gospel reading. **_All_** other liturgical elements of the Paschal Divine Liturgy remain **_exactly_ the same** as celebrated on Pascha!

The only other element that is different is that, usually on Bright Monday (in the **Greek** practice, **_every_** day of Bright Week where a Divine Liturgy is celebrated), there is a procession with the Holy Cross around the outside of the church (weather permitting) at the conclusion of the Divine Liturgy. During this procession, the people sing the full Paschal Troparion ("Christ is Risen...!") as they move along. The procession stops at the center of the four sides of the church (south, east, north, and west), at which time a Resurrectional Gospel reading is chanted, with the usual responses sung. Then, the procession continues, with the resumed singing of the full Paschal Troparion. The four Resurrectional Gospels, in order of celebration, are: Matthew 28:1-20; Mark 16:1-8; Luke 24:1-12; and, John 20:1-10. (*Some* parishes, instead of chanting this final reading from John, substitute Luke 24:36-53. This, however, seems *inappropriate* because, utilizing instead the reading from John, the Church manifests the fullness of all four Gospels.) In the **Greek** practice, **only** *one* Gospel Reading is taken at the end of the procession before everyone re-enters the church building.

On Bright Monday, the Prokeimenon, sung in tone 8, is "Their proclamation has gone out into all the Earth, and their words to the ends of the universe!", with its accompanying verse, "The Heavens are telling the glory of God, and the firmament proclaims His handiwork!". The Epistle reading is Acts 1:12-26 (or, in *many* parishes, Acts 1:12-17, 21-26). The "Alleluia!" verses, in tone 1, are: "The Heavens will confess Your wonders, O Lord, and Your truth in the congregation of the saints!", and, "God is glorified in the council of the saints!". The Gospel reading is John 1:18-28.

On Bright Tuesday, the Prokeimenon, sung in tone 3, is "My soul magnifies the Lord, and my spirit rejoices in God, my Savior!", with its accompanying verse, "For, He has regarded the low estate of His handmaiden! For, behold! Henceforth, all generations will call me blest!". The Epistle reading is Acts 2:14-21. The "Alleluia!" verses, in tone 8, are: "Arise, O Lord, and go to Your resting place, You and the ark of Your might!", and, "The Lord has sworn to David a sure oath, from which He will not turn back!". The Gospel reading is Luke 24:13-35.

    On Bright Wednesday, the Prokeimenon, sung in tone 6, is "I will remember Your Name in all generations!", with its accompanying verse, "Hear, O daughter! Consider, and incline your ear!". The Epistle reading is Acts 2:22-36. The "Alleluia!" verses, in tone 3, are: "My soul magnifies the Lord, and my spirit rejoices in God, my Savior!", and, "For, He has regarded the low estate of His handmaiden! For, behold! Henceforth, all generations will call me blest!". The Gospel reading is John 1:35-41.

    On Bright Thursday, the Prokeimenon, sung in tone 3, is "Sing praises to our God, sing praises! Sing praises to our King, sing praises!", with its accompanying verse, "Clap your hands, all peoples! Shout to God with loud songs of joy!". The Epistle reading is Acts 2:38-43. The "Alleluia!" verses, in tone 4, are: "Go forth, and prosper and reign, because of truth and meekness and righteousness!", and, "For, You love righteousness and hate iniquity!". The Gospel reading is John 3:1-15.

Since Bright Friday is also **_always_** the feast of the Life-Giving Spring of the Theotokos, there are **_two_ _Prokeimena_** called for, celebrated as follows: The **_First Prokeimenon_**, sung in tone 8, is, "Their proclamation has gone out into all the Earth, and their words to the ends of the universe!". After the reader chants the accompanying verse, "The Heavens are telling the glory of God, and the firmament proclaims His handiwork!", the people **_again_** sing the **_full_ _First_ _Prokeimenon_**, in tone 8, "Their proclamation has gone out into all the Earth, and their words to the ends of the universe!". **_Then_**, the reader chants the **_Second Prokeimenon_**, sung in tone 3, "My soul magnifies the Lord, and my spirit rejoices in God, my Savior!". The people then sing this **_full_ _Second_ _Prokeimenon_**, in tone 3, "My soul magnifies the Lord, and my spirit rejoices in God, my Savior!". (In the **_Greek_** practice, the Prokeimenon [in tone 4] is, "O Lord, how manifold are Your works! In wisdom, You have made them all!", with the accompanying verse, "Bless the Lord, O my soul!".) The reader then chants **_two_** Epistle readings, Acts 3:1-8 and Philippians 2:5-11. **_Note:_** The reader announces **_only the first_** Epistle reading ("The

Reading is from the Acts of the holy Apostles!"), beginning the reading, as usual, with, "In those days!". At the beginning of the **_second_** Epistle reading, there is **no** announcement. The reader simply begins with, "Brethren!", and **then** continues with the reading. (In the Greek practice, the **one** Epistle reading taken is Acts 3:1-9.) Since there are **three** "Alleluia!" verses instead of the customary two, the chanting of these verses is as follows: When the celebrant intones, "Peace be with you, Reader!", then, the reader chants, **as _one_ unit**, "And with your spirit! Alleluia! Alleluia! Alleluia! The Heavens will confess Your wonders, O Lord, and Your truth in the congregation of the saints!". The people then sing a **triple** "Alleluia!" in tone 1. The reader then chants, "God is glorified in the council of the saints!". The people then **again** sing a **triple** "Alleluia!" in tone 1. The reader then chants, "Hear, O daughter! Consider, and incline your ear!" (this is **omitted** in the **Greek** practice). The people then sing a **triple** "Alleluia!" in **tone 3**.

In the **Antiochian** tradition, the singing of "Blessed be the Name of the Lord!" is **replaced** with the quick singing of a triple "Christ is Risen!" all during Bright Week.

Bright Saturday

The one unique element of the Paschal Divine Liturgy of Bright Saturday that differs from this service celebrated previously throughout Bright Week is that, on Bright Saturday, the artos (*άρτος*, meaning, "leavened loaf), the special bread baked with a sweet icing glaze on top and left in front of the opened Royal Doors between the services all during Bright Week, is blessed, broken, and distributed to the people.

After the Prayer Before the Ambo, at its exclamation, the people sing, "Amen.", and then, "Blessed be the Name of the Lord, henceforth and forevermore!" **_twice only!_ _Then_**, the deacon intones, "Let us pray to the Lord!". The people sing, "Lord, have mercy.". The celebrant then chants the prayer to bless the artos. At the conclusion of the exclamation, the people sing, "Amen.", and **_then_**, **_immediately_**, "Blessed be the Name of the Lord, henceforth and forevermore!" a **_third_** and **_final time!_** The rest of the Paschal Divine Liturgy concludes as it did during the rest of Bright Week.

BIBLIOGRAPHY

Liturgical Books

The Great Book of Needs, Expanded and Supplemented, St Tikhon's Seminary Press, South Canaan, PA. Very crisp and clear presentation of the texts. In four volumes: ***Volume I: The Holy Mysteries*** (1998); ***Volume II: The Sanctification of the Temple and other Ecclesiastical and Liturgical Blessings*** (1998); ***Volume III: The Occasional Services*** (2002); and ***Volume IV: Services of Supplication (Moliebens)*** (1999).

Hapgood, Isabel Florence, ***Service Book of the Holy Orthodox-Catholic Apostolic Church***, 4th Edition, Syrian Antiochian Orthodox Archdiocese, Brooklyn, New York, 1965. Although the translations are quite archaic, the book does present all the services of the Church.

Mother Mary and Ware, Archimandrite Kallistos, ***The Festal Menaion***, Faber and Faber, London, 1977. A little cumbersome with the heavy use of the "Thee-and-Thou" translations, it still is a very thorough presentation of the liturgical services of the Twelve Great Feasts.

_____, ***The Lenten Triodion***, Faber and Faber, London and Boston, 1978. Again, although still cumbersome with the translations, it presents a complete rendering of the services from the Sunday of the Publican and the Pharisee through Holy Saturday.

Nassar, the late Reverend Seraphim, ***Divine Prayers and Services of the Catholic Orthodox Church of Christ***, Antiochian Orthodox Christian Archdiocese, Englewood, New Jersey, 1979. Also archaic in textual usage, it nevertheless presents the rubrical propers of the liturgical services.

Books

Hopko, Thomas, **The Lenten Spring**, SVS (St Vladimir's Seminary) Press, Crestwood, NY, 1983. A collection of 40 meditations, one for each day of Great Lent, with much useful information from Scripture, patristic texts, and stikhera from the Lenten services.

Schmemann, **Great Lent: Journey to Pascha**, SVS Press, Crestwood, NY, 1974. A treasure trove of detail regarding the liturgical services of Great Lent, as well as explanations of Great Lent as preparation for Baptism, the different meanings of fasting and Communion, the liturgical meanings of Saturday (the Sabbath) and Sunday (the Lord's Day), as well as a wonderful Appendix on Confession and Communion.

_____, **Of Water and the Spirit: A Liturgical Study of Baptism**, SVS Press, Crestwood, NY, 1974. A great analysis of Baptism and Chrismation, and their meaning in the Orthodox Church.

www.ingramcontent.com/pod-product-compliance
Lightning Source LLC
Chambersburg PA
CBHW052041220426

4366JCB000128/2395